2020

2020

World of War

Paul Cornish & Kingsley Donaldson
and others

HODDER &
STOUGHTON

First published in Great Britain in 2017 by Hodder & Stoughton
An Hachette UK company

A CIP catalogue record for this title is available from the British Library

Hardback ISBN 978 1 473 64032 0
Trade paperback ISBN 978 1 473 64033 7
Ebook ISBN 978 1 473 64034 4

Typeset in Plantin Light by Palimpsest Book Production Limited,
Falkirk, Stirlingshire

Printed and bound by CPI Group (UK) Ltd, Croydon CR0 4YY

Hodder & Stoughton policy is to use papers that are natural, renewable
and recyclable products and made from wood grown in sustainable forests.
The logging and manufacturing processes are expected to conform to the
environmental regulations of the country of origin.

Hodder & Stoughton Ltd
Carmelite House
50 Victoria Embankment
London EC4Y 0DZ

www.hodder.co.uk

For Fiona, Emily, Archie, Charlie and Duncan.

Paul Cornish

To Helen for her love and support throughout and
to those friends and colleagues who never came home.
We have our tomorrow because they gave their today.

Kingsley Donaldson

To the memory of General Sir John Hackett GCB,
CBE, DSO and Bar, MC, DL, BLitt, MA, LLD

Soldier and Scholar

Contents

CONTENTS

AUTHORS' NOTE AND ACKNOWLEDGEMENTS

We who have put this book together know very well that the only forecast that can be made with any confidence of the course and outcome of another world war, should there be one, is that nothing will happen exactly as we have shown here.

These are the words with which General Sir John Hackett and his co-authors concluded *The Third World War, August 1985: A Future History*. Having set out to write an adaptation of Hackett's imaginative and provocative book, one more suited to the security challenges of the present day, we have all along sought to emulate Hackett's caution regarding strategic prediction and over-confident 'futurology'.

If events *could* turn out as described here, then that is reason enough to ask whether that possibility has been contemplated seriously and whether preparations have been made. Where security, defence and national strategy are concerned, what is not acceptable is to abandon thought, analysis and preparation until the future reveals itself.

Where we differ from Hackett's approach is that we do not contemplate the possibility of 'another world war' or any other form of global cataclysm. Instead, *2020: World of War* depicts twenty-first-century international security as a complex of interwoven pressures, challenges, hazards and threats.

In the course of this project, we have drawn upon countless conversations, discussions, seminars and conferences in the UK, Europe, the United States and elsewhere around the world. Our friends and colleagues in government, the armed forces, research institutes, universities and the media are all owed our thanks. These discussions informed the selection of topics and scenarios that form the core of this book. *2020: World of War* was conceived and delivered as a collaborative effort and these scenarios could not have been written without expert contributions from the following:

- Professor Kerry Brown: Professor of Chinese Studies and Director of the Lau China Institute, King's College, London; Associate Fellow, Chatham House, London.
- Mr Anthony Cornish: author and editor, Longmead Publishing.
- Professor Christopher Donnelly CMG: Director, Institute for Statecraft, London.
- Professor Julian Lindley-French: Vice-President of the Atlantic Treaty Association, Distinguished Visiting Research Fellow of the National Defense University in Washington DC, and a Fellow of the Canadian Global Affairs Institute.
- Dr Rajiv Nayan: Senior Research Associate, Institute for Defence Studies and Analyses, Delhi.
- Ms Prabha Rao: Senior Fellow, Institute for Defence Studies and Analyses, Delhi.
- Mr Nathan Ryan: Defence and Security Analyst, RAND Europe, Cambridge.

- Dr Uttam Kumar Sinha: Fellow, Institute for Defence Studies and Analyses, Delhi; Distinguished Fellow, Institute for National Security Studies, Sri Lanka.
- Professor Gareth Stansfield: Al-Qasimi Chair of Arab Gulf Studies and Professor of Middle East Politics, University of Exeter.

Following the example set by Hackett and his fellow authors, no contributions to *2020: World of War* are signed since strict attribution would not be easy in so cooperative an enterprise.

Our final word of thanks must go to Rupert Lancaster, our publisher at Hodder & Stoughton and to Barry Johnston for his meticulous and patient editorial guidance.

Paul Cornish & Kingsley Donaldson
March 2017

INTRODUCTION

Our world rapidly worsens.
Nothing now is so horrid
Or silly it can't occur . . .
W. H. Auden, 1972

Cold War Strategy

With the Cold War at its height, 1978 saw the publication of *The Third World War, August 1985: A Future History* by General Sir John Hackett and others. *The Third World War* was a work of fiction centred upon a scenario in which the armed forces of the Soviet Union and the Warsaw Pact launched a major offensive into NATO's Central Region, crossing the Inner German Border separating the Federal Republic of Germany (West Germany) from its estranged close relative the German Democratic Republic (East Germany). The uneasy stability of the Cold War collapsed into full-scale conflict as both sides committed their land, air and maritime forces to the struggle for Europe.

Sir John Hackett was a highly decorated veteran of the Second World War, who had fought in the Syria–Lebanon campaign and in North Africa, where he was awarded the Distinguished Service Order. Having begun his career as an armoured soldier, Hackett was only thirty-three when he commanded the 4th

Parachute Brigade in Operation Market Garden, the unsuccessful attempt in September 1944 to capture vitally important bridges across the Maas and the Rhine. Badly injured in the operation, Hackett was awarded a second DSO for his service at Arnhem. After the war, Hackett rose to command both the British Army of the Rhine and NATO's Northern Army Group, before retiring from the British Army in the late 1960s.

Hackett was subsequently to become the epitome of the modern 'soldier-scholar'. A graduate of Oxford University, he was fluent in many languages and a noted author and lecturer in military history and strategic analysis. He concluded his academic career as Principal of King's College London from 1968 to 1975. Known for the sharpness of his intellect as much as his physical courage, Hackett was a man of trenchant opinions concerning national strategy and defence. In 1968, while controversially still a very senior serving officer, Hackett wrote a letter to *The Times* newspaper in which he criticised the government's complacency over the capabilities of NATO forces in Europe. Hackett's critical edge was to re-emerge in 1978, in the form of *The Third World War*.

This was 'future history' driven by a very straightforward idea; it was one scenario, developing along a singular path to one conclusion (including the end of Birmingham, the UK's second largest city, in a nuclear strike). This linearity was characteristic of Cold War strategic thinking at the time. The Cold War had begun in the late 1940s and for the following thirty years or so there had been no shortage of 'hot war' around the world. But none of these conflicts captured the Cold War strategic imagination, of which the core concern was the outbreak of war along the European Central Front (as it was known throughout the middle decades of the twentieth century), leading to the use of nuclear weapons between East and West.

The Third World War captured both the public imagination and that of Cold War politico-military experts; the book achieved popular and critical success in the United Kingdom and it was serialised in several newspapers in the United States. The success of the *Third World War* was attributable in part to Hackett's reputation and in part to the convictions underpinning Cold War strategic thinking. The book also drew heavily upon the perceived certainties of recent history, conveying, as it did, that at some point international insecurity would probably lead to major war, the conduct of which would probably be fought – initially at least – along the lines of the Second World War in Europe. In that vein, *The Third World War* reflected growing disquiet that Cold War strategic certainty was not being matched by military readiness.

National Strategy for the Twenty-First Century

To a considerable extent, national security policy-makers and defence strategists are concerned with the passage of time; past, present and future. A national strategic outlook is rooted in a political, cultural and geostrategic past, perhaps several centuries old. The more recent past offers a bank of military, intelligence and other experiences, connecting to the deeper historical context and providing much-needed 'lessons' in the application of national power – both successes and failures. One of those lessons is that even the most compelling analysis, and the most reasonable scenarios can prove to be inaccurate. The Third World War did not begin in August 1985; by then Mikhail Gorbachev had been General Secretary of the Communist Party of the Soviet Union for five months. Gorbachev's coming to power instead signalled the beginning of the end of the Cold War in a manner very different from that imagined by Hackett and his fellow authors.

With the benefit of hindsight, the immediate post-Cold War period was also the point at which national strategy and defence began to decline both in substance and in relative political significance. During the 1990s, governments across Europe grasped the opportunity to make major savings in defence expenditure in both manpower and equipment, using such expressions as 'new world order' and 'peace dividend' to validate their decisions. After all, no serious case could be made for NATO members to retain large numbers of well-equipped troops in order to fight the Soviet Union and the Warsaw Pact, both now defunct.

Yet while it must draw lessons from the recent past, national strategy must be concerned primarily with the present and the future; with articulating a view of the world, its strategic challenges and opportunities, and with organising national resources so as to achieve the optimal balance of capabilities – diplomatic, policing, development aid, military, trade, intelligence, cultural outreach and so on.

The obvious difficulty is that the future is by definition unknowable and therefore unpredictable. The economist J. K. Galbraith reportedly divided forecasters between 'those who know they don't know, and those who don't know they don't know'; an aphorism which at least makes it possible to distinguish between those so-called 'futures analysts' who have wisdom in their ignorance and those who do not. But the most that can be said of Galbraith's words is that they describe the problem of the future without offering a solution to it. For those concerned with national security and defence strategy, the problem of the future is that it is not only vast and protean, but also inescapable; the most complex of problems to which a solution must nevertheless be sought, and to which scarce resources must nevertheless be committed.

When national strategists look to the future, they might be

excused for finding it a rather bleak prospect; a dystopian world of competition, contest and conflict in which security and stability will be challenged in every conceivable way (economic, environmental, technological, criminal and ideological) and on every conceivable level (global, inter-state, intra-state, commercial and individual). This analysis could result in an exaggerated sense of crisis – if not impending apocalypse – crowding out the likelihood that the future will also offer plentiful opportunities for peace and prosperity around the world. But a pessimistic view of the future might also be accurate, and it is that possibility which cannot be overlooked, least of all by strategic decision-makers and military planners.

While national strategy is concerned with the future – including the worst of futures – it is also characterised by process and expenditure. National strategy requires assessment, decision, planning, purchase and implementation; all of which demand a protracted engagement with the future, in all its uncertainty. Development aid, for example, if it is to result in sustainable improvements, might involve investment and assistance plans spanning a generation or more. Taking a similarly long view, effective intelligence-gathering might require new technologies to be devised and deployed, information networks to be cultivated, and officers to be trained to high levels of proficiency in certain languages. And unless armed forces are to be given unlimited resources to undertake any sort of operation, anywhere in the world, they too must engage with the future; they must train for certain types of operations in certain regions using equipment that might have taken as much as a decade to design and acquire.

If national strategy is expected to be *informed* by the past, to *manage* the present and to be *responsive* to the future, and if that future could be as complex, intractable and dangerous as suggested above, then it is at least possible that strategic decision-makers and planners might revert to their 'comfort zone' and concentrate on what they know best – the past and the present. Yet to do so would be to succumb to the most non-strategic form of confirmation bias: *since we do not know the future, we will assume the future to be what we know.* How then can national strategy, and particularly military leaders, analysts and planners, remain engaged with a future that they cannot know, and make expensive preparations for contingencies that they cannot predict?

The international security picture of the twenty-first century is far from linear and straightforward. There is no singular, predictable adversarial relationship, as there was during the Cold War; governments around the world now face a more challenging combination of diversity, complexity and urgency. Current trends suggest that the international security future will be neither black nor white; the UK and its allies might not be at war, strictly speaking, but they might not be at peace either. Security threats might not be 'existential' but neither will they be trivial. It will be difficult to set priorities among a wide range of security challenges – both (natural) hazards and (man-made) threats. Twenty-first-century international security is likely to involve security threats and challenges that are largely unpredictable in their source, timing and consequences. And it will be difficult to discriminate between short- and long-term challenges to security and wellbeing.

National strategy must nevertheless be prepared to confront these multiple challenges to security. Challenges may or may not reinforce each other, whether unintentionally or as the result of deliberate collaboration, or as the result of unintended consequences in our own planning and reaction (for example, the crisis in Syria, where military operations have precipitated huge population displacement, which has in turn contributed to the migration crisis currently being experienced in Europe.)

The response to this complexity has so far been disappointing. With some rare exceptions, investment in broad-spectrum research and deep analysis of global security trends has become unfashionable or at best repetitive. Wikipedia, Google and online crowd-sourced 'intelligence' (something of a misnomer) are now considered authoritative and definitive sources through which many senior decision-makers are being given their information – ideally in the form of a two-page briefing note with accompanying 'lines to take' for use at press conferences. The wide availability of very shallow knowledge has led to the illusion of profound understanding. Certainly, more is known about the contemporary world than could be said for any previous generation. But our critical understanding and strategic wisdom are arguably much weaker than those of our forebears. They may not have had access to 24-hour news from across the globe, but that which they knew, they understood.

2020: World of War

While the attitudes of politicians to defence-spending reductions might not have changed much in the forty or so years since Hackett published *The Third World War*, the world has changed dramatically in that time. In order to gauge the depth and breadth of this change, *2020: World of War* takes a fundamentally different, much less linear approach to contemporary challenges in international security.

Our first chapter examines the strategic challenge posed by Russia and asks how Hackett and his co-authors might interpret Russia's capabilities and intentions, were they alive today and contributing to the policy debate. The second chapter shows that in the early to mid-twenty-first century, security policy and defence strategy must take account of a breadth of non-traditional, non-military dynamics such as climate change, resource scarcity and health security; all of which Hackett *et al.* might have considered peripheral or exotic, or both.

We then discuss the international security environment in terms of various scenarios. The first three scenarios take a broadly geopolitical approach to security in Southeast Asia, South Asia and the Middle East respectively. These are followed by two thematic scenarios – the first dealing with crime and terrorism and the second with cyber security – before we turn to UK domestic security. Our final 'omni-scenario' makes the essential point that international security challenges might very well not behave themselves and arrive one at a time, at our convenience.

It is important to understand that our scenarios are illustrative; they have been designed in order to underpin the central argument of this book. That argument runs as follows: instead of waiting patiently for some new, large-scale and largely military equivalent of Cold War strategic certainty to reveal itself, national strategists must instead engage with international security as it is, in all its diversity, complexity and uncertainty. Used in this way, scenarios are simply an analytical device; they are not attempts at prediction and least of all do they seek to exaggerate or inflame situations or give offence to any government, people or organisation depicted.

There will, nevertheless, be those critics for whom *2020: World of War* is 'worst-case analysis' or even 'scaremongering'. We would reject the latter criticism, but welcome the former. This book is knowingly and deliberately an exercise in worst-case analysis and as such it is, arguably, precisely how security and defence policy-makers and analysts should be spending much of their time in a chaotic and often confusing world. Given the complexity and diversity of the international security outlook, it is only through well-reasoned, scenario-based analysis that strategic risk can be properly (and periodically) quantified and managed. This is never more important than when decisions are being taken *not* to act in a particular instance. Gaining an insight, through scenario-based analysis, into both the intended and unintended consequences of deliberate choices to intervene or desist, is crucial in making assured strategic decisions.

The scenarios are also bounded in time. *2020: World of War* deliberately takes a very short-term view of the international security landscape, in order to accentuate the volatility with which national strategy must engage. In this regard, the book provides a counterpoint to the 'ten year no war rule' adopted by the United Kingdom in the 1920s and 1930s, and its 'five plus five' variant adopted in the 1940s. In a sense the 'rule', in either variant, amounted to a willing suspension of strategic judgement; in all three decades, the 'rule' was, arguably, a reasonable response (not least in times of austerity) to a linear threat projection – Germany in the first instance, the Soviet Union in the second – which seemed to suggest that a 'strategic holiday' could be taken, at least for some years. Conversely, we argue that this is the least appropriate moment to resort to a strategic/psychological comfort blanket of this sort; to suspend strategic judgement while adversaries' intentions and capabilities are allowed to clarify. Strategic threats and challenges are no longer of one type (such as largely military) and in the UK and elsewhere, a national strategic outlook can no longer be narrow and linear.

Each of the chosen scenarios is sufficiently plausible and

credible, and sufficiently complex to provoke serious strategic consideration. Taken together, they convey the sense of a strategically chaotic future. Although chaotic, *2020: World of War* stops short of presenting an image of international strategic pandemonium. To do so would be alarmist, passive and ultimately self-defeating, describing a strategic future for which nothing can be planned, no preparation can be made and no action can be undertaken. To reiterate: these are scenarios, but they are not predictions; they are not required to be true, although they must be authentic; and their purpose is simply to provoke thought and analysis – and a little humility.

Whereas Hackett and his co-authors used what they considered to be the strategic certainties of the Cold War to warn against the lack of military preparedness, *2020: World of War* conveys an image of global strategic uncertainty – even chaos – and warns against a lack of general strategic engagement (of which military preparation is only one part). The scenarios presented in this book are not intended to be taken literally, in quite the same way as Hackett's 'future history'. But if these scenarios, and the concerns that underpin them are not at least taken *seriously*, this will be the result of strategic complacency more damaging even than that feared by Hackett.

Simply because nothing on the scale of the Cold War seems currently imminent is no reason to lose interest in, and commitment to, strategic analysis. As the popular aphorism goes, 'the absence of evidence is not the evidence of absence'; in matters of international security and national strategy, the argument from ignorance is surely the least satisfactory of all.

CHAPTER 1

FROM COLD WAR TO HOT PEACE

The Russian Strategic Challenge

Introduction

How would Hackett and the co-authors of *The Third World War* interpret Russian behaviour today? And more to the point, what response would they recommend? Hackett's aim in publishing his seminal book was simple enough; he knew how terrible war was, and he did not want to see another happen unnecessarily or by miscalculation. As a way to manage adversarial international relations, Hackett understood that deterrence was preferable to war. But he also understood that deterrence does not obviate military preparedness. Far from it; deterrence requires military strength if it is to succeed, and it cannot be allowed to mask military weakness. Hackett also saw that nuclear deterrence needed a strong conventional military force to give it credibility, to create an escalatory ramp so as to provide an opportunity for reflection in event of hostilities, and to prevent war by miscalculation or accident. He could see with great clarity that, more than anything, deterrence depended on a demonstration of unflinching political will. It was a combination of both having the tools and demonstrating the will to use them that did the job. He wrote his book because he saw that, in the Britain of his day, both will and tools were failing.

If there is such a thing, the 'national mood' in Britain during the 1970s was far from buoyant. A very unpleasant and costly civil conflict had begun in Northern Ireland. National morale and self-confidence were very low following a series of crippling strikes that had led to the introduction of a three-day working week, a very destructive political crisis and staggering inflation. A change of government did nothing to improve the situation until, at the end of the decade, the 'winter of discontent' and a new election brought Margaret Thatcher to power.

The cost of health, education and social security, which until the mid-1970s had together consumed about a third of government spending, began to rise and the maintenance of the UK's conventional defence forces – principally in Germany – was progressively neglected. The British Army was focusing on fighting the Northern Ireland campaign; strategic and operational thinking about how to fight and win in Germany against a peer enemy was virtually abandoned. The feeling was of a Britain in hopeless, perhaps terminal, decline. It was against that backdrop that Hackett delivered his warning.

Superpower confrontation collapsed at the end of the Cold War with the demise of the Soviet Union and the Warsaw Pact. At that point the Western model, which rejected armed force as an acceptable tool for resolving disputes between European (and, by association, all) nations, was deemed to have triumphed and, it was assumed, would become universal. The supposed 'triumph of liberal democracy' was the basis of Francis Fukuyama's celebrated book *The End of History and the Last Man*, published in 1992.

But things have turned out otherwise.

Britain today is not suffering as it was in the 1970s. Despite the impact of the 'Credit Crunch' and economic downturn of 2008–9, there is a high degree of political stability and economic prosperity. Yet the impact of rapid and profound global change has been to trigger widespread crises of governance across the world, including in the advanced democracies. Across Europe, established political systems are experiencing a crisis in public confidence, resulting in the rise of anti-establishment figures, parties and movements, as evinced in extreme right-wing movements gaining popularity, in the Scottish referendum and in the UK 'Brexit' referendum in June 2016, and the US Presidential Election later the same year.

However serious the impact on established, prosperous democracies, the effects of this global change are far more acute in countries with ineffectual, brittle governments (for whatever reason – tradition, ideology, corruption, technical or political incompetence, or a combination of these) that lack responsiveness to their peoples' aspirations. The result can be sudden governmental collapse, as in the Arab Spring, Eastern Europe's 'colour revolutions' or Ukraine's 2014 Maidan. The threat of such developments can be used as a justification for strong, dictatorial rule to protect a national leadership from destabilisation. Using language with which Hackett and his fellow authors would have been familiar, this has been the reaction of the Russian leadership, which has chosen to interpret the three examples listed above as deliberate Western plots, the ultimate target of which the Russians presume to be the Kremlin itself.

Understanding the Russian Strategic Challenge

Following the collapse of the USSR, traditional ideas of large-scale industrial warfare no longer provided the most convincing explanation for conflict involving major powers. The reason was simple: US technological predominance, which made it futile to challenge the West in areas where it was strongest. Those countries and organisations which, for one reason or another, did not see fit to accept the Western economic, diplomatic and strategic preferences, and wished to challenge Western global dominance, had to search for alternatives to classic war if they were to have any hope of success in their challenge.

The result is that what Hackett would have understood as the nineteenth- and twentieth-century model of conflict as being between two clear belligerents (countries, alliances, ideologies) has been replaced today with a system – if it can be called that – which is far more fractured and often confused. Violent conflict now seems to be an option for a multiplicity of actors, organisations and even small groups, each pursuing their own goals on their own terms. In that respect the world might even be said to be reverting to type; a 'war of all against all', as the English philosopher Thomas Hobbes put it, in which violent conflict is the norm rather than the exception.

In this more complex global system, where all significant players (countries, corporations, or sub-state groups such as al-Qaeda, Islamic State and Hamas) are competing simultaneously against each other, as well as against the environment in which they are operating, the resulting *hyper-competition* is the underlying, basic element in the new paradigm of conflict.

Many in the West had come to see theirs as the only world model after the competing Soviet system failed in 1990.

However, the failed wars and financial crisis of recent years have undermined the credibility of the Western model in the eyes of much of the world. This has given credibility and even, in some eyes, respectability to those who, for various reasons, now wish to challenge the Western liberal international order and establish their own version as an alternative, or even as the dominant model. China and Russia both challenge the West's predominance in this way, as of course do Islamic State and similar groups. The challenge to the West is fundamental and certainly requires a coordinated, strategic response.

But how good is the West at adapting and responding to a strategic challenge on this scale? In crude terms, liberal democracies equip themselves best for the environment they prefer and can be reluctant to invest in, and prepare for adverse conditions. In time of peace and stability, the tendency of liberal democracies is to select leaders – politicians, corporate CEOs and Boards and even senior military officers – who will do best in a peaceful, stable environment. In 1939, for example, of the British battalion and divisional commanders who were in command of their units and formations when the UK joined the war on 3 September, only a small number were still in command six months later. This was because the skills, abilities, attitude, mentality and behaviour needed from the peacetime military leader proved to be radically different from those required in wartime. When the war ended, conversely, many officers who had experienced outstanding military careers could not cope with peacetime conditions and became ineffectual misfits whose post-war civilian careers failed, because their wartime skills did not suit peacetime conditions. Hackett was a notable exception.

In a period of rapid and possibly profound strategic turbulence, the requirement is for leaders who have the abilities to meet the challenge for what it is, not for what they might prefer it to be. Liberal democracies are not at war – at least not in the sense of the Second World War – but neither can they be said to be enjoying a period of stable peace. In these circumstances, the requirement is neither for wartime nor for peacetime leaders; what is needed are strategic leaders.

Vladimir Putin is a good example of a leader with a strategic mentality, in marked contrast to most of his current Western counterparts. With his KGB background and exposure to the corrupting influence of money in East Germany, combined with his cleverness, ruthlessness and ambition, he rose to the top during the turmoil, vicious free-for-all and extreme violence that characterised Russia in the 1990s.

This process of natural selection rewarded Putin's competitive mentality – his ability to deal with complexity, instability and uncertainty, his readiness to deploy violence where necessary to achieve his aims, his capacity to think and act strategically, exploiting and creating opportunities. Putin's ability to achieve his policy objectives in today's turbulent international system differs notably from that of many Western leaders, as does his willingness to use all forms of power in pursuit of his aims. Putin needs a 'zero-sum' competitive environment if he is to thrive. He has not hesitated to create such an environment when it suits him.

To understand Putin's position it is necessary to return to Russia in the mid-1980s. Gorbachev came to power when the USSR was failing economically, unable to match the West. Massive investment in military power had not only failed to give a return on investment, it had contributed significantly to the economic disaster. No longer could the state control the flow of external information to its population, as had been the case in the past. The Moscow Olympics, arguably, had done much to open the information floodgates. The

election of a highly popular Polish Pope had triggered nationalist movements in the Eastern European satellite countries.
Terrible social and public health conditions afflicted the
USSR and nationality problems gripped many of its constituent republics. The ruling Communist Party everywhere
suffered a precipitous decline in public trust and confidence.

Gorbachev's answer was reform: liberalisation of the
economy; defusing the tension with the West; drastic reductions in military spending; moving away from confrontation;
opening society to Western ideas; relaxing power over Warsaw
Pact allies, and loosening strict Communist Party control.
The result was catastrophic for the Soviet system. The USSR
disintegrated, 250 million people losing not only their country
and their ideology in the turmoil, but also their pensions. In
the tumultuous decade that followed for Russia, extreme
instability, societal violence and 'jungle capitalism' destroyed
the reputation of 'democracy' as a political answer.

Vladimir Putin came to power during that same decade.
It should be scarcely surprising, therefore, that he has
described the collapse of the Soviet Union as the greatest
catastrophe of the twentieth century. After some years
attempting to rebuild Russia's position in the world, Putin
found himself leading a Russia once again with a failing
economy, unable to match the West and China, and with
desperate social problems and growing national minority
issues that drastically affected his own popularity and popular
faith in his leadership. What was his response to be? To follow
Gorbachev's discredited model of reform, or to adapt and
compete?

It should be no surprise that Putin chose his own, not
Gorbachev's path, rejecting the Western blueprint, reversing
Russia's decline and presenting Russia as a proud, strong
and even moral alternative on a path to confrontation with

the West. He is not the first ruler to restore his waning popularity by creating adversaries and provoking grievance and conflict. But what is especially notable is the way Putin has gone about it, creating a form of strategic competition that is neither peace nor war, but somewhere in between.

The Emergence of Ambiguous or Hybrid Warfare

There is no standard vocabulary with agreed definitions to describe Russia's evolving strategic posture. Simply importing the language of traditional, 'kinetic' industrial and high-technology warfare can have misleading results. Different Western authors use different terms, and Russian writers use different terms again, most commonly *nelinneynaya voyna* – non-linear warfare. In much of the West's political and military leadership, the new and elaborate strategic outlook developed under Putin's leadership is known as *Hybrid Warfare*. Whatever vocabulary is used, the core principle of this form of strategic competition and conflict is that it can and does turn *everything* into a weapon. Hybrid warfare could encompass some, or even all, of the following sectors and practices at different moments and at different levels of intensity:

- Cyber crime, espionage, intrusion (and possibly electoral manipulation)
- Disruption of energy supplies
- Preference given to Russian popular culture and language
- Appeal to the authority of religion, ideals and ideology
- Economic measures and counter-measures
- Manipulative financial investments
- Financial crime including bribes, corruption

- Serious and organised crime
- State-approved business practices
- Political assassination
- Traditional, 'Cold War style' subversion and espionage
- Strategic communications: information, influence and lobbying
- Psychological operations and deception

It would be wrong, however, to see these necessarily as *alternatives* to the use of classic 'kinetic' military force. Ambiguous or hybrid warfare combines the tools and methods of hypercompetition described earlier with the use of military force in its many forms, including:

- 'Plausibly deniable' military force such as proxies, supposedly civilian contractors, ostensibly civil militias as well as the 'little green men' and troops in disguise which were deployed by Russia in Ukraine in recent years
- The classic use of conventional forces (land, air, sea and space)
- The threat to use nuclear weapons

The Ukraine crisis saw Russia experimenting with the various tools at its disposal and learning accordingly. In many ways Ukraine exemplifies the strategic challenge to the West, in which the hybrid warfare 'weapons' listed above were combined with a more traditional use of lethal military technology. It would be a mistake to assume that this challenge is limited in time or space; Russia has been using the weapons of hypercompetition against the West for years. It is a general *strategic* challenge rather than a challenge over the future of Ukraine, serious though that challenge undoubtedly is. But because this is only poorly understood in Western capitals, European governments today consistently underestimate the effort Russia has been putting into its strategic challenge through influence, information, and the other 'non-kinetic' weapons or tools listed above. In Eastern Europe, by contrast, both the nature and the gravity of Russia's strategic challenge are much better understood.

The Prussian General Carl von Clausewitz once observed:

> *The aggressor is always peace-loving. He would prefer to take over our country unopposed. To prevent his doing this, we must be both willing and prepared to make war.*

In modern terms, preparing to make war means war using all the forms of power available, including kinetic means. To try to define these simply as 'hard' and 'soft' power is really not adequate and can even mislead. There is nothing *soft* about any of these powers when used as a weapon, least of all information.

The information weapon, is now coming to be acknowledged as a problem by some Western governments. Ironically, in concentrating on understanding Russia's use of information as a weapon or tool of hypercompetition, and rather belatedly at that, we have tended to play down the corresponding, growing relevance of classic military power in Europe.

The political imperative in many Western countries for the last quarter of a century has been to cut defence spending. In the UK, government spending on health, social security and education together now consumes not one-third but over two-thirds of government spending, leaving only one-third for *everything* else, defence included. It has thus become difficult, if not embarrassing for politicians to acknowledge

that classic kinetic warfare is still important, even if its relative utility has changed.

New forms of power have *not* rendered conventional military force obsolete. Indeed, in some parts of the world, such
as in the Indian sub-continent, it still retains much of its
twentieth-century significance. In Europe, it is a key – and
increasingly significant – element in Russia's overall strategic
outlook. Yet within the British Army, for example, the
exhausting effects of more than two decades of intense operational commitments, coupled with stringent cuts in the
defence budget and the impact of defence-cost inflation,[1]
have meant that commanders have ceased to think seriously
about how to defeat a peer enemy. The UK arguably no
longer has the equipment needed to do so, nor the industry
and acquisition systems necessary to create that equipment
quickly and at the necessary scale. Some analysts claim that
with a fleet of just nineteen frigates and destroyers the Royal
Navy is today below the critical mass needed to survive, let
alone expand quickly and regenerate. Similar things are said
of the British Army and the Royal Air Force.

Advocates for increased defence-spending in the UK face
a hard struggle in political circles. It is as though the national
mechanisms for strategic thinking, decision and preparation
have been lost, with some in Government even questioning
the need for a national strategy.

It is this situation that makes the warning given in *The
Third World War* so relevant today. And this is despite the
obvious differences in weaponry, the growth of 'hybrid
warfare' and the complexities of the international situation
that make it so difficult to be confident of future security
trends and forthcoming threats. Neither is it solely the UK
that is affected. All European countries have reduced their
forces, and defence-cost inflation has cut their size even

further, making equipment and manpower unaffordable on a large scale.

European societies have shown themselves to be ever more unwilling to suffer losses in lives, finance and lifestyle. And international institutions such as NATO have been overtaken by events, becoming ineffectual and in urgent need of reform and rejuvenation. For NATO, having spent almost all of the twenty-first century campaigning against a third-world enemy, calls to confront the Russian strategic challenge are inconvenient and awkward. When reality proves too difficult to manage, it can be tempting to indulge in some modish displacement activity such as the deployment of battlegroups here and there, or the construction of new headquarters, none of which are in any way adequate to meet or mitigate the Russian threat.

Yet the task faced by Western governments is clear enough: to rediscover how to employ traditional, coercive military force – albeit available now on a much smaller scale – as part of our own ability to fight hybrid warfare and to prevail. This includes the revival of an 'adversary agnostic', comprehensive and credible deterrence posture, ranging from low-level to high-level, including conventional as well as nuclear forces, involving all levers of government power and influence – diplomatic, economic and cultural – and able to meet all levels and types of threat. But with conventional armed forces having been so much reduced since the end of the Cold War, Western deterrence is in danger of lacking continuity (and therefore credibility) – a challenge for NATO.

From the Kremlin's perspective, the weakness of the West's military response to Russian aggression in Ukraine presented an opportunity to step up their strategic challenge. This brought the Russian military more into the frame in Syria, where the West's response has been weak and incoherent. Strategically, it could be said that while Western governments might claim the moral high ground in these and other situations, Russia maintains the initiative.

The Difference that Hybrid Warfare Makes

Like any other form of conflict and warfare, hypercompetition and hybrid warfare have evolved from earlier concepts and are continuing to evolve. As they involve the use of all forms of power, they do not sit naturally within any single government department. Yet for maximum effect these many forms of power must be used coherently. To do this, to be able to generate, deploy and employ all these forms of power effectively, it is essential to be able to think and act strategically, across all departments of government.

In recent years, and in common with many other European countries, the UK's capability for national strategy-making has atrophied. Many politicians today have gone so far as to oppose the idea of a national (or, as some prefer, *grand*) strategy, often it seems for reasons of party-political expediency. To restore this capability for strategy the UK and Western governments in general will need to take a number of steps:

- Recognise the nature of today's strategic contest
- Have a clear understanding of national and allied interests and objectives
- Create new mechanisms for focused and rapid strategy-making
- Educate and promote strategic thinkers
- Create an appropriate command system for implementation of strategy

- Ensure popular understanding of, and support for the strategy adopted

Only strategy, in its fullest politico-military sense, will enable Western governments to manage the complexity and dynamism of the twenty-first-century international ecosystem in which they find themselves. It is only strategy that makes it possible to understand and engage with the fact that allies in one area might be competitors in another. Russia's ability to work with China is a good example of two countries that, although not natural friends, are able to put strategy into practice, building collaboration where mutual interest coincides.

It is clear from *The Third World War* that Hackett thoroughly understood strategy and that, when dealing with Russia, to compartmentalise a problem such as Ukraine and to look for solutions specific to that problem will only result in being outmanoeuvred strategically. In early 2017, Russia has many ways in which it can counter Western moves: by taking action in the Arctic (a crucial region in current Russian strategic thinking); through restricting its supply of energy to Western countries; by taking advantage of the situation with migrants; by making it difficult to achieve a durable solution in Syria or with Iran; by withdrawing financial investments from national capitals; or in a variety of other ways, even by creating anti-Western feeling in Latin America, where RT (formerly *Russia Today*) is already the most widely watched and trusted foreign media outlet.

The implications for the future design of Western armed forces are considerable. Even if governments increase defence spending, it will never be possible to hold permanently within our armed forces all the people and skills necessary to wage hybrid warfare using all the forms of power now available.

Even if all NATO defence budgets met the target of two per cent of GDP, it would not be possible to defeat all the conceivable military (and other) threats that might arise.

The issue of defence spending across Europe, usually discussed in terms of the arbitrary two per cent target to which NATO member states have agreed, is symptomatic of the structural bias towards peace and stability within liberal democracies, even in the face of evidence to the contrary. There has thus been no serious, authoritative assessment of the optimum level of investment in national defence that a state should make for greatest effect, whether it is two per cent of GDP or more, or less. But if historical example is anything to go by, states that really fear for their security have generally been prepared to spend much more than that to ensure it. In this way, discussion returns to the problem of governments being unwilling or unable to recognise that they are facing a strategic challenge.

To deal with this challenge, armed forces should evolve to be genuinely and effectively adaptable. That means understanding what constitutes a critical mass for each function and maintaining it in a way that allows rapid expansion when needed, and contraction again when the need has passed. It means understanding that a capability is only militarily usable when it is sustainable, having adequate capacity to survive losses. As someone who was responsible for a root-and-branch reorganisation of the Territorial Army, formerly the British Army's reserve force, so as to keep it fit for purpose in a changing world (something for which many officers criticised him in his day), Hackett would have understood well that in the circumstances of the early twenty-first century, expansion must be possible for all forms of power, not just for kinetic force.

An adaptable and effective strategic outlook must also meet

two other requirements. The first is the need for a new understanding of reserves as crucial for all future operations, with new structures put in place to harness talent from all corners of civilian society. To fight hybrid war, it will be essential to combine and use new forms of influence, power and coercion, integrating civilians, reserves and regulars effectively, and to be able to dismantle and rebuild these power structures as many times as necessary, in whatever format is most appropriate to the challenge being faced.

The second requirement is for a significant increase in intelligence capability and capacity to give maximum possible warning of new threats to counter, or opportunities to exploit, in the national or allied interest. In the twenty-first century, strategic intelligence must cover a much broader spectrum in order to deal with all elements of ambiguous warfare, while maintaining a close overwatch of both conventional and nuclear military capabilities. More so than in other sectors of the national strategic posture, intelligence organisations must be able to expand and contract quickly, accessing the expertise needed – expertise (capabilities and capacities) that the military could never afford to maintain within a regular force structure.

Old models of the intelligence process are no longer sufficient. Concentrating on finding the nuggets of secret intelligence that will provide a conclusive answer to a strategic problem is no longer likely to be possible, and most certainly will not be sufficient. Classified material must be supplemented by the ability to exploit the mass of open-source material available. This in turn may require the ability to identify, harness and empower those on the ground who have the knowledge and skills to understand and navigate open-source material, distinguishing what is important and decisive from what is not. To organise this will require different structures, processes and skills. In many circumstances it will require deep cultural knowledge and the trust of those communities which, are the focus of interest.

Russia's Strategic Challenge

The extent to which Russia's strategic challenge to the West can be laid entirely at Putin's door can be debated. But there can be no doubt that, in defining Russia as different from the West, as not needing the West, and as morally superior to the West, Putin has set Russia's course for the foreseeable future.

His information and influence campaign has nowhere been more successful than in Russia itself. As evinced by the often vituperative rhetoric coming out of Moscow, Putin has let the genie out of the bottle. He has successfully made an enemy of the West in the eyes of many of his people and in the eyes of virtually all of Russia's defence and security establishment – the so-called 'Power Ministries', Army, Interior Troops, Emergency Troops, Intelligence and Security Services. Their sense of affront and resentment of the West today is palpable.

Any successor to Putin would find it difficult to change this quickly, even if he wanted to. The West is seen as hostile to Russia; Russia will be secure only when it controls its neighbours; zero-sum gain has become the only measure of successful relations with the West.

Putin's objectives are generally agreed by analysts to be twofold: to stay in power, which includes maintaining his wealth; and to retake lost ground, to restore Russia's position of influence and prestige in the world, lost with the disintegration of the USSR. For a West that has spent much of the last twenty-five years trying to include Russia, to make it a partner, to persuade Russia to 'become like us' and embrace Western values, this is particularly difficult for Western leaders to acknowledge.

It will be hard to undo the organisational changes that NATO made to bring Russia closer to the Alliance to the extent that it did. And it will be even harder for governments to reverse the spending patterns that have been established for the past twenty-five years.

~

Ukraine is the crucial element in Putin's vision to restore Russia, for two reasons in particular. The first concerns the re-establishment of Russia's pre-eminence in countries on its borders (sometimes known, tellingly, as Russia's 'near abroad'). The calculation is that if Russia can dominate Ukraine then other, smaller countries in the Caucasus and Central Asia will lose heart and succumb more easily – these countries are all watching Ukraine as a test case. The second reason is that if Ukraine were to join the West, it might be seen as a viable model for Russia itself, demonstrating an attractive alternative to Putin's world view and undermining his plans for Russia. At present the only realistic opposition to Putin comes not from the democratic movement, but from oligarchs who do not want to be cut off from Europe. A westernised Ukraine could be attractive to ordinary Russian people, who can currently see no alternative to Putin's vision.

Ukraine is now set to be a very long-term problem between Russia and the West. Putin's invasion has done more than any Ukrainian government to create a sense of nationhood and mobilise civil society in Ukraine. When the crisis began, it seemed that the problem hinged on the fact that the kind of Ukrainian government that would be acceptable to Putin would never be acceptable to the West. Today, it is clear that the kind of Ukrainian government that would be acceptable to Putin would never be acceptable to the majority of the Ukrainian people.

But Ukraine is only one element in Russia's strategic challenge to the West. Russia's pressure on the Baltic States has been a serious concern for some years. This is not so much a threat of armed intervention or all-out invasion; as long as such an action could credibly trigger a reaction from NATO and the EU, it would make armed intervention counter-productive. Rather, Russian policy is aimed at cowing the three Baltic republics into accepting that they should take no action without first taking Russia's interests into account – a kind of self-censorship. That said, recent years have seen a rapid evolution of thinking, attitude, and now action in Russia. The Army is back on the scene as an important player in Russian foreign policy.

When Putin first became President of the Russian Federation in 2000, he laid much of the blame for the collapse of the Soviet Union on the uncontrolled drain on the economy caused by the Armed Forces. Russia maintained a military that was large in comparison to its immediate neighbours and could still intimidate them, but it was only a fraction of the size of the Soviet Army and did not have the latter's massive mobilisation capacity. Not surprisingly, it maintained much of the Soviet doctrinal thinking and concepts of weapon design and acquisition – a valuable heritage. But it lost much of its former sense of purpose and political influence. Putin preferred to conduct his strategic challenge to the West by developing and learning to use other weapons of hybrid warfare and hypercompetition.

In other respects, Putin's attitudes betray his Soviet origins. He recognises that, as in Soviet times, the West is vastly stronger than Russia overall – in economic terms, in technology and cyber, in the health and robustness of its societies and its political systems. Moreover, the gap is getting wider. He also, of course, recognises the West's weaknesses and divisions, and has played his poor hand of cards very well in order to exploit these. But as a good student of Marx, he knows that in any extended conflict with the West in which the latter has time to mobilise and operationalise its many advantages, Russia will lose. In vain do EU officials protest that the EU has no military arm. To Putin, that is exactly the role NATO plays at the grand strategic level.

The last Russian ruler to try to improve Russia's competitiveness was Gorbachev. He attempted internal reform and it cost him his position. Putin will not make this mistake. He is trying to improve Russia's competitiveness by changing the environment – the ecosystem in which both Russia and the West exist. Putin is intent on breaking the rules of the post-war world, in order to remake them in Russia's interest. He is out to challenge the European security system that he, and now much of Russia, sees as 'encircling, suffocating and trying to dismember' Russia, as was the case in Soviet times.

Russia's domestic ailments and foreign policy reverses, such as the Maidan events in Ukraine, the Colour Revolutions, the Arab Spring and the drop in the oil price are portrayed not as being a result of Russia's own incompetence, or as the incidental effects of globalisation, but as a direct result of Western hostility. Conspiracy theory wins every time in the Kremlin.

At the same time, the Western liberal order is itself looking increasingly fragile. Western interventions to impose order in Iraq, Afghanistan, Libya and Syria have resulted in disorder.

Putin is thus offering a new kind of order that some national leaders (such as the former Argentinian President Kirchner) seem to prefer. In Russia, this manifests itself as traditional xenophobia and extreme nationalism, and in the strategic challenge to Western interests and values that we have been describing. It is into this framework of thinking that the Russian military have inserted themselves and, in doing so, have found a new sense of purpose.

~

The Russian military have now firmly re-established themselves in Putin's eyes as having a real political utility. Firstly, in cooperation with the FSB (Federal Security Service – the successor to the KGB), they have made a significant contribution to the success of Russia's campaign in Ukraine, and are the leading tool in Russia's policy in Syria. They have evolved and refined the use of military forces as an important element of hybrid warfare. They have successfully experimented with (and even advertised on YouTube) new weapons and tactics in both Ukraine and Syria.

In recognition of this usefulness, Putin has given the task of organising the employment of all forms of power, and developing doctrine for their use, to the General Staff, who have set up a special HQ in Moscow to this end – the National Defence Command Centre. Their understanding of 'doctrine' includes not just best practice, but also future concepts; it is a disciplined framework of thought, not a stultifying process of applied dogma as it is often depicted.

Secondly, and most significantly, is the evolution of a new operational concept for the Armed Forces. The General Staff are revisiting classic military power as an important element of hybrid warfare. Putin, it seems, appreciates this new role the Russian Armed Forces can play in advancing his objectives and helping to 'break out' of Russia's perceived 'encirclement' by the West. We are now seeing the result in Russia: greatly increased defence spending; new weapons prototypes; aggressive rhetoric; demonstrative tactical challenges, such as bomber flights entering our airspace, or a Russian carrier task force in the Channel.

This new military concept owes a great deal to Soviet strategic and operational thinking, but must always be understood as being an important element of modern hybrid warfare, combined with the hypercompetition designed to break up the integrity of NATO and the EU. This increased strength of the military in policy does not mean that Putin will let the military dominate Russian strategic thinking, as they did in Soviet times. But it does mean that the Russian military are now seen by the Kremlin as a useable weapon and tool of policy once again. It is this new dynamic that poses a very serious challenge to the West.

The best recent example of this new Russian strategic thinking can be seen in two recent exercises – internal and external – which, taken together, deliver an interesting message.

Internal: Between 2 and 10 April 2015, Interior Ministry troops (seventy per cent of whom are now regular rather than conscript) conducted a large-scale, operational-strategic exercise, code-named *Zaslon* ('backstop' or 'barrier') *2015*. Announced as being held to deal with circumstances similar to Ukraine's Maidan, it included defence of state borders, supporting civil order, and the protection of built-up areas and infrastructure objectives. It covered most of European Russia, including the North West, Central, Volga, North Caucasus, Southern and Crimean Federal Districts. For the exercise scenario, the situation 'developed as it has recently done in a neighbouring country', necessitating the deployment of troops on public order, anti-terrorist and anti-extremist duties, where they faced hostile crowds throwing bottles and stones.

Coordination of the troops with the civil authorities, the FSB and the Federal Narcotics Control Service was exercised, as were their whole range of special weaponry, including individual equipment, tear gas, water cannon, conventional military equipment and weapons, and non-lethal weapons. This whole 'anti-Maidan' exercise could equally have applied to suppressing civil disturbances in the Baltic States, Belarus or Russia itself.

External: A month earlier, in March 2015, the Russian Armed Forces had been put through an even larger-scale, no-notice 'snap' exercise, a wash-up report of which was delivered to Putin by the Russian Minister of Defence, Sergey Shoygu, and the Chief of the General Staff of the Armed Forces, Valeriy Gerasimov, on 24 March. This evaluation of the snap test of the Russian Armed Forces' combat readiness demonstrates that it was a truly strategic exercise involving multiple theatres. Moreover, there was no scripted scenario; the forces' reaction times were in minutes and hours; the CPX (Command Post Exercise) that accompanied the FTXs (Field Training Exercises) in the Military Districts involved the whole Armed Forces; the different theatres were deployed for different tasks. And importantly, Belarussian forces were integrated into the Russian command system.

The strategic thinking behind the exercise seems to have been to deny the West access to key strategic areas; a kind of 'pre-emptive forward defence'. One of the main implications of Russia's growing interest in 'anti-access and area denial' is that, in the event of any escalating crisis, Russia would deploy its military at a very early stage in the crisis, giving the West a much shorter reaction time than perhaps might previously have been expected.

This stratagem – to move so quickly that the Russian Forces can seize and hold strategic objectives before the West can react, thereby presenting a *fait accompli*, is entirely consistent with traditional Russian and, before that, Soviet military doctrine. The occupation of Crimea is an excellent example. That operation was conceived as a defensive measure designed to neutralise the West's perceived superiority in modern technology and its domination of the global economic and political system.

It is also, therefore, a deterrent to the West's attempting, or even threatening to use armed force in the event of such a crisis. This deterrent posture is backed up by nuclear weapons to neutralise the West's resort to the nuclear card. It is also consistent with other aspects of Russian doctrine that were on display in Ukraine, such as the manipulation of the form, scale and tempo of an operation, so as to keep below the West's reaction threshold.

The more effectively this pre-emptive forward conventional and nuclear shield can be established, as against NATO's ability to deploy forces rapidly forward, the more initiative an emboldened Russia will feel it has to press its challenge across the board, taking advantage of what Putin sees as the West's divisions, its lack of appetite for confrontation, its preoccupation with other concerns, and its unwillingness to contemplate or prepare for war over 'a small country, far away, of which we know nothing'.

Were he alive today, Hackett would have been at pains to point out that, unfortunately, the West no longer has the tools available in the Cold War to track and respond to Russian actions. The West has lost much of its intellectual 'critical mass' with which to understand and rationalise nuclear and conventional strategy and deterrence, and has lost too much of the physical mass of the conventional military posture without which deterrence – nuclear and conventional – lacks credibility. NATO has no 'Indicators and Warning' mechanism with which to monitor adversaries' preparation and escalation and to keep political leaderships aware of changing circumstances. More broadly, the West has also lost the capability to educate and exercise political and military leaderships together in strategic thinking and acting.

It is important to appreciate that the reaction of the West's political, military and economic/financial establishments, both national and international, to every Russian military and diplomatic activity is closely monitored by Russia. The West has traditionally underestimated the effort Russia puts into this activity, much as the effort Russia puts into trying to shape our perception of events is consistently, and grossly underestimated. During the Cold War, the West understood itself to be in a strategic competition with the Soviet Union and the Warsaw Pact. Putin's actions make it clear that a deadly serious strategic competition is once again underway, even if the global environment and weapons employed are in many cases different. But neither the populations nor, it seems, the political and strategic leaderships of the West understand this; or perhaps they simply prefer not to do so.

The means and ways may be ambiguous, but the end is not. The West is facing a direct strategic challenge from Russia/Putin to which it is not yet responding adequately, and which some in the West are not even willing to recognise. The West's consequent *failure* to react adequately may be interpreted in Moscow as the West's *inability* to react, and may encourage further Russian action, which could make things even worse.

The West should heed the warning contained in *The Third World War*. Unpalatable as it might be, it is no longer unthinkable in the second decade of the twenty-first century that just as the Cold War was succeeded by the Hot Peace we have described in this chapter, so the Hot Peace might in turn give way to Hot War.

CHAPTER 2

STRATEGY IN BREADTH
The Global Insecurity Complex

Introduction

The previous chapter asked how General Sir John Hackett and his co-authors, were they still alive and active in the strategic debate, might consider the behaviour of Vladimir Putin's Russian Federation, the successor state to the Soviet Union of the Cold War. For Hackett *et al.*, the strategic problem was not only single source – emanating from the Soviet Union and its allies in the Warsaw Treaty Organisation – it was also of a certain type; a volatile mixture of territorial ambition and ideological conviction, to be pursued using the means of industrial warfare.

The possibility of territorial/ideological confrontation did not, of course, vanish into history with the ending of the Cold War. Yet rather than simply gather new evidence for the persistence of an all-too-familiar type of conflict, the purpose of this chapter is to suggest that the origins of confrontation in the twenty-first century will become increasingly diverse. Drawing upon authoritative published research, we argue that strategic challenges might arise in many more places than were considered significant during the Cold War, and for a much broader range of reasons.

The evolution of these challenges might also be far harder to identify and anticipate. The Cold War confrontation was a reliably perennial feature of strategic analysis, for several decades. If the origin of that confrontation did indeed lie in competing territorial claims and in deep-seated ideological differences, then these were influences that had long since had their effect by the time Hackett *et al.* wrote *The Third World War.* The confrontation was set, in other words, and Cold War strategists could reasonably concern themselves with preventing the deterioration of confrontation into open conflict if they could, and avoiding defeat if they could not.

Strategic assessment is unlikely to be quite so straightforward in the twenty-first century. In this chapter we describe five main dynamics, each of which could, in one way or another, be the source of challenge, confrontation and perhaps even conflict: climate change, demography, resource security (water, food and energy), health security, and financial security. It is no easy task to assess how competition and tension in these areas might give rise to conflict, who or what might be the parties to such conflict and for what reasons, and what level of risk the respective parties might be willing to accept. What is clear, however, is that these tensions could become critical in a matter of months and years, rather than decades.

It would therefore be unwise for governments to expect the strategic implications of, say, urbanisation to become clear at a steady, manageable pace in keeping with the liberal democratic policy cycle. Everything described in this chapter is already happening and is already shaping the strategic environment of the twenty-first century, for better or for worse. The difficulty for policy-makers and strategists is that they cannot be sure when, why and how these dynamics will give rise to strategic challenge. What they should know, however, is that these mounting tensions cannot be ignored.

Climate Change

Climate change is taking place and the planet is warming up. Data published by the US National Oceanic and Atmospheric Administration suggests that in 2015 the average of all land and ocean surface temperatures was 1.01°C higher than it was in 1880.[2] According to the Intergovernmental Panel on Climate Change (IPCC), a scientific body acting under the auspices of the United Nations, the thirty-year period from 1983 to 2012 'was *very likely* the warmest thirty-year period of the last 800 years (*high confidence*) and *likely* the warmest thirty-year period of the last 1,400 years (*medium confidence*)'.[3] (Emphasis in original).

These and other reports reflect a global scientific consensus that can only be described as overwhelming. Yet the causes of climate change continue to provoke controversy and dispute. Is climate change anthropogenic, attributable to the human production of vast quantities of greenhouse gases during the modern industrial period? The IPCC's answer to that question is unequivocal: 'the science now shows with ninety-five per cent certainty that human activity is the dominant cause of observed warming since the mid-twentieth century.'[4] From this perspective, climate change and global warming represent a global strategic challenge like no other in history, dwarfing all other strategic concerns such as terrorism and nuclear proliferation. By this view, mankind as a whole must address the ecological crisis it has created.

Conversely, could it be argued that climate change is a natural geological phenomenon and that the world heats up and cools down cyclically? For those 'climate change sceptics' (or 'deniers' as they are often described) who are more persuaded by the latter argument, the most that might be said is that the world is undergoing one of its periodic warm phases rather than warming up irreversibly. Then there are those whose views on the subject come closer to the more radical analysis seemingly favoured by US President Donald Trump. During the 2016 presidential campaign, Trump reportedly described climate change and global warming as 'bullshit' and a 'hoax' perpetrated upon the United States by China as a form of industrial and economic sabotage.[5] From these perspectives, the strategic challenge of managing and reversing climate change does not arise; nature is simply taking its own course.

As analysts of security policy and defence strategy, we do not have the standing to make a constructive contribution to the climate change debate; least of all to adjudicate any simmering confrontation between believers and deniers, proponents and sceptics. Our interest, instead, lies in the strategic effects of climate change – whatever its causes. These effects include the increasing frequency of more-or-less transient meteorological phenomena such as heatwaves, droughts, floods and storms.[6] The human and economic costs of extreme weather events cannot be overestimated, but it is longer-term climate-related change, such as desertification and the loss of Arctic sea ice, that will arguably have a more structural influence on the global security environment.

Desertification, whereby fertile land becomes nutrient-depleted and ceases to be able to support life (whether wild or cultivated), perhaps through a combination of climate change, over-use (intense farming) and misuse (unregulated logging), is proceeding at an alarming rate. The United Nations estimates the loss of arable land to be taking place at up to thirty-five times the historical rate.[7] In the judgement of the International Fund for Agricultural Development (IFAD), a United Nations specialised agency, some 12 million hectares of cultivable land are being lost each year; land on which 20 million tons of grain could have been grown. With 2.6 billion people around the world dependent on agriculture, desertification seems certain to have very severe consequences for local, regional and international security. IFAD calculates that over the next decade as many as 50 million people could be displaced, resulting in mass movements to urban areas and/or a considerable increase in international migration.[8]

The international security landscape will also be affected by the loss of Arctic sea ice. The US National Snow & Ice Data Center gauges the extent of Artic sea ice in November 2016 to have been the lowest for that month in the satellite record.[9] The loss of Arctic sea ice can cause a vicious cycle; as the amount of ice reduces so less sunlight is reflected, the Earth absorbs more of the Sun's heat, and yet more ice is melted. As the Arctic becomes warmer, so Arctic land ice (and specifically, the Greenland ice sheet) also begins to melt, causing sea levels to rise – an existential security challenge for the world's low-lying islands. The depletion of Arctic sea ice is also expected to have more immediate, practical and strategic effects. Further development of the Arctic sea routes – the North-West Passage through the Canadian Arctic Archipelago and the North-East Passage running along Russia's Arctic coast – would be of immense economic and geostrategic importance, but might also give rise to tension and disputes over territorial sovereignty and transit rights. Equally, declining sea ice could permit access to more of the Arctic sea bed and its possibly considerable reserves of oil and, particularly, natural gas. Competition for these strategically significant mineral reserves has been described by *The Economist* magazine as a new 'frozen conflict'.[10]

Demography

Population Growth

According to the Population Division of the United Nations Department of Economic and Social Affairs, the global population will rise from 7.3 billion in 2015 to 9.7 billion in 2050; a rate of increase of roughly 83 million annually.[11] Unless resources such as energy, food and fresh water grow at a commensurate rate, which seems singularly unlikely, the increase in global population can only result in increased competition for resources, and even for survival itself.

Population growth is likely to be unevenly distributed, with higher growth rates experienced in regions that already face resource-scarcity; by 2050, over fifty per cent of global population growth is expected to have occurred in Africa, with Africa's share of the global population rising to approximately twenty-five per cent.[12] More broadly, the UN study also expects high population growth rates to be experienced by the world's forty-eight Least Developed Countries (LDCs), with the population of this group doubling in size between 2015 (954 million) and 2050 (1.9 billion). The UN's assessment of the implications of these statistics is sobering:

> The concentration of population growth in the poorest countries will make it harder for those governments to eradicate poverty and inequality, combat hunger and malnutrition, expand education enrolment and health systems, improve the provision of basic services and implement other elements of a sustainable development agenda to ensure that no one is left behind.[13]

Migration

In Africa and elsewhere, the unhappy prospect of a growing population relying upon limited (or even dwindling) resources could see pressure being released in the form either of internal displacement (such as the movement to urban areas), or international migration. Between 2015 and 2050, as many as 91 million people might have moved to high-income countries (largely in Europe, North America and Oceania) from Africa, Asia, Latin America and the Caribbean. When set against the expected ratio of births to deaths in high-income countries, net migration could consequently account for as much as eighty-two per cent of population growth in these countries.[14]

For those unable to migrate in pursuit of improved economic and/or living conditions, within their own country or internationally, the pressure might become intolerable and unsustainable. Malnutrition and public health crises could prompt demand for vast levels of development aid and frequent humanitarian intervention from the international community.

Regional Population Change

Changing regional age profiles could also influence the international security environment in indirect ways. The population of Europe, estimated at 738 million in 2015, is expected to increase slightly to 740 million by 2020 and then to reduce dramatically to 707 million by 2050. That declining population is also ageing; in 2015 some eighteen per cent of the European population was aged sixty-five years or more, increasing to nineteen per cent by 2020 and to twenty-eight per cent by 2050. At the other end of the demographic spectrum, however, by 2050 the proportion of Europeans aged under twenty-four years is expected to fall to twenty-five per cent of the population, from twenty-seven per cent in 2015. In Africa, by contrast, some fifty per cent of the 2050 population is expected to be aged up to twenty-four years, with just six per cent aged sixty-five years and older.[15]

The ageing of European and other high-income populations will affect the economic security of the countries concerned, particularly as the proportion of national GDP committed to public benefits for the elderly and economically inactive continues to rise. And as the proportion of young, economically and physically active people continues to decline, so there will be fewer people both to generate wealth, and to serve in the armed forces and police. As the taxpaying population reduces in size, so it will also be increasingly difficult to meet the costs of both development aid and highly capable, armed forces.

Urbanisation

Research published in 2016 by the UN Department of Economic and Social Affairs (Population Division) suggests that in 2016 approximately fifty-four per cent of the global population lived in urban areas, increasing to as much as sixty per cent by 2030. At that point, one in every three people will be living in a city with at least half a million inhabitants. Many of these urban concentrations will be significantly larger, however. In 2016 there were 512 cities around the world with at least 1 million inhabitants; by 2030 there could be 662 cities of this size. In some cases, the urban population will be high enough to qualify for 'megacity' status – a city with at least 10 million inhabitants. According to the UN, there were thirty-one megacities in 2016 and there could be forty-one by 2030, with some 730 million residents between them. In 2014 the vast majority of the

world's cities (up to eighty-nine per cent) were considered
vulnerable to mortality and/or economic losses associated
with natural disasters such as cyclones, floods, droughts,
earthquakes, landslides and volcanic eruptions. Cities in less
developed regions were more exposed than those in the
developed world, and larger cities more exposed than smaller
cities.[16]

The prospect of urban concentration on this scale, particularly with its uneven distribution between developed and
less-developed regions, prompts a string of fairly obvious
questions. Will the inhabitants of the world's cities have access
to the water, food and energy resources they will need? In
regions already experiencing resource scarcity, is it conceivable that the growing urban population might compete with
the dwindling rural population for access to fresh water? In
2030, how will the 730 million occupants of the world's
megacities occupy themselves? Will there be sufficient work?
What might they do for leisure and pleasure? In short, what
will it be like to live in these places, and how safe and secure
will their inhabitants be? And when a megacity becomes
bankrupt or its infrastructure collapses, whether as a result
of economic failure or natural disaster, who will have the
responsibility to intervene to restore sustainable living conditions, and if necessary, law and order? In the words of the
otherwise constructive and optimistic UN-Habitat *World
Cities Report 2016*:

The fear of crime and violence continues to be pervasive
in cities and is one of the top concerns in citizens' everyday
lives. [. . .] sixty to seventy per cent of urban residents have
been victims of crime in those developing or transitional
countries where rapid urban population growth is at its
highest. New and pervasive risks affecting cities include

terrorism, urban warfare, heightened securitisation, and disease and pandemics. Insecurity and risk undermine the long-term sustainability of cities worldwide.[17]

Resource Security

Water

After breathable oxygen, the second prerequisite for human survival is water. A healthy human being requires over two litres of water per day, whether drunk directly or ingested in food. Water is also essential to successful agriculture and food production – the third item on humanity's survival check list. Counter-intuitively perhaps, it is often assumed that access to water is not a cause for armed conflict; as if mutual dependence on water will in some way persuade competing groups to collaborate rather than to compete, taking diplomatic steps to ensure mutual access to this essential resource. One celebrated illustration of the impulse to collaborate took place in December 2013, when Israel, Jordan and the Palestinian National Authority all reached agreement on the construction of a desalination plant in Jordan, supplying fresh water to all three signatories.[18] As Wendy Barnaby has argued, 'Countries do not go to war over water, they solve their water shortages through trade and international agreements.'[19] This is not the place to test the robustness of this assessment, other than to suggest that before much longer, it might be more the exception than the rule.

Drawing upon research undertaken by the OECD and other organisations, the World Economic Forum's *Global Risk Report 2015* observes that the global demand for water might exceed sustainable supply by forty per cent in 2030 and that 4 billion people might be living in water-scarce areas by 2050.[20] In Africa, roughly ninety per cent of all surface water is held in about eighty trans-boundary lakes and rivers, yet, as the High Level Panel on Fragile States noted in 2014, 'so far, only a few of these shared water resources have any intergovernmental agreements or institutional arrangements for their integrated development and protection.'[21]

The global and regional consequences of chronic water shortage on this scale can scarcely be imagined. As clean water becomes increasingly scarce, so more and more people will be forced to drink filthy, disease-ridden water with predictable results for personal and public health. Agriculture will become increasingly hard-pressed. The pressure to migrate, internally and internationally, seems certain to increase. And this outlook, pessimistic as it already is, takes little account of the possibility that a major water crisis might come about rapidly and without warning, leaving people with no choice other than to fight for water if they are to survive: 'A fairly sudden acute shortage of arable land and fresh water would [. . .] show up many of the optimistic liberal assumptions and expectations of today for the illusions that they are.'[22]

Food

In *Global Risks Report 2016*, the WEF observes that 'the risk to food security is especially great, because agriculture is already straining to meet a rapidly growing demand from a finite resource base.'[23] If the agricultural capacity of vulnerable regions is being degraded by desertification and by the loss of nutrient-rich topsoil, and if at the same time the world's population is increasing rapidly, the result can only be malnourishment; a food security challenge with which we are already becoming very familiar. The 2015 edition of

The State of Food Insecurity in the World (a joint publication by the UN Food and Agriculture Organization, the International Fund for Agricultural Development and the World Food Programme) claims that 'about 795 million people in the world – just over one in nine – were undernourished in 2014–16'.[24]

As is so often the case, misfortune follows misfortune; the incidence of malnourishment is worse in regions of the world that already suffer from population pressure, environmental degradation, and other challenges to sustainable living. Analysis published by the Population Division of the UN Department of Economic Affairs suggests, for example, that the population of Sub-Saharan Africa could just exceed 1 billion by 2020. A recent UN Food and Agriculture Organisation projection indicated that by 2016 as much as twenty-three per cent of the population of that region would be undernourished.[25] The 2016 projection represented a very significant reduction from the 1990 figure of just over thirty-three per cent. If that encouraging trend were to continue out to 2020, and perhaps even to improve, then the percentage of undernourished people among the population of Sub-Saharan Africa might fall to perhaps fifteen per cent. But that simple statistical extrapolation nevertheless suggests that as many as 165 million inhabitants of Sub-Saharan Africa could lack basic nutrition in 2020. These people might very well be in need of periodic assistance in the form of food aid and humanitarian assistance, on a scale that could dwarf anything so far undertaken.

Energy

The United States Energy Information Agency predicts a forty-eight per cent increase in global energy demand from

2012 to 2040. The bulk of the increase in demand (seventy-one per cent) will occur among non-OECD developing nations, a consequence of these countries' economic growth, burgeoning populations and increased urbanisation. By 2040 liquid fuels, natural gas and coal will account for about seventy-eight per cent of the world's energy supply.[26]

Oil, gas and coal are all finite resources. Yet for the fore-seeable future, any insecurity associated with the increasing demand for energy is likely to have more to do with the effects of sudden price rises and with the security of supply, than with scarcity. According to BP's *Statistical Review of World Energy*, in 2015 global reserves of recoverable coal stood at 892 billion tonnes (sufficient for 114 years of global production); oil reserves stood at 1,698 barrels (fifty-one years of global production); and natural gas reserves stood at 187 trillion cubic metres (fifty-three years of global production).[27] These reserves are not evenly distributed around the world, however – some countries and regions have abundant energy reserves while others are much more dependent upon external supply. India, China and other fast-growing countries will doubtless compete – possibly very vigorously – for access to these supplies. Where nuclear-power generation energy is the preferred energy source, there are likely to be concerns over the safety and security of nuclear materials and technology.

Health Security

Humanity's battle with micro-organisms continues, and not without significant success – polio could very soon become the second disease after smallpox to be eradicated. The eradication of malaria – the cause of hundreds of thousands of deaths around the world each year – is again being contemplated, thanks in large part to the support of the Gates Foundation. Yet this is no time to be complacent: HIV/AIDS is still prevalent in Sub-Saharan Africa; typhus, tuberculosis, cholera and other epidemic diseases continue to have devastating effects. Humanity is also proving susceptible to previously unfamiliar microbes, such as Ebola and Zika; possibly the result of human intrusion into new areas, exacerbated by living in close proximity, and by the ease with which disease carriers can travel locally, regionally and even globally. Malaria, Ebola and Zika are all examples of zoonotic diseases; microbes that are transmitted across the human/animal 'barrier', which subsequently mutate to exploit their new, unprotected host.

These diseases challenge national and international security processes in terms of the research-and-development response to a newly discovered disease or variant, and in terms of the logistics of drug manufacture and distribution. The UK is generally considered to be well prepared for major public health crises, yet it could take as long as six months to identify a new microbe, research and develop an antidote, produce sufficient quantities of the drug, and inoculate enough of the public 'herd' to prevent large-scale infection.

The lack of surge capacity in the production of drugs can only be described as a national and international strategic challenge. A far more significant challenge, however, lies in the form of anti-microbial resistance, whereby the bacteria, viruses, parasites and fungi causing relatively common diseases are becoming increasingly resistant to the antimicrobial drugs that have long been used to treat them. In their *Global Tuberculosis Report 2016*, the World Health Organization estimate the number of TB cases around the world in 2015 to be 10.4 million. Of these, 480,000 cases are classified as Multi-Drug-Resistant (MDR-TB).[28] The higher level of microbial resistance is known as Extensively Drug-Resistant (XDR), while the highest level of drug resistance is termed Pan-Drug-Resistant (PDR). The WHO estimates that approximately nine per cent of MDR-TB cases worldwide – some 45,600 cases – could be classified as XDR-TB.[29] TB killed 1.4 million in 2015. Since it is a disease that spreads relatively easily in confined spaces such as aircraft and trains, and in close human accommodation, the public health implications are clear enough. Other disease-causing microbes known to have developed MDR strains include streptococcus, HIV, salmonella, malaria and influenza.

Anti-microbial resistance is the consequence of loose controls over bulk drug manufacture, the overuse of anti-biotics in agriculture, animal and fish farming, and the casual use of antibiotics in human medicine. Even so-called 'last-line antibiotics' – antibiotics that have not yet been undermined by anti-microbial resistance – are being compromised by easy availability and over-use.[30] India is often considered to be the 'epicentre' of the AMR problem, although this is, of course, a global challenge confronting the whole of humanity. In 2015, the WHO developed a 'blueprint for tackling AMR' – the *Global Action Plan on Antimicrobial Resistance*. In her foreword to the *Action Plan*, the Director-General of the WHO described the AMR challenge in language that could not have been more stark:

> Systematic misuse and overuse of [antimicrobial] drugs in human medicine and food production have put every nation at risk. Few replacement products are in the pipeline. Without harmonized and immediate action on a global scale, the

world is heading towards a post-antibiotic era in which
common infections could once again kill.[31]

The AMR challenge has risen to the highest levels of international diplomacy. In September 2016, the UN General
Assembly endorsed a 'Political Declaration of the High-level
Meeting of the General Assembly on Antimicrobial Resistance';
only the fourth occasion on which the General Assembly has
discussed a matter of international public health concern.
The implications for human security are clear. The fear that
what were once common and largely treatable infections
might now become untreatable and fatal, could impinge upon
social and economic interaction at all levels, in all places.
More narrowly, it might also be prudent for advanced urban
economies to give more thought to the societal and infra-
structural effects of a major disease outbreak; for the time
being at least, critical national infrastructure continues to rely
upon healthy workers and might have too little redundancy
in the face of a major epidemic.

Financial Security

Financial security – or rather *in*security and poverty – features
prominently in the broader international security landscape.
Poverty can be defined in both qualitative and quantitative
terms. In 1995 the United Nations World Summit for Social
Development defined 'absolute poverty' as 'a condition characterised by severe deprivation of basic human needs,
including food, safe drinking water, sanitation facilities, health,
shelter, education and information.'[32]

The more compelling definition, we suggest, is quantitative. 'Extreme poverty' is defined in cash terms. In 2015 the
World Bank, the international body whose mission is 'a

World Free of Poverty' – announced 'a new international poverty line' of 1.90 US dollars per day.[33] Although global poverty is steadily being reduced, hundreds of millions of people continue to live in conditions of extreme poverty. In 2013 some 767 million people were still living on less than $1.90 per day, including about 389 million living in Sub-Saharan Africa.[34]

The increasingly uneven distribution of wealth between the world's 'haves' and 'have nots' also means that the wealthier regions of the world are enjoying a standard of life unimaginable to those elsewhere, who face grinding poverty with all the challenges and risks that entails. In a recent report, Oxfam claimed that in 2014 the richest eighty-five people in the world 'owned as much as the poorest half of humanity'.[35]

It is not difficult to see how the maldistribution of wealth might affect the international security environment. The persistence of extreme poverty suggests an equally persistent case for humanitarian assistance and intervention in the worst-affected areas of the world. Governments in the economically developed world might be compelled by their electorate to commit resources and capabilities to development assistance and humanitarian relief. Poverty could increase the susceptibility of some individuals to the solutions offered by radical and extremist groups. And in a world in which information and images can be transmitted with relative ease, the 'have nots' might become militantly aggrieved by the sight of the lifestyle enjoyed by the 'haves'.

Conclusion

This chapter has provided no more than the briefest summary of highly detailed research undertaken over many years by various organisations. Our summary is also partial, insofar as it takes a deliberately worst-case approach; little if any mention is made of advances in health research, for example, or of progress towards the elimination of world poverty, or the social and economic benefits that could accompany life in modern, planned urban developments. Our purpose, instead, is to show that the international security environment of the early twenty-first century is far more diverse and complex than that of the late twentieth century, when Hackett wrote *The Third World War*.

We do not suggest that urbanisation, or the scarcity of fresh water, will inevitably lead directly to conflict and war. What we do argue, however, is that these and the other dynamics we describe will be far less peripheral to international security than might have been supposed in the late Cold War. The effect on international security need not be direct and tangible, either. As the US National Intelligence Council noted in 2008, 'worries about climate change effects may be more significant than any physical changes linked to climate change. Perceptions of a rapidly changing environment may cause nations to take unilateral actions to secure resources, territory, and other interests.'[36] In other words, international security and national strategy have become very much more complex than relatively straightforward assessments of actual military capabilities and likely intentions.

Policy-makers and strategic planners might react to these trends in one of several ways: they could ignore them altogether; they could focus on one security challenge (public health, for example) to the exclusion of all others; they could seek to respond to all challenges, at all levels and in all places. Or they could take a more rational approach; positioning themselves to be agile and adaptive, able to react in a timely and effective manner as scenarios become more real than theoretical and as security crises develop.

CHAPTER 3

UNRAVELLING IMPERIUMS
China and the US in the Southeast Asian Region

The History

In 2020, the People's Republic of China (PRC) is on the cusp of pulling off one of the greatest achievements in modern human history – the creation, from the fires of international and civil war and the devastation it wrought on their country from 1937 to 1949, of a socialist-run country, accounting for a fifth of humanity, which is now finally restored to its historic space at the centre of the world.

In the mid-2010s, the leadership around Xi Jinping had articulated this goal by fixing it firmly to the destiny of the Chinese Communist Party (CCP) itself. 2021 would mark the hundredth anniversary of the CCP's foundation. Labelled the first of two 'centennial goals' (the second, in 2049, would mark the foundation of the PRC itself and was accorded the label 'achievement of Chinese democracy'), it would be the moment when, as a middle-income country with a per-capita GDP of 13,000 US dollars, China would stand once more as a modernised country, with a globally recognised importance and status.

Underneath this rhetoric, however, there was something much less tangible – the sense that 2020–21 marked a landmark for the journey of the Chinese psyche in the modern world.

China, in the narratives constructed by the CCP since it came to power in 1949, had been a victim of Western colonial aggression and Japanese imperialism. It had been unjustly victimised and ostracised. From the grand centrality of the country in imperial times, it had been relegated to impoverishment, the victim of bullying and interference, with its sovereign integrity violated by Great Britain, the US, Japan and others.

From 2005, Chinese thinkers like Zheng Bijian, with great influence on the Party leadership, had talked about an era of China's renaissance and 'peaceful rise'. But this embraced a more visceral appeal to the emotions of a Chinese people, taught by heavy state propaganda that they were about to witness a moment, the key moment in Chinese modern history, when finally, national rectification could occur. 2020 would see the dawn of this – of a China that, in the words of nationalist bloggers two decades before, could finally say no to the world, treat the world on its own terms, be assertive and dominant, and freed from the cloying grasp of the US, with its dense network of treaty alliances all around the Pacific region.

This Chinese psychic resurrection and the hope it held out for their people was something Chinese leaders had known was a major mobilising political asset since the era of Deng Xiaoping in the 1980s, when the reform and opening-up era had first started and the Chinese economy had experienced its initial phase of explosive growth. The ideology of Maoism, with its corrosive class struggle and mass campaigns, was like a bad memory recollected from another world, or a different country from the one most Chinese could remember. From now on, the mantra was that the Party placed economic development at the heart of all that it did and based its legitimacy on that. It did not want some remote Utopia, but a heaven on earth, here and now.

The only real problem arising from this change in leadership and governing philosophy was that the Communist Party,
which had once energetically pursued these events in the
Maoist bad old days, now stood at the heart of an economy
and a social world within the PRC that looked as red-bloodedly
capitalist as anything the world had ever seen. Under the
leadership of Party Secretary and PRC President Xi Jinping,
the message grew ever more stark and clear: love or loathe
the Party, the Chinese people had one bet, and one bet alone,
to realise the Chinese Dream of strength, power, global respect
and renaissance – and that was through unified rule and
stability under the Party. Take away this, and the whole project
stood a good chance of faltering and collapsing into the
dreaded chaos, disunity and instability of the past.

Nationalist currents in domestic Chinese politics intensified
throughout the 1990s and into the 2000s, as a result of various
state-led 'patriotic campaigns' stressing the notion of
Chineseness. In many ways, this was simply a testament to
how insecure was the idea of a single ethnic and national
unity. However, by 2020, the concept of a restored, powerful
China had become akin to a state and Party religion. Not
believing in it for Chinese citizens was akin to heresy, or
spiritual self-harm. But more reflective observers could also
see that the nationalist tropes masked something deeply useful
for the Party state – distracting from the deteriorating state
of the economy, plummeting from the heady days of double-
digit growth in the 1990s and 2000s to an underwhelming
six and a half per cent by 2016, and falling even further up
to 2020, when it reached a mere three per cent.

This fall was due to a mismanaged economic transition
from a manufacturing-led, export-orientated growth model
used in the early decades of reform, to a more service-sector,
high-consuming one. The simple fact was that by 2017, the

attempts to stimulate and channel this change ran into deeper problems. Chinese consumers would not spend, despite rising wages and attempts to stop them perpetually saving. Lack of a functional healthcare system and good pension provision, despite many attempts to construct them, still impacted on public confidence, meaning that they were always saving for a rainy day, rather than trusting more to the present.

Attempts to create a national, more predictable, finance and services sector were stymied by the disunity between provinces, and the vested interests that did not buy into a national, uniform banking and insurance system. Finally, there was the ongoing problem of taxation, and the battles to try to raise more from individuals, and less from state enterprises, who, until then, had given almost half of all central and local government income. The government remained loath, despite falling state-enterprise profits, to lay too much of a tax burden on the people themselves directly, for fear of the political conse-quences – demands for a more direct, participatory say in decision making. The problem was therefore a situation in which a rising middle class wanted more public goods, without being willing to pay.

The falling growth, more than anything else, preyed on the CCP elite leadership's minds, because it struck at their legitimacy as no other issue did. Every step of the way since 1978, when the reform and opening-up era started, successive generations of leaders had staked everything on producing good growth and prosperity. This, more than solemn lectures about socialism with Chinese characteristics, was what bought people's compliance, if not their heartfelt allegiance. Dissidents remained marginal and opposition muted when growth was ten per cent a year or more. People were too busy making money to protest.

But by 2015, the 'new normal' talked of by leaders around

Xi, and his Premier, Li Keqiang, became code for low growth, and began a search for Party state legitimacy elsewhere. The failure to address these economic challenges from the mid-2010s meant that the Party needed a replacement strategy that would appeal to the public and maintain its support. A natural place to find this was in arousing nationalistic sentiment amongst the public, and in securing a stronger and higher profile for China in its own region. China's global ambitions were muted. They did not want to be exposed to US suspicion and all the pressures and responsibilities of being a great power and global policeman in the wider world. This was despite the appearance of a more isolationist America under Donald Trump. But in the Asian region, they did want a greater role. Here the dream of the Chinese leadership and people was the same – to have dominance.

Strategically, from 2009 onwards, China started making incremental moves to achieve this – ratcheting up pressure on the contested maritime borders in the South and East China Sea, which reached deep into the Asia-Pacific Region, coming close to the coast of Malaysia, two thousand kilometres from China's most southern land-edge, by using proxy agents like lifeguards and fishermen to push against opponents in dominating islands across the vast sea region. Most egregiously, at least for the US, they endeavoured to change the 'facts on the ground', building permanent structures where once only submerged rocks and tiny promontories had been.

Adjudication by the International Arbitration Court in the Hague in 2016, in favour of the Philippines, refusing to recognise the historic basis of China's claims in favour of ones based simply on modern law, only inflamed Chinese anger even more. For them, it was, and would always be, not an issue of international law with its ahistorical nature, but of justice for China merited through its history. The world owed restitution to China for the sufferings it had inflicted on it in the past. This, at least, was the mindset in Beijing.

Underlying this, too, was the subliminal objective of all the movements and counter-movements through the region – final reunification of China through resolution of the outstanding territorial issue of Taiwan. The Republic of China on Taiwan, created at the end of the Chinese Civil War in 1949 when Nationalist opponents of the Party fled to the island, still asserted *de facto* independence, its daily existence a humiliation for a Xi leadership that wanted to declare to the world, and have acknowledged, its primacy and power. Taiwan undermined this – a vibrant, modernised democracy, which still lived under the close security mentorship of the US through the Taiwan Relations Act of 1979. For Xi, with his sense of historic mission and his evident desire to go down in history as a great leader, providing a framework for finally resolving Taiwan's status and seeing it, under some terms, come back to the fold of the motherland, would ensure that he achieved this. The 'One China Policy', which asserted that there was only one nation, and that the People's Republic and the Republic of Taiwan were parts of that nation, not separate entities, only defended the status quo. Xi was clearly agitating for something more.

Thus his words to a visiting Taiwanese dignitary in 2015 that the two sides could not put off political discussions indefinitely and leave problems for the next generation to solve. Thus the risks he took in meeting with the President of Taiwan, Ma Ying-jeou, in Singapore in late 2015, the first time that any contact at this level had been made since 1949. Thus his support for increased adventurism by Chinese forces in the region. Taiwan was not, as Mao and Deng had said decades before, something that could be dealt with far into the future. The time to deal with it had arrived now. And for the Chinese public, this would be a huge achievement for Xi, and something that would cement his hopes for a perpetual presidency, with a third, fourth, or even fifth five-year term.

With the Trump presidency and his provocative contact with Taiwan's newly elected leader, Tsai Ing-wen, this only raised the temperature – contact like this had never happened before. But it also created space for China, and the idea that there might be a deal, where the People's Republic could trade economic issues and some of its claims to the South China Sea for the space to offer a resolution of the Taiwan issue.

For all the language of nationalistic bravado and great achievements, however, there was one other piece of the jigsaw that needed to be factored in. During the vast celebrations in September 2015 in Beijing to mark the seventieth anniversary of the end of the Second World War in Asia, seventy per cent of the military kit displayed before the world's eyes was new. China had increased its defence expenditure by factors of fifteen to twenty per cent year-on-year from the 1990s, when the Chinese army had been ordered to get out of business and professionalise.

By 2016, it was the second-largest spender on weapons and high-grade kit in the world, after the US. Under Liu Haiqing, regarded as the father of the Chinese modern navy in the 1980s, China had taken an interest in blue-water capacity for the first time in modern history, acquiring one aircraft carrier, and seeking to build a second. In 2015, it had even opened a naval offshore base in Djibouti, East Africa, close to its important logistic supply lines from the Middle East.

Neighbours looked at China's new military prowess with impressed fear. But there was one factor that was often missed:

no Chinese soldier had seen any combat experience since 1979, when the Chinese People's Liberation Army (PLA) had a brief, but unsatisfactory clash with Vietnam. Before this date, paradoxically, in an era when China was poor, isolated and weak, it had been bellicose, clashing with UN forces in the Korean War from 1950 to 1953, with the Indian army on the Sino–Indian border in 1962, and with the Red Army in a nasty battle with the USSR on the north-east border in 1969.

After 1979, as it had become stronger and richer, it had engaged in no major conflicts. A wealthy China did seem to be a peaceful one. This belief was countered by the ominous statement in the 1980s by Deng himself, then paramount leader, who referred to the country 'keeping a low profile, building up its capacity and going about its own business'.

The question became whether China had simply been biding its time, and was now ready to truly step onto the world stage. Doing so meant it had an awful lot of soldiers handling large amounts of kit, which they had never used in real combat situations. This ate at the confidence and inner belief of the political and military elite, creating a contradictory attitude of over-confidence and under-confidence at the same time.

The Search for 'Friends'

China's aspirations to have a stronger regional role, moving towards something approaching dominance, face a number of hurdles, but have one immense asset on their side. On the disadvantageous side is the simple military fact that the PRC is surrounded, at least on its Pacific side, by a 'great wall' of US treaty alliances. From Japan, down to the Philippines, to Malaysia, Indonesia and across to Australia and New Zealand, the US has a set of links, military installations, and military capability, which are still leagues ahead of anything China could dream of in the next few decades.

To its one aircraft carrier, a refitted vessel bought from Ukraine in the 1990s, there are fifteen US models, technically far more advanced than anything possessed by the Chinese. The US has troops and assets based in Japan, in South Korea, and a close alliance with Australia where, since 2010, it has been able to rotate marine troops in the Northern Territory capital of Darwin. But with the Obama 'rebalancing', or pivot, back to Asia since 2009, the pushback against Chinese attempts to develop more strategic space around them has intensified. Even with the Trump ascendancy and the promise to ask for more financial support for America's military presence in the region by allies, along with remarks made by the President of the Philippines, Rodrigo Duterte, elected in 2016, to side more with China, the fact remains that the US has by far the greatest sea capacity in the whole region, and sound interests for wanting to maintain freedom of navigation against a usurper like the PRC.

By 2016, China's frustrations were clear enough. As the world's second-largest economy, and as an emerging great power, it needed space at least in its own backyard where it can operate more freely. It also felt intensely the vulnerability of its energy and logistic supply routes through the Malacca strait, policed, largely, by US navy vessels and easily blocked off should conflict ever arise with China. For this reason, with the Belt and Road Initiative, since 2015 China has sought to develop routes via her land borders to the west, seeking to build train lines across Central Asia, and sign off major energy deals with Russia to diversify its supply.

The Belt and Road Initiative has received some infrastructure through the creation of the Asian Infrastructure

Investment Bank at China's instigation, a $200 billion entity created in 2014 to help the region develop better roads, logistics and connectivity. This has been backed up by a proposed free-trade agreement covering twenty-two Asian countries. Such thinking is also behind the attempt to wean China off the use of too much imported oil, over half of which comes from the Middle East, and to develop its own domestic supplies.

For all the eagerness to gain from Chinese economic links, diplomatically, the Southeast Asian and South Asian region is one marked by a deep ambiguity towards China. On the one hand, there is receptivity to the benefits that linkages with its economy give. For many countries, China is the chief trading partner, but there are deep residual suspicions. With Vietnam, China has been experiencing conflict for two millennia. With Malaysia and the Philippines, it contests the South China Sea. With Japan, its memory and resentment of the horrors it suffered in the Second World War seem to intensify, not recede, as the years pass. Historically, too, the region has never seen a strong Japan and a strong China reside peacefully side by side with each other.

The Chinese leader's mindset seems to be an increasingly imperious one. Former Foreign Minister and now State Councillor Yang Jiechi stated at an Association of Southeast Asian Nations (ASEAN) meeting in 2010 that China was a large country, and that it did not need to heed too much the complaints and voices of 'small nations'. Many commented on the legacy of a 'vassal' state attitude by Beijing, where its prominence meant it could ask for subservience and obedience from its neighbours. Such an attitude grated against the feelings of other countries in the area, where sovereignty had been hard won, and China's imperious attitude bespoke a cultural, political, and in some cases even racial, sense of superiority.

China's slogan for its neighbours, particularly those located in the Belt and Road Initiative, is for them to engage with it on a 'win-win basis'. The inducements for this are the economic opportunities that engagement with China supplies. For some, China grants preferential access to its domestic market; for others, it showers investment. With the Asian Infrastructure Investment Bank, China's economic dominance is likely to increase rapidly in the short-to-medium future – even with a more modest annual growth to 2020, it is still on track to double the size of its economy in the decade from 2011, leaving competitors like India far behind. In 2016, it signed $46 billion of aid deals with Pakistan alone, most of them in construction and infrastructure. It also started to attempt to export its highly regarded high-speed train technology.

In this context, Asian region countries have to balance daily the need to enjoy harmonious economic relations with the regional superpower, while keeping a close eye on their security interests. The dichotomy is a simple one to state: look to Beijing for material prosperity, trade, investment and physical things; look to Washington for security. The problems arise when these clash – when, for instance, China asserts its economic importance for a partner country alongside its security needs. Such a calculation seems to have persuaded the Philippines' President Duterte to shift his allegiances to Beijing. Others look likely to follow. It is unclear, however, just how deep these new alliances are. And what happens, if and when the money runs out.

The most important of China's security needs are its desire to resolve the issue of Taiwan and to have naval and operational dominance across the vast expanse of the South and East China Seas and, in some cases, beyond this. Taiwan remains a matter of existential importance for the Beijing regime, and one on which it cannot soft pedal or compromise. With the Trump presidency, too, there is a feeling in Beijing that a moment of strategic opportunity has arrived. The question is not so much about what to do, but how quickly, and how powerfully. The aim is simple: to get a reunification track set in place. The problem is also easy to articulate: this will run against the clearly stated wishes of the 23 million inhabitants of the island.

The Build-Up

Mao Zedong called Australia the 'lonely continent'. Its distance from China meant that until the 1990s, it barely figured as more than the supplier of some of its beef and grain. But during the era of China's great construction boom after it entered the World Trade Organisation in 2001, iron ore, coal and copper sourced in Australia were sent in seemingly endless fleets northwards to build Chinese cities, appear in Chinese manufactured goods, and fuel Chinese energy needs. This quickly created a dependency between the two economies, with the fall in GDP growth in the vast northern economy from 2013 having an immediate impact in the southern hemisphere.

China's influence over Australia occurred not just in the flow of dollars and material goods. Chinese investors started to appear in real estate, in agribusiness, and tourism. A Free Trade Agreement signed in 2014 during President Xi Jinping's visit to Canberra was heralded as a major development in allowing the two economies to operate more harmoniously with each other. Similar symbolism was read into the creation of a Chinese RMB currency-swapping agreement set up between Sydney and Shanghai in 2013. But the reality concealed by all this diplomatic nicety was that the relationship was an asymmetrical one, with China's hunger and need for resources, markets and intellectual property, and its imperative and ability to satisfy these, being far more intense than Australia's.

It was this suspicion on the part of the Australians that was behind their refusals to grant permission for Chinese telecoms provider Huawei to bid for the national broadband network, for the Chinese State Grid to be part of a consortium to supply New South Wales with power, and for a Chinese company to acquire the Kidman Estate, a vast territory adjacent to military land in north Australia. For all of these, there were no strictly legal impediments – only political ones. And they made clear the level of distrust felt in Australia over too much Chinese influence.

This played to the area where there was the greatest asymmetry – in the realm of security. Since the Second World War, when Australia's primary diplomatic relationship shifted decisively from the UK to the US, it was Washington to which Australia had looked for security. Vulnerable because of having the largest coastal line to protect of any country in the world, with only 27,000 active service people, and aware of the potential for major illegal migrations from its closest neighbours, particularly Indonesia, in 1951 Australia signed the Australia New Zealand US Treaty (ANZUS), which set in place one of the post-war cornerstones for security in the Pacific Region.

Australia's fidelity to the US was partly based on pragmatic calculations about how to best serve its own interests. With no nuclear weapons, and nothing close to the US naval capacity, it was intensely aware of its dependency on the US Seventh Fleet and its operations in the Asian region, policing the waterways, and defending the alliance system there.

Until the 2000s, there was little to undermine or test this

commitment. Australia was able to have the best of both worlds, creating warm relations with an emerging China, but untainted by the stain of a colonial past (unlike the UK), or the taunting status for the Chinese of being the world's sole superpower (for the US). Everyone loved Australians – to such an extent that, after the accidental bombing by NATO of the Chinese embassy in Belgrade in 1998, foreigners in China went around wearing T-shirts declaring that they were Australian, to avoid potential reprisals then being directed at Europeans and Americans!

With leaping investment and trade with China, however, the dynamics changed. For the first time ever, in 2010 China replaced the US and the EU as Australia's largest trading partner. A Mandarin-speaking Prime Minister, Kevin Rudd, was elected in 2007. Chinese international students in Australia increased so quickly they became China's second largest overseas contingent by 2012. In two White Papers issued by the Australian government, one in 2009, the other in 2013, the schizophrenia this development created was dramatically spelt out.

In the 2009 Defence White Paper, the second in as many years, China was painted as both a trade ally, but also a potential security threat. The strategic response to this was to agree with the US to the rotation for the first time of American marines through the northern port of Darwin, and to impose a blockage on the Chinese telecoms company Huawei.

On the other hand, the 2013 'Australia in the Asian Century' paper produced by the Gillard government conveyed a rosier picture, where deeper integration with partners like China (particularly China, because of the potential size of its economy and growth prospects) would lead to a future where, alone amongst developed nations, Australia would be able to sustain long-term positive growth largely through its fortunate geographical location, and the need by its neighbours for its resources.

China's sharp response to the 2009 paper indicated just how aware it was of its opportunity to work in Australia in new and potentially very assertive ways. Xi Jinping's visit in late 2014, soon after the G20 meeting held in Brisbane, typified this. Boldly standing in front of the Australian parliamentarians in Canberra, he demanded that Australians show more 'vision and imagination' in their relationship with China. On a visit to Hobart, right at the southern edge of the country on the island of Tasmania, he was able to look over to the region of the South Pole where China was already managing four research stations, with a view to gaining even more influence in the area. With underwhelming growth in Europe and the US, Australia's opportunities seemed overwhelmingly with China – a fact symbolised more powerfully by the signing of a Free Trade Agreement, which most agreed was more generous to Australia than China.

~

Australia in the second decade of the twenty-first century might have been enjoying the benefits of being a power in the Asian region, but it was easy to find evidence for the deep ambiguity amongst the public, most of whom traced their ancestry to European roots, about this relatively new development. Since 1950, Australia had produced over sixty different official reports on its role as an Asian power and what this might mean, testifying to the immense debate it perpetually had within itself about what sort of power it really was. But its security heart remained firmly rooted in the 'old world' back in Europe, or the new one across the Pacific in the US – not in the Asian region itself.

Public unease at the country's isolation and exposure never shifted, despite the fact that twenty-five per cent of the population were born outside Australia, and that every credible report showed that, with falling birth rates, and rising skill needs, Australia needed to continue being a migrant nation, attracting the best talent it could. Much of that would come from Asian neighbours, and particularly from China.

The public debate about migration was one of the most toxic, with the Tony Abbott government in particular from 2014 claiming that they would reassert control over this area. Attempts by his predecessors Kevin Rudd and Julia Gillard prior to this had ended in agreements by Papua New Guinea and other neighbouring countries to host 'refugee outposts', where those caught trying to make it into the country across the treacherous and vast seaways were sent to be processed and assessed, the majority being refused on the grounds that they were economic migrants.

Contentious internationally and within Australia, where many condemned it as being inhumane, the Abbott government was still able to make the case that it, and it alone, would clamp down on rising levels of efforts to illegally enter the country, particularly by those travelling from the Middle East, who took Indonesia as their last port of call before trying to arrive in Australia itself.

Once gaining power, Tony Abbott introduced draconian measures, made a new deal with the Indonesians, and managed to clamp down on the arrivals so that they dropped in 2014 to only 8,500. Despite this, it still wasn't enough. Public pressure on protecting Australia's vast borders from new arrivals grew. Memories of the catastrophe visited on former Prime Minister John Howard in the late 1990s, when a boat of refugees capsized with the death of dozens, and the impact this had on Australia's relations with its neigh-bours and its international reputation, haunted the country's leaders.

But there was now a new dynamic – the terrorist threat posed by some of the entrants, with the first-ever case of a terrorist attack in Sydney itself, in the coffee-house hostage taking and murder by a radicalised Muslim, originally from Iran, in late 2014. Terrorism was no longer a remote issue, but had come right into Australia's own territory. More cases were reported.

Never an easy issue, now the immigration debate for Australia carried deeper security worries. And on this issue, Australia could, and sometimes did, clash sharply with its regional neighbours, because domestic consensus over what to do was fractious, and the public debate often led by visceral feelings of threat and vulnerability, rather than reason and logic. For all his more liberal veneer, Malcolm Turnbull, when appointed prime minister after replacing Abbott in early 2016, pursued the same harsh policies. This was only reinforced by a general election result in late 2016 that saw a raft of populist, anti-immigration parties gain seats.

The Scenario

Australia is the lucky country – lucky in its prosperity, secur-ity and its alliances. But it is also a vulnerable one – isolated, hard to defend, with a delicate ecosystem. For China, Australia's assets, its location and its links are all of interest. So too are its weaknesses.

One of those weaknesses, unexpectedly, is its domestic politics. For the decade from 2011, no prime minister has managed to see out more than three years, with swift changes between leaders in the same party. Gillard had politically assassinated Rudd, to be dispatched in turn by him in 2013. Abbot had removed Rudd later in the year through a general election, only to be felled himself by Malcolm Turnbull in 2015.

Now Turnbull's underwhelming performance in the election in 2016, eighteen months later, will lead to a second return by Abbott, who has lingered on the parliamentary back benches, waiting for his turn to be summoned back to complete the unfinished business of his truncated first term.

Abbott's prime argument against Turnbull is a simple one: that Turnbull has lost control of Australia's borders. Since 2016, plummeting economies in the Asian region have supplied a whole new dynamic, with vast increases in migrants from Indonesia, Malaysia, and, surprisingly, China – where the conditions have deteriorated more rapidly than anyone expected, flattening out growth to close to three per cent, and leading to a crisis in the leadership of Xi Jinping.

The issue that breaks Turnbull's back, only one year from an election in 2019, is the relentless rise of migrants, on boats, across the northern straits from Indonesia. This is something, as the 2016 election result made clear, that touches a deep, visceral nerve for the public and on which their minds are made up. There can be no influx of new arrivals. This is deepened by the cases, loudly paraded in the press, of radical, recently arrived migrants with Muslim backgrounds, who are caught either planning, or carrying out, attacks on Australian soil. Australia's migration reception system is stretched to its limits even by mid-2018. By the end of the year, the system has imploded, with the offshore centres largely redundant, their effectiveness wholly undermined by the numbers that they are expected to cope with, but clearly cannot, and by the rising number of cases of poor treatment of those incarcerated there, along with the reputational loss that this gives to Australia internationally.

Abbott's response on being appointed prime minister, under the mantra that 'Turnbull isn't working', is a simple one – to use Australia's military capability to turn boats back, or block them from coming into Australian maritime territory. It is a 'zero tolerance' approach. In the majority of cases, after ugly and sometimes extended confrontations, the tactic works. But the numbers, and the fractiousness of the confrontations, continue to rise through 2019.

Standing on a ticket of 'Australia for Australians' in the most right-wing platform of modern Australian history, since the White Australia policy of over half a century before, Abbot manages to succeed in gaining the best electoral result for a government in over two decades. Part of his tactic has been to steal the harsh anti-migration rhetoric of the One Nation and more extreme parties. Zero tolerance on migrants, unless they are part of tightly managed government schemes, becomes the central plank of Abbott's government and its strategy.

Despite the fierce language, and the deplorable treatment of refugees who do endeavour to get through, the Abbott approach falters on one miscalculation: the truly desperate economic conditions that have propelled so many people to make such a hard, thankless journey in the first place. For them, the lives they are leaving are worse than anything they might end up going to. Wave after wave of boats, ranging from small vessels to significant passenger liners, continue to probe the Australian lines, their resistance getting increasingly resilient.

By early 2020, however, after bitter complaints in Jakarta and Beijing, Abbott's intelligence service and security advisers are given evidence that the seemingly haphazard nature of the attempts is not as it seems and there is a far more sinister story unfolding. The sheer numbers getting through, and the sophistication of the vessels they are now using, along with signals intelligence indicating some level of coordination, imply that they are part of a concerted, deliberate attempt, via proxy agents, to destabilise and undermine Australia.

There is evidence of deliberate cooperation between China and other partners it has recently found in the region, who are tied to it more deeply now by economic interests and calculations. The mindset quickly takes root, in a Canberra more paranoid and vulnerable than normal, that the country is in the midst of a phony war, one where not a single shot has so far been fired, but where the air is full of aggression and ill intent, and that the Australian people are seeing something they always feared but hoped would never happen – a strong, effective, but covert onslaught on them by China and its regional allies through the one area where it can truly be made to hurt – uncontrollable migration.

~

Coming towards the Centennial moment, the leadership of Xi Jinping is facing its own unique constellation of challenges. Since the Nineteenth Congress in late 2017, Xi's people have filled the Politburo, with his iron grip increasing on almost every area of policy. Xi's relentless focus on political and military issues at the expense of economic ones, the most distinctive aspect of his leadership, has led to a country with vast issues of inequality and a system so complex and hybrid that no one seems to fully understand how it works. The transition to a new economic model based more on service and consumption has hit the skids. There is a dearth of new ideas, because the Party state refuses to allow more marketisation and freeing up of economic space.

Careering growth in some areas stands against stagnation in others, with issues around the environment, healthcare, and the quality of life in Chinese cities – all themes that Xi seemed originally willing to address – sidelined because they appear either too difficult, or because the government is creeping into a crisis mode and does not have the attention and political capital to address them.

The overarching appeal is a very simple one – something that has appeared more strongly since the early 2010s – a blatant manipulation of nationalistic sentiment. Such a feeling raises its head in the South and East China Sea clashes. Through 2017 and into 2018, as China's economic challenges rise, so too does its adventurism, paying heed to no other power as it stakes out, constructs, and builds increasing assets on the ground across the vast maritime region. The isolationist nature of the Trump presidency and its relentless focus on transactional diplomacy and economic returns has created the space for China to be far more active and dominant in the region. What has not been foreseen, however, is that its diplomacy will be so effective in exploiting this opportunity. With deteriorating economic conditions within the country, China shows that it is in no condition to start negotiating nice deals that might be seen by its own people as in favour of other countries.

Their muscular deconstruction of the alliance system within the Asia region is brutally effective, if only because China makes it clear that it is too big to fail, and that should its political and economic structures ever totter or even fall apart, the impact on those around it will be devastating. Throughout 2018 into 2019, therefore, China undertakes deals with each of the contesting parties in the maritime disputes, isolating them, negotiating bilaterally, and hammering out what is called 'a new Asian arrangement'. This comes quickly to be called part of the 'New Chinese Diplomacy', where China deals with the world on its own terms.

For some partners, it demarcates new lines that accord them at least some territory, recognising a more flexible area than the vast Nine-Dash Line, which has been the cause of so much argument in the years before. For others, it works out resource-sharing and cooperation deals. In almost every case, it sells the arrangements back in Beijing as a new sign of the country's prowess and strength in the world, and evidence that it is winning against the American skein of alliances that has been set up around China to entrap and inhibit it.

With State Department muted and the US undergoing a complete reappraisal of its role in the world as a result of the election of Donald Trump, and with an even more unpleasant encounter imminent in late 2020, its commitment to the whole system of treaty alliances within the Asian region has been questioned. The American public, enduring their own economic and inequality woes – and continuously furious at their elites, especially in view of an unexpected, and deep, recession from mid-2019 – has grown weary with any forms of involvement or intervention that do not have an immediate relationship with their own interests.

A 'rescale' from 2019 communicated to countries like South Korea, Japan, the Philippines, and even Australia, states clearly that more is expected from them to support their security. Anger in the US at what have come to be called 'Asian free-loaders' means that China is able to spot a new strategic space. The question that has always been posed about whether the US will really come to the defence of partners in the region, if there is a potential conflict, now seems to have an increasingly clear answer – highly unlikely.

This is compounded by the fact that despite its poor

economic performance, China, like its neighbour and ally
Russia, has maintained steady commitments to its military;
it is confident now that it has one of the best prepared, most
advanced technically, and most effective fighting forces in
the world – a conviction not based on any recent combat
experience, and therefore all the harder to shift. The decades
of under-confidence are replaced in the military elites by an
almost light-headed conviction that they can do anything.
Behind this is also an eagerness by a generation of soldiers,
who have never properly seen a battlefield, to prove that they
are able to perform.

Australia – the Back Route to Taiwan

Xi Jinping's advisors have been focused on the issue of 'a
great historic prize' – something that proves irrefutably that
China is indeed, despite its stumbling economy, finally able
to sit once more at the centre of world affairs, as a respected,
feared and admired entity. In 2020, with the weight of expectation of the 2021 centennial goals only a year away, their
minds are grasping for one huge 'historic' hit – an event of
immense significance, which will show vividly and powerfully,
within and outside of China, the great renaissance of the
Chinese nation. An endpoint of its 'peaceful rise' talked of a
decade and a half before, a moment to close off the two
decades of strategic opportunity referred to by previous president Jiang Zemin at the turn of the millennium, and the
culmination of the language of historic destiny that Hu Jintao
had articulated.

Having cleared away all possible opposition within the
upper levels of the Chinese elite with a series of savagely
effective anti-corruption campaigns, and with no obvious
competitor, Xi's 'perpetual presidency', with his ability to

continue in power beyond 2022 when he is due to retire, becomes increasingly inevitable. But it needs a big event – one that will cement his place in history. But also one that has to be beyond the realm of economics. It has to be, his key advisors feel, something of historic proportions, which symbolises the end of the era of humiliation and its aftermath. Reunification is the core theme – and Taiwan sits at the heart of it.

Strategically, the Xi leadership has cleared the space around them for directly addressing Taiwan. The Belt and Road Initiative has symbolically mapped out the territory over which China wants to demonstrate increased hegemony, from its land neighbours to the vast maritime region. For Chinese strategic thinkers, it is the perfect means to demonstrate two key things: that the economic future of countries around it lies in the potential for assisting in creating further growth within China and benefiting from it, despite the recent challenges, and that China has the ability to cause them real damage if they do not consider its security demands more carefully.

They have the choice of investing in a future where their region is increasingly dominated by the stability, growth and power of China – or simply clinging on to a past where the US has been relied on, but where its real impact and commitment is weaker and weaker. US appetite for supplying vastly expensive public goods in Asia with no tangible direct benefit to its home population has waned. Increasingly there is talk of the US simply withdrawing from the region, scaling back its alliances system, and recalibrating its Pacific region policy.

The Belt and Road Initiative has involved building up a meaningful financial and investment architecture in the region. This means that, either openly or subliminally, China's name is everywhere, and its influence, negative and positive, is on everyone's minds. Countries in the Association of Southeast Asian Nations (ASEAN), and in South Asia, have to calculate the cost of displeasing their vast northern neighbour, with the increasingly popular theory that Xi is a man who really would press the red button if he felt thwarted or threatened. There are still more cautious people around Xi, however, who counsel against any bold moves – particularly on the issue of Taiwan. For them, it is unclear if the US would, or would not, move to protect the island.

Over the course of early 2020, a consensus among the Xi advisors starts to form. Military intervention in Taiwan, so close to home, against a people they regard as their own flesh and blood, is unthinkable. No one around Xi, except the most purblind and reckless, suggests taking this path. Not the least of the problems is that, despite all the bravado and hubris in the military, there is still too much uncertainty about whether they would even have the military capacity to undertake an air and amphibious attack across a hundred-kilometre stretch of water.

Instead of this crude approach, the suggestion handed to the Politburo for full discussion in mid-2020 is to use multiple levels of pressure. The region has been settled – there are larger and larger numbers of countries who have real doubt in their heads that the US will stand by its traditional security commitments. The Belt and Road Initiative, the huge investments, and the interlinkages and co-dependencies reinforce this. Attacking China would end up being the same as attacking themselves.

For Malaysia, Indonesia, and even the Philippines, struggling with their own interminable domestic issues, getting China off their backs by ceding it the one thing everyone knows it wants – control over Taiwan – is less and less ridiculous. In fact, in the ministries of foreign affairs across the capitals of these and other countries, it is regarded as a palatable way of delivering security. The real fear is that with the US withdrawing more, Japan rather than China will step in to fill the spaces – resurrecting deep antipathetic emotions from the war era decades before.

At the end of June, Xi Jinping meets with his core advisory team in Zhongnanhai, the central government compound in Beijing. They have received some intelligence at the highest level, which they wish to discuss with the normally reticent, paramount Chinese leader. As usual, he sits on his chair in the centre of the round table, with the other attendees from his closest foreign-policy advisor, Wang Huning, downwards, studying a brief report sent in from the embassy in Washington.

The Chinese ambassador had attended a formal dinner for the Chief Executive of the Hong Kong special administrative region arranged by the State Department, and had been placed next to the US Secretary of State. During the course of the dinner, the Secretary had confided in the ambassador the recent thinking in Washington as a result of a thorough review, on behalf of the President, of foreign-policy options for the upcoming election in 2020, where they were seeking a further four-year term.

It had become clear that domestic politics remained as angry and disenchanted with America's continuing prominent global role, and the costs on its economy, and that this was to play as big, if not a bigger role, in the campaign as it had in the fractious and ill-tempered one four years earlier. The notion was increasingly that America needed to rebalance and repivot – but towards itself and its own interests, rather than away from them.

When asked by the Chinese ambassador whether treaty commitments in the Pacific were included in this review, the Secretary of State had simply said, Yes, everything was included. He had looked at the Chinese ambassador while making this statement, leaving the diplomat with the conviction that this language about all treaties included the Taiwan Relations Act. This had been compounded a few days later, when requests for an upgrade of weaponry from the US to Taiwan were stalled by the administration in Washington.

The ambassador's words in the top-secret cable are unequivocal. There has been a clear sign that the US is wavering, and might even seek to downgrade its security commitments around Taiwan, as long as they can gain clear economic benefits from greater access to the Chinese market. 'Trump is a man who only understands the bottom line,' one advisor says. The implication is clear. Taiwan and its status are negotiable. This is a major opportunity.

Xi has remained characteristically opaque during this discussion over the cable's contents. For Wang Huning, whose expertise on the US was gleaned in a visit there thirty-five years before, the interpretation is simple – the Chinese have been given a clear sign that space is now opening up for them. This is the opportunity they have been waiting for. It is now incumbent on them to do everything they can to pressurise Taiwan to accept negotiations, with the clear outcome of a framework over fifty years for complete reunification. The model of Hong Kong and its one country, two systems, will be used.

Discussion of this evidently excites Xi and he interrupts.

'It is a great goal,' he says, 'one befitting the moment of China's renaissance and rebirth, a clear sign of the national regeneration dreamed of by all 1.4 billion Chinese. But,' and he pauses, catching everyone's attention, 'we cannot get this one wrong. If we miscalculate, if we misunderstand, the Americans will seize their chance to deal with us the way they dealt with the former Soviet Union.'

Then Xi admonishes his team, 'Remember, the soul of an American, underneath the smiles and friendliness, is the soul of a killer. Look what they did to their native population. Look how they behaved in Vietnam. Don't underestimate them.'

His words chill the meeting. But after a few seconds' pause, an elderly official, who has been brought back into the leadership advisory system as an academic and specialist advisor, breaks all protocol by speaking from the further end of the round table.

'There is an ancient Chinese saying, "If you want to hit the target in the west, make a sound in the east [声东击西 – *shendgong jixi*]",' he says.

Xi looks at him puzzled.

'To get Taiwan resolved, the road lies to the deep south, in the Pacific, where there is weakness now. Creating troubles there will mean resolutions back here.'

'Australia,' someone says.

Once more there is a long silence. But a meaningful, not a perplexed one. Australia's economic dependence on China has risen for a decade. It is seen as the American ally with the most exposure, because of its total reliance on the US for its security. It is also regarded as complacent, a place once so remote that it only ever saw a few skirmishes in the Second World War, the worst being the bombing by the Japanese of the northern city of Darwin.

'The Australian character is to think they are untouchable, living in their paradisical remote eyrie,' someone comments. Xi nods. He has been to every single state in the country. It is a place he feels he knows. A place regarded in the rest of the Asian region as an aberration, a white-dominated enclave, one that has the best of everything, and which has grown increasingly jealous of its position.

'What is more,' another advisor chips in, 'our intelligence shows that the Canberra government are already convinced we are working to destabilise them through supporting refugee ships coming from Indonesia. If we are being blamed, we may as well do something to merit the blame.'

Xi says nothing to this comment, but simply gives a wry smile.

New Alliances, New Moves

The final consensus of the meeting is simple to summarise. Aggression by China towards Australia would catch the rest of the world, and particularly the US, on the back foot. It would be something no one had ever expected. But it also makes strategic sense. It is adventurism far enough away from China to have little chance of adversely affecting it in its core area of interest. In stirring up trouble in this area, it will be able to focus the minds of the US and its fair-weather alliance system on what they are really willing to sacrifice in order to maintain their most important interests. It will be a safe way of testing the true resolve of the American Pacific system. Even more appealingly, it offers a chance for the Chinese navy and its splendid new kit to prove what they are really capable of.

This is truly a win-win situation – one where China stands to win twice! Once it has demonstrated its military capability, China will be able to put a deal with Taiwan on the table that it demands to have taken seriously – a deal the rest of the world, and especially the US, will find deeply appealing when they see the potential scope of China's abilities and how much chaos it could cause in the deep Pacific if its interests are not listened to.

A few weeks later, the stand-off over a large vessel with as many as 700 refugees caught in the region around the Arafura and Timor Sea, between Indonesia and the northern coast of Australia, becomes global news. For the Abbott government, looking to burnish its reputation as being the toughest ever on illegal migration, this is the case that it cannot lose. But the fact that as many as three-quarters of those on the vessel are apparently from Indonesia itself is a major problem. So too are the accusations by the Australian government of complicity amongst Indonesian security officials and high-level politicians in the event. It is regarded as flagrant provocation, with the more right-wing parts of the Australian parliament vehemently denouncing any moves to accommodate the ship, which is running low on fuel and food, but refuses to turn back.

Indonesia has never enjoyed a trouble-free relationship with China. But the suggestion, through the visit by a delegation of top Chinese military officials to Jakarta in late July, that in this case China stands on the side of Asian interests, and that Australia is violating and insulting Indonesia's national integrity and sovereignty, has deep resonance in the country. China has already committed large amounts of investments there through the Asian Infrastructure Investment Bank. It has donated increasing amounts of aid, and has proved generous in its developmental advice and assistance.

For most Indonesians, the growth of living standards and the rise of Chinese power are something they have increasingly admired. China's overtures in mid-2020 fall on fertile ground. The idea of a unified response to the outrageous, provocative behaviour by the Abbott adventurist government is welcomed – especially as there is a conviction that with Chinese diplomatic and military support, the Australians will immediately back down and grant concessions, relaxing some of their intrusive behaviour and reviewing their migration policy.

These views are only reinforced when two more ships,

with smaller groups of people, are simply rammed back to the direction from which they have come, with the smaller of them capsizing, leading to the necessity of local ships having to rescue the drowning passengers. The greatest impetus, however, comes from a similar incident some days later, when another smaller vessel, this time with refugees who have transited Indonesia from the Middle East, many of them Syrian and Iraqi, gets into trouble and then sinks, killing all thirty on board.

The Indonesian and Australian press scream that what is happening on the seas is a war in all but name. On the morning of 30 July 2020, the worst outcome happens, with the largest of the vessels, the one carrying 700 people, developing a large leak in its hull, which causes the whole ship to sink within a few minutes, taking its living cargo with it to the sea's depths. No one survives.

The cacophony of international condemnation following this tragedy convinces the leadership in Beijing that now is the time to move. Readying five of their eight new-generation, 'Shang' nuclear-attack submarines and their refitted Liaoning aircraft carrier, along with three of their brand-new Luyang destroyers, the Chinese move swiftly into the area. The other vessels of the People's Liberation Army Navy are put on high alert, with frigates, destroyers and missile boats massing in Hainan, the southernmost island from China's coast, then moving slowly down the South China Sea.

The sight of China's new naval assets sends a shock wave across the world – a vivid image of its newfound prowess. Campaigns to whip up public support are run across China, with demonstrations in Beijing, Shanghai, and every major city, demanding that other Asians show heartfelt commitment to the struggle by each other to be freed of the yoke of US interference, and to show solidarity with Indonesia as it faces down the bullying, illegal, threatening behaviour of America's chief 'lackey' (as the official Chinese press call it) in the region, Abbott's Australia.

Tony Abbott is soon contending, not just with the escalating regional crisis, but with a series of massive demonstrations against the inhumanity of his government's attitude towards refugees. Suspicions amongst the Australian security services that many of these are infiltrated by pro-Beijing forces is partly verified by evidence of massive transfers of money to a Sydney businessman of Chinese ethnicity, who is regarded as being profoundly patriotic – to his ancestral country.

The issue of the divided allegiances of Australia's Chinese community becomes a constant feature of press commentary and discussion. A rise in ugly, racially motivated attacks and tensions focuses on the amount of real estate and property that the Chinese have bought in Australian cities. Some of these houses are firebombed. One ethnic Chinese student is murdered by a group of racist thugs in Sydney. In China, there are massive demonstrations outside the Australian embassies and consulates across the country.

For the USA, the initial response is disbelief. How, strategists ask, has China managed to forge this unlikely alliance with a power like Indonesia? How has it managed to placate, silence and mollify players across the Asian region, who simply sit on the sidelines as the face-off between Australian and Indonesian–Chinese forces intensifies?

The real issue, however, as commanders and analysts quickly recognise, is that America is now, for the first time since the Korean War seventy years before, directly facing Chinese military and naval forces. Sending its key Seventh Fleet aircraft carrier and submarines into the area, the predominant attitude of the administration is to avoid, at all costs, being sucked into a conflict that can get out of hand.

The assumption is that once the US come to the side of Australia, the Chinese will back off.

~

The Chinese do not back off. The support whipped up amongst the public in China means that the government in Beijing has no way of climbing down. Victory for the US in this encounter would mean that they had not cleared the final hurdle lying between them and the Great Nation Renaissance planned the following year. It would also put back claims on Taiwan by decades. These are seen as existential threats to the regime, and ones it has to oppose whatever the cost.

On the night of 9 August, President Xi Jinping is woken at three in the morning. He has been briefed on the tense stand-off between American and Chinese–Indonesian forces in the region. It is a huge surprise. The American position has been misunderstood, and the level of their commitment underestimated. Eight of their aircraft carriers have now arrived. Their military assets are now massing in Australia. They have demanded support from Japan, South Korea, Taiwan, Malaysia down to Indonesia – and have imposed immediate travel, trade and finance restrictions after what they have labelled 'unprovoked acts', and which one senior official has come close to labelling as 'war'. A new Pearl Harbor is being talked about in the US, with an immediate swing in public opinion to support Washington dealing with Beijing once and for all.

'President Xi,' the aide says, standing by his bed. 'We have just had a report in. One of our submarines has fired on an American vessel. We aren't sure of the details. We only know it was a strike. Washington has declared war. We are getting reports of them shelling our carrier. Their forces are moving into our waters around Taiwan island. There are Japanese vessels coming close to our waters near the Northern Ports. The British, too, are saying that they will stand by their security alliance with the Americans and the Australians, and are sending aircraft across from their bases. They are saying that they will demand NATO also act. We need a command, Mr President, we need a command to act.'

The President does not respond at first, but sits up in bed, then simply says, 'Get the Politburo. Get all of them immediately.' When the aide goes, he looks down at his wife, who is now also awake.

'What is it?' she asks.

He pauses for a moment, before he replies, 'We have just got something terribly wrong.'

CHAPTER 4

THE AFGHAN FACTOR
Indo-Pakistani Confrontation

The History

Parts of Afghanistan and Pakistan have been steeped in violence for centuries. Knowing something of the region's long history is a prerequisite to understanding the area and the tensions for which it has become infamous. In terms of conflict and empire-building, Afghanistan can boast a veritable 'Who's Who' of invaders including Darius I, Alexander the Great, Mahmoud Ghazni, Genghis Khan, Muhammad Ghori, Tamerlane and Babur, who crossed through the Khyber Pass in 1526 *en route* to establishing the Moghul empire in India.

The modern state of Afghanistan was founded in 1747 by Ahmad Shah Durrani, a former commander in the Persian Nader Shah's army. At its high point, Ahmad Shah's own empire would become one of the largest in the world and extend from the Amu Darya River in Central Asia to the Indian Ocean and from Khorasan into Kashmir, Punjab and Sindh.

Following a series of conflicts during the nineteenth century Afghanistan acquired the rather dubious soubriquet 'graveyard of empires', having been a focal point in the 'Great Game' in which Britain and Russia vied for supremacy. Three Anglo-Afghan wars were fought (1839–42, 1878–80 and

1919) and the USSR would, of course, face defeat in its own Afghan adventure of 1979–89. In the course of the latter, Pakistan would seek to exert its own influence under the umbrella of the CIA's Operation Cyclone, intended to build up local resistance to the Soviet occupation and reportedly funded to the tune of $20 billion or more from various sources. The Pakistan Inter-Services Intelligence (ISI), supported by the Home Minister, also recruited a large number of Pashtuns from among the refugees who had fled the conflict and about 100,000 militants were trained and dispatched to Afghanistan. This gave Pakistan unprecedented inroads into the internal politics and governmental mechanisms of Afghanistan, but had a secondary destabilising effect by introducing a Takfiri form of Islam alien to the country.

Modern-day Afghanistan's plethora of internal divisions are an enduring legacy of such foreign 'hard' and 'soft' interventions, with adjacent countries and local warlords having carved out spheres of influence in the region. Iran cultivated the Tajiks and Shia Hazaras in western Afghanistan using Ismail Khan from Herat; Uzbekistan nurtured General Rashid Dostum and Commander Mohammad Atta; and Pakistan incubated several fiefdoms in the Pashtun areas including the Taliban, the Haqqani Network and others. All of this activity and competition resulted in the fracturing of the country into numerous, frequently inimical ethnic groupings including Pashtuns, Uzbeks, Tajiks, Hazaras, Takfiris and others, leading to deep-rooted mutual suspicions and endemic instability.

~

With the Taliban unbowed and locked in a power struggle with the government in Kabul, Afghanistan is rife with instability. Pakistan's ISI continues to exercise covert control and direct the Taliban forces in Afghanistan, using it as a proxy and thereby allowing the Pakistani military to maintain its conventional strength along its eastern border with India, where the relationship with its neighbour remains highly militarised.

Perhaps the most enduring consequence is the enmity between the Afghan government in Kabul and Pakistan dating largely from two episodes. The first of these was the drawing of the Durand Line as long ago as 1893 – a 2,500-kilo-metre-long border with Pakistan that arbitrarily divided the Pashtun heartlands, separated Baluchistan from the Pashtuns and, crucially, deprived Afghanistan of any access to the Arabian Sea. The Line is disputed by Afghanistan to this day, having already fuelled the Third Afghan War of 1919 and causing Afghanistan to oppose Pakistan's accession to the United Nations in 1947. For its part, Pakistan is under-standably hostile to any suggestion that its border should be redrawn to appease Afghanistan, as to do so would be to surrender around sixty per cent of its present territory. The second catalyst for hostility came during the Cold War era when Islamabad, a key US ally, created and financed the Taliban to subvert the Soviet occupation.

A cornerstone of Pakistan's foreign policy has been to ensure that Afghanistan remains a weak, client regime. Pakistan's intelligence agencies, both the ISI and its Intelligence Bureau, have allegedly used Afghanistan to equip and train terrorist elements and deploy them west into Afghanistan and east into India to agitate the Kashmir issue. The years of chaos following the fall of the Najibullah regime in Kabul in 1992 were used by Pakistan to emerge as the Taliban's primary patron, enabling the free movement of the likes of Osama bin Laden, Ayman al-Zawahiri and the Arab Mujahideen.

Predictably, Afghanistan emerged as a veritable crucible for terrorism, sponsoring the Islamic Movement of Uzbekistan, the

East Turkestan Movement and various franchises of al-Qaeda. Mohammad Zarqawi honed his skills in Herat before returning to Iraq to establish al-Qaeda in Iraq (AQI), the precursor of the so-called Islamic State of Iraq and the Levant (ISIL) or Daesh. Zarqawi's assistant in Herat was none other than Abu Bakr al Baghdadi who became leader of ISIL in 2014. Their global terrorist network became so deeply entrenched in the Afghanistan–Pakistan (Af-Pak) region that even Operation Enduring Freedom, the US response to the 9/11 attacks, would eventually fail to dislodge it. One need only look to the Mumbai attack on 26 November 2008 by Lashkar-e-Taiba and the assault on the Indian Embassy in Kabul on 7 July 2008 for evidence of quite how effective the various regional terrorist groupings and operations had become.

Further evidence for Pakistan's involvement in Afghanistan came on 2 May 2011 as Osama bin Laden was killed in Abbottabad, a military cantonment of Pakistan and then, in May 2015, when the National Directorate of Security (NDS) in Afghanistan announced that Mullah Omar, declared Amir-ul-Momineen of the Taliban, had died in Peshawar in 2013 – the ISI having conducted an elaborate charade about his activities for over two years. Pakistan's international credibility thus weakened, its ties with the US began to fray, culminating in the refusal of a US $300 million package to fund the supply of F-16 combat aircraft. The US report on Pakistan states unambiguously that:

> Pakistan did not take substantial action against the Afghan Taliban or the Haqqani Network (HQN), or substantially limit their ability to threaten US interests in Afghanistan, although Pakistan supported efforts to bring both groups into an Afghan-led peace process. Pakistan has also not taken sufficient action against other externally focused groups such

as Lashkar-e-Taiba (LeT) and Jaish-e-Mohammad (JeM), which continued to operate, train, organise, and fundraise in Pakistan.

Despite this, Hafiz Sayed, a known terrorist with a bounty of $10 million on his head, is able to move around Pakistan with impunity while openly acknowledging his links to terrorists in India. To the west, the President of Afghanistan, Ashraf Ghani, who had tried hard to normalise ties with Pakistan, has claimed that the attack on a Hazara procession in Kabul in July 2016 was jointly planned by the ISI and LeT. Internally, there are persistent accusations of complicity among Pakistan's armed services, a prime example being the aborted September 2014 attack on PNS *Zulfiqar* in the Karachi dockyard. It was subsequently revealed that the attackers' plan had been to hijack the warship and use it to attack US Navy patrol vessels in the Indian Ocean. Five Pakistani naval personnel were apprehended and charged with mutiny and having links to Islamic State and their interrogations revealed the extent of radicalisation within the Armed Forces.

Even so, the ISI's relationship with the Taliban remains uneasy, the latter remaining resentful of Islamabad's manipulations. A faction under the leadership of Baitullah Mehsud broke away to form the Tehreek-e-Taliban Pakistan (TTP) in 2007, headed by Mullah Fazlullah after 2013 when Mehsud was killed in a drone strike. Since then Mullah Fazlullah has been uncompromising about striking at Pakistani interests. Further factions have emerged, such as Jamaat-ul-Arhar, headed by Omar Khalid Kharasani and the Tariq Gidar group headed by Umar Mansoor. These groups have perpetrated acts of terror against Shiites and Ismailis, on educational institutes, on a military school in Peshawar, on Bacha Khan University, Peshawar and on Jinnah International Airport, Karachi.

In response Islamabad activated the anti-terrorist Operation Zarb-e-Azb in June 2014 in the North-West Frontier Province (NWFP) and a nationwide initiative against terrorism, all concentrating on groups mounting operations in Pakistan while largely ignoring those active in Afghanistan. Consequently, the Haqqani Network, the LeT and the Taliban have been left almost unscathed to continue their operations in Afghanistan, while hundreds of Uighurs, Islamic Movement of Uzbekistan and TTP cadres have been killed or pursued across the Durand Line only to provoke armed conflicts with the established local Taliban and create a fertile recruiting ground for IS. At the same time, the pressure being applied to IS in Iraq and Syria has led to an influx of battle-hardened cadres into the region.

The theological basis of a popular Hadith endorsed by Prophet Mohammad states that the apocalyptic final war, the Ghazwa-e-Hind, will begin in portions of Iran, Uzbekistan, Turkmenistan, the entirety of Afghanistan and Pakistan as well as the north-west portion of India. A relative newcomer to the scene, Wilayat Khorasan (ISIL-K), has absorbed battle-hardened Central Asian and Uighur cadres and has been able to capture and hold small pockets in the Nangarhar and Kunar provinces of Afghanistan.

In concert with the volatile mixture on the Pakistan–Afghanistan border, the persistent tensions between India and Pakistan in the Kashmir region are yet another source of tension. Pakistan-backed separatists have fed a confrontational narrative into the valley, espousing the same Takfiri form of Islam that contributed to Afghanistan's destabilisation. There is also evidence of financial irregularity: India's National Investigation Agency (NIA) has tracked some twenty-two bank accounts in south Kashmir that have received money from unaccounted sources. A case in point is JKART (Jammu

Kashmir Affectees Relief Trust), a Pakistan-based organisation floated by Syed Salahuddin and sponsored by the ISI.
According to the NIA, around Rs 80-crore (£6 million) were
routed through JKART to India into various accounts over
an eight-year period.

The Nuclear Factor

Set against this backdrop is the ever-present issue of nuclear
weapons. Estimates by reputable bodies suggest that Pakistan
has one of the fastest-growing nuclear arsenals in the world.
India is likewise a nuclear power, but Pakistan alone has a
first-use policy, flaunting the Hatf-IX Nasr (Vengeance-IX
Victory) short-range, surface-to-surface missile designed
specifically for battlefield use. If India should attempt to
reclaim disputed territory then the possibility is that Pakistan
might reply with nuclear weapons, especially in view of India's
superiority in conventional weapons. With the received
thinking being that an all-out war with its eastern neighbour
would present it with an existential dilemma, Pakistan is
convinced that the use of short-range tactical nuclear weapons
may be its only recourse in the event of a determined Indian
assault.

Pakistan maintains that it operates a highly centralised
command-and-control system when it comes to the use of
nuclear weapons. Nevertheless, the use of these weapons by
relatively low-level field commanders has reportedly been
visualised by the Pakistani military leadership. And in the
face of various domestic and international threats there could
be strong domestic public support for the use of tactical
nuclear weapons. The inherent risks are clear: terror groups
that have infiltrated the Pakistani Army could potentially
instigate a nuclear weapons launch.

The Water Factor

Of the five river basins in Afghanistan the Kabul River basin is of critical importance, covering twelve per cent of Afghanistan and providing for thirty-five per cent of the population, covering about twenty-six per cent of the country's overall needs. Kabul's lifeline, the basin also has very advantageous topography for the development of water storage and hydropower projects.

India, a significant donor to Afghanistan's reconstruction and humanitarian aid, assisted in building the Salma Dam (officially the Afghan–India Friendship Dam) on the Hari River in Herat province and this now provides both electricity to thousands of homes and essential irrigation for its agricultural needs. But India's assistance has also had the effect of weakening Pakistan's lower riparian position. With renewed efforts to build dams on the western rivers in Kashmir and its footprint on the Kabul River, India is now in a position to limit the flow in the rivers reaching Pakistan from both sides. With World Bank funding and technical support from India, four dams are currently under construction in the Panjshir sub-basin of the Kabul River, including the 200 MW Totumdara, the 100 MW Barak, the 100 MW Panjshir and the 210 MW Baghdara. Each of these projects also provides substantial storage capacity. Without its own dams, Pakistan will soon be forced to buy electricity from Afghanistan.

Pakistan and Afghanistan share nine rivers including the Kabul and the Chitral. The latter has its source in Pakistan and after entering Afghanistan it joins the Kabul River near Jalalabad before re-entering Pakistan. The Kabul and Kunar eventually become part of the Indus River system and are critical drivers in relations between the two countries. Within the disputed territory of Kashmir the rivers flowing through it are the subject of military planning. The 1960 Indus Waters Treaty (IWT) governing the apportioning of the Indus River system is under pressure. Given Pakistan's dubious record concerning regional terrorism, India is reportedly considering whether to withdraw from various bilateral agreements, and perhaps even to abrogate the IWT.

In the interim India argues that it is seeking ways to improve the application of the IWT and fulfil its provisions. India has accelerated its programme of dam building and creating storage facilities on the western rivers (Jhelum and Chenab). Interpreted by Pakistan as a hostile act, India has also terminated the Permanent Indus Commission – a dispute-resolution mechanism which Pakistan had previously used to oppose the hydro projects in Kashmir. Likewise, on the eastern rivers (Beas, Ravi and Sutlej) and following the provisions of the Treaty, India has started creating infrastructure to optimise use of the river water, including the desilting of canals and improving structures at the headworks of the eastern rivers. Pakistan's vulnerability is obvious in that the volume of water flow in the rivers' lower reaches may come under threat as a consequence of India's actions.

The Build-Up

With Pakistan–Afghanistan relations at a low ebb and the TTP wreaking havoc in Peshawar, Lahore and even Islamabad, the Army is also facing considerable public criticism. Vertical splits emerge and several officers have even defected to the Taliban. More significantly, with IS having lost territory further afield, thousands of Mujahideen now enter the Af-Pak region and merge with al-Qaeda, thereby entrenching terrorist groups not only in NWFP, but even in Karachi and Lahore. The Army attempts a coup and chaos ensues. Sensing an opportunity, al-Qaeda is attempting to gain territory in Pakistan-occupied Kashmir and the Kashmir valley, working closely with the LeT.

Also taking advantage of the turmoil, Indian forces retake Muzzafarabad, the second-largest city in Azad Jammu Kashmir, with little effort and now threaten Gilgit-Baltistan via Kargil. This proves more difficult as Pakistan complains to the UN Security Council and a subsequent resolution requires the immediate suspension of hostilities. Indian military operations result in large parts of Pakistan-occupied Kashmir being taken, with the exceptions of Aksai Chin and the Shaksgam Valley.

Combined cadres of the Taliban and al-Qaeda in the Peshawar Shura have moved to neutralise the Durand Line in an attempt to create a Caliphate along strict Islamic lines in the Pashtun-dominated areas. They name the West, Russia and India as legitimate targets and the potential of lone-wolf or wolf-pack attacks rises exponentially. The US moves to secure Pakistan's nuclear arsenal, most of which is located around Islamabad, but they do not move quickly enough: the fledgling Caliphate has already seized several low-yield tactical nuclear weapons from Kahuta, Punjab, with the help of Army regulars and the LeT. The weapons are used to blackmail India into ceding Kashmir.

The Scenario

15 December 2020, Kabul. Two powerful blasts kill over 200 people, one in front of the National Directorate of Security (NDS) and another between the ISAF HQ and the US Embassy. The US First Secretary's car is found damaged and abandoned near the Soccer Stadium.

Kabul in December is cruel. The winter winds from the Hindu Kush Mountains bring sleet, snow and slush, creating treacherous stretches of mud and ice on the roads. Come evening there is a frantic rush to catch the buses taking office staff home from the National Directorate of Security (NDS), the Ministry of Interior Affairs and the presidential palace, the Arg.

With people so distracted by the cold, the SUV flying the Afghan flag – but with no windscreen or rear glass – passes by without attracting attention. Its driver and passengers have assault rifles sticking out of the vehicle, and are carrying bulky backpacks. The vehicle stops and the gunmen fan out. When it comes the violence of the attack is appalling, culminating in a series of explosions as each man detonates his backpack. Dealing with the casualties and damage is one thing, but the source of the attack and its political fallout are the incident's most significant after-effects.

It's not over yet. As the Kabul police and Army rush to the spot the terrorists, using the shift in focus, strike again at 17.35 Kabul time, in a narrow lane adjacent to the US embassy. Using an Afghan military vehicle, they breach the US Embassy's perimeter defence and kill the troops on guard duty. The vehicle explodes close to the fuel terminal, causing carnage. Fire rages through the embassy living quarters. The result is pandemonium – and a very high number of casualties.

The present Afghan President is a Pashtun from Nangarhar Province. The Director of the NDS, dishevelled and bleeding with minor cuts, sits opposite him beside the Interior Minister. Afghans have learnt to accept loss of life with stoicism, but they also know that the wrath of the international community carries a heavy price.

The President recalls a conversation with his US counterpart four years previously, in the course of which the hard-line Western leader had warned him, 'Keep in mind the current Asian tradition: China, Japan and India put in power authoritarian centralisers, who present themselves as strong leaders, and who rely on ultra-nationalism for legitimacy. You could say that we, and to an extent some of our allies in Europe, have followed the Asian tradition. Both India and China have no choice but to undertake major internal restructuring of their economies – they are at a crossroads, a moment of transformation. Understandably, their core interests come first.

'So, expect to see China deepening its commitment to Pakistan: look at Xinjiang and the China–Pakistan Economic Corridor. China is now interested in Pakistan's stability, not to counter India, but for herself. India's economy is facing growing pains, Kabul is emotionally and politically important, but the Indian economy has no space for an "albatross". And in Washington, head-hunting is the new political sport. We need to look inwards now. Tolerance for body bags is at an all-time low, and I am seriously reconsidering our support for NATO, and whether to wind down the remains of the US mission in Afghanistan. You need to take charge of your own country and your own future.'

Paling beneath his thick, grey beard, the Afghan President had protested, 'Mr President, your withdrawal now would mean the end of Afghanistan as we know it. "Take charge of your country" is hollow advice. Pakistan has nourished and sponsored not only the Taliban, but a host of other recidivist groups, who control over forty-five per cent of our territory. Tribal leaders along the Durand Line are assassinated if they do not pay due homage to the Haqqani Network, who operate like a Sicilian clan and are beyond reproach.

'Our Afghan National Security Forces are still at little more than a constabulary level, yet we are expecting them to confront battle-hardened terrorists, armed to the teeth, often with stolen US arms, and trained by the Pakistan army. No country in the history of the world has faced an attrition rate like the ANSF. Mr President, please also keep in mind that extremism cannot be kept in a container, held by terrorists. The public is becoming influenced. The situation in Afghanistan has deteriorated since the US and Saudi Arabia began Operation Cyclone and established the Taliban and al-Qaeda as a counter to the Soviets.

'Narcotics smugglers are the new, parvenu warlords. Pashtun nationalism is fuelled by Takfiri Islam. This is going to affect us badly, as well as Pakistan. Mullahs are using an apocalyptic discourse about the "end of times", quoting the Quran. Anti-US and anti-India diatribes are in all the *khutbahs* during the Friday prayers. We need help now; we have an existential threat; a threat you have a responsibility to contain, for history cannot just be washed away.'

The US President subsequently agreed to revitalise the US military presence in Afghanistan until 2022, and thereafter to continue its support of the Afghan Government with airpower, but not with a large-scale deployment of ground forces. The outcome was analogous to life support via an intravenous drip; keeping the patient alive, but only barely.

By this time the NDS chief has learned that four of his officers from the Pakistan Desk were killed in the blast. Was this a targeted killing? The officers had penetrated the Taliban/al-Qaeda's elite group the 'Lashkar-e-Qamiyah' (Army for Resurrection), which comprises cadres from the now-defunct Islamic State, Taliban, al-Qaeda and LeT (Pakistan). The group is educated, does its money transactions in crypto-currency from Dubai and Karachi and has an excellent communication system, which can be operated on Bluetooth.

The NDS team said that they were planning a *Naqbah* – a devastation – and it did not sound as if this was the usual apocalyptic rhetoric.

The Afghan President rues the West's lack of vision, and the fondness of its commentariat for ignorant clichés such as 'You cannot buy a Pashtun, but you can rent one.' They do not understand the conflicting Pakhtunkhwa traits of cunning, necessary for survival in the inhospitable Hindu Kush area, and the tradition of blind loyalty ingrained in tribal culture.

As expected, an agitated US ambassador arrives at the presidential palace, but with much more than the attack on his mind: the deputy chief of the CIA unit in Afghanistan, working under the cover of a First Secretary, Consular, has been kidnapped, and his car abandoned at the Kabul football stadium; the same place that witnessed the public hangings during the Taliban regime in the late 1990s. A message has been placed by the terrorists saying that if they wish to see the officer again, the US is required to: (i) withdraw forthwith from Afghanistan and stop interfering in Pakistan; (ii) cease transshipments of nuclear reactors to India; and (iii) force India to give up Kashmir. All this, or face an ordeal by fire. The message is accompanied by pictures of the officer photo-shopped onto the image of Daniel Pearl, the *Wall Street Journal* journalist murdered in Pakistan in 2002.

Claims for responsibility do not come from the usual suspects and chatter referring to any of the three incidents has not been picked up by the monitoring agencies. This is not surprising as the jihadis are adept at adding encrypted add-ons to existing platforms, making messages difficult to decipher in real time and forcing the intelligence agencies to rely on the often-discredited human intelligence (HUMINT).

In Chicken Street, the busiest market in Kabul, the

Intelligence wing of the Indian embassy is working overtime. The CIA officer had been kidnapped just after meeting his Afghan counterpart and the information he had given, a message from a contact in the NDS, was confused: a shadowy group, the Lashkar-e-Qamiyah (LeQ) was planning an attack 'which will bring the Kafir to his knees, cringing for mercy. The power of the "Zlatoy Khram" will be over.'

'No idea what this means, if this is a code . . . we need time,' the NDS contact was reported to have said. Immediate alerts are sent to the security establishments in New Delhi.

17 December
The bombings and the kidnapping of a US diplomat on 15 December quickly fade from public memory, overshadowed by the possibility of yet more terrorist attacks: Port Qassim in Pakistan has been attacked and terrorists in double motor-driven dhows have used the shallow and difficult routes through the adjacent mangrove forests, up the Phitti and Khuddi creeks, to overcome and kill an unprepared contingent of Coast Guard and Naval personnel. They have seized a tactical nuclear weapon as it was being unloaded from a North Korean ship, the *Ru Hyong*. The US and Indian agencies pick up agitated chatter on the Pakistani Coast Guard link referring to the loss of a high-value item from the ship.

Pakistan's Inter Services Public Relations (ISPR) tries to explain away the incident as a minor scuffle between local thieves. But a rapid contradiction comes from the al-Qaeda mouthpiece, *as-Sahab*, declaring triumphantly that the terrorist group the LeQ now possesses a nuclear weapon. They publish a photograph of the warhead, showing it to be about one metre in height and half a metre in diameter, in a machined ballistic casing.

18 December

An urgent inquiry conducted by the International Atomic Energy Agency, in conjunction with various international intelligence agencies, uncovers the supply chain. The bill of lading described the weapon as a power-plant part with the end-user shown to be Pakistan's Water and Power Development Agency (WAPDA). The consignment was shipped from Beijing to Pyongyang and then on to Karachi, to be sold on to WAPDA.

American and German intelligence agencies believe the tactical warhead to be part-payment for the Pakistan Atomic Energy Commission (PAEC)'s supply to North Korea of specialised nickel-alloy metals (Inconel and Monel), which are non-corrosive and used in centrifuges and vacuum-induction melting (VIM) furnaces.

In New Delhi, the Indian security establishment hastens to complete the jigsaw, establishing linkages between the three incidents in Afghanistan and the Port Qassim theft. India's head of External Intelligence reports in sober terms: 'We need to understand that the Pakistani security establishment is not a monolith, but split vertically with over forty per cent of its personnel radicalised. Previously, service officers have colluded with terrorists in the attack on the Mehran base and the attempt to commandeer the ship PNS *Zulfiqar*, which was carrying cruise missiles. The US claim that nuclear weapons were safe in Pakistan was never accepted. Now the LeQ has stolen a warhead from the most vulnerable point, when it was covertly entering the country. This means that sections of terrorists have links into not only the Navy, but also in the PAEC and the Prime Minister's office.'

The Indian Prime Minister asks for advice as to likely developments. 'Do you have information on this group the

LeQ? Have you been able to break the code – what does "Zlatoy Khram" mean?'

The exhausted External Intelligence Chief regrets that he cannot provide adequate responses. The Foreign Secretary speaks up, 'Sir, while I have no knowledge of codes, the term means "Golden Temple" in Russian. Perhaps the LeQ intends to target Amritsar?'

The shocked silence is broken by the External Intelligence Chief. 'After ISIL lost Mosul in Iraq and Raqqa in Syria there was a movement of highly trained cadres to the Af-Pak region, including Caucasians. We were especially worried about Gulmorod Khalimov. He is Tajik and was the former head of the Tajik Special Forces, before he chose to defect to ISIL. He assumed command of ISIL after Omar Shishani, another Caucasian, was killed. Gulmorod is reputed to be very tech-savvy and has even been trained by the US and NATO armed forces. He worked in southern Tajikistan and is well aware of all the infiltration routes through the Wakhan corridor. We have uncorroborated reports suggesting that he is now in Af-Pak, possibly in Kurram Agency, which would give him the best access to Kabul.'

The Prime Minister and his advisors then discuss the nuclear threat and the possibility that India might decide to launch a second strike in response to any nuclear attack from Pakistani territory. The Army Chief recommends a close watch to monitor the deployment of Hatf-IX missiles on the border.

The discussion is interrupted by a CNN news flash. The American First Secretary, with hands bound behind his back and kneeling in front of four masked men carrying Kalashnikovs, speaks to the cameras in a dazed voice. 'I request that India withdraws all its troops from Kashmir and allows its merger with Pakistan. Fail to do this and we will destroy the Indian State. There will be no further warnings. You have twenty-four hours to respond, after which I will be killed.'

'Put me on the Hotline,' insists the PM.

Indian Military Intelligence reports unusual movements within Pakistan's 6th Armoured Division, based in Gujranwala, Punjab Province. An artillery battery, or part of one, has been detected moving towards the Indian border in the Ramgarh sector.

'We cannot wait like sitting ducks for them to strike,' declares the Air Force Chief. 'But there will be huge international pressure on us to act responsibly and with restraint. Pakistan will claim that it has no involvement and will remind the world that it has already lost many men in Port Qassim.'

The Defence Minister is thoughtful. 'Our No First Use policy is concerned with the prospect of a state attack. But if we are dealing with a renegade element of some sort we cannot apply the same rules. I would suggest, Prime Minister, that we rethink the No First Use policy and launch a pre-emptive strike.'

The room falls silent.

CHAPTER 5

THE CALIPHATE RESURRECTED
Cairo in Chaos

The History

Looking back from 2020, three years have passed since what many, erroneously, described as the 'end of the Islamic State', as the cities of Mosul and Raqqa were liberated from their vicious rule. The military side of the operation to remove the Islamic State from the stronghold of Mosul, in Iraq, which had started in October 2016, had proceeded well enough. Against all the odds, the US and her allies had managed to persuade, cajole, and threaten Iraq's multiplicity of political interest groups – including government forces, Kurdish *peshmerga*, and Shi'i militias mainly loyal to Iran – to act in coordination with each other to remove what was seen by the US, if not by Iraqis, as the prime enemy. Raqqa was more problematic, due to the sensitivity of having US and Western forces work closely with the Syrian Democratic Forces (SDF) and their pre-eminent outfit, the Kurdish People's Protection Units (YPG). Turkish opposition meant that the progress to liberate Raqqa was haphazard but, ultimately, the city would fall.

By mid-2017, Mosul had fallen to the Golden Division of the ISF less than 100 days in to the Trump presidency, much to the aggravation of former President Obama, who had hoped it would happen before he left office, granting him one more military success to match his neutralising of Osama bin Laden. The timing, though, could not have been better for newly inaugurated President Trump, who quickly positioned himself to take the glory.

Conclusive though the retaking of Mosul was, it was not an easy undertaking. Islamic State fighters were doughty in their resilience, their command and control was exceptionally well organised, and their evacuation planning – perhaps designed in conjunction with one, if not more, regional powers – was expertly conceived. True, many hundreds of Islamic State fighters were killed during the heavy street-to-street fighting that engulfed Mosul in those dark days of November and December; but nowhere near the numbers that Western analysts believed would have perished. And, tellingly, the key leadership figures of the Islamic State – including the most capable of the *walis*, the key intelligence figures, the former Saddam generals, and the key confidants of the self-proclaimed Caliph, were never accounted for. Displaying all the skills and attributes that had led his fighters, CIA analysts, and Shi'i militiamen alike over the years to nickname him 'The Ghost', no sighting was ever made of Caliph Ibrahim, otherwise known as Abu Bakr al-Baghdadi.

The Israelis were adamant that Abu Bakr had been spirited out of Tal Afar, a town to the west of Mosul, earlier in November 2016 by Iranian special forces of the Al-Quds brigade. Operating within the ranks of the brutal Shi'i *Asaib ahl al-Haq* militia, as their most highly valued agent, Abu Bakr's role was to shatter any possibility of Sunni Arab unity, before turning against the State of Israel herself. Similarly, the Iranians were utterly convinced that US covert forces, with Israeli and Turkish connivance, had spirited Abu Bakr and his cohorts out of Mosul, perhaps many weeks before the October 2016 assault had even commenced, such was the absolute lack of visibility of him and his key compatriots.

Other eyewitness reports suggested that instead he found a way to return to Raqqa, in Syria, before simply evaporating into thin air. Whatever opinion is held on the matter, the fact remained that Mosul had been retaken by mid-2017, but the leadership of the Islamic State stayed elusively free thereafter. And if the Arabic for the Islamic State was correctly translated, given its original meaning from the time of the Abbasid Caliphate, as the *dynasty* rather than the *state*, then the Islamic State, albeit now without territory, still had very potent and real meaning. It could be sown once again among Sunni Muslims, who had been marginalised, dispossessed, disenfranchised, and humiliated by successive decades of US and Western support of regimes that were corrupt and ungodly in the eyes of those over whom they ruled.

The collective bandwidth of Western intelligence services and their political masters was overwhelmed by the scale of the challenge that had begun to emerge in what was rather over-confidently referred to as 'the post-Islamic State world' in Western policy circles. The situation in the north of Syria became an even greater maelstrom of conflict, with territory being contested between at least five sets of combatants. Over to the east, the north of Iraq rapidly deteriorated into intense intra-state territorial contestation as Sunnis, Shi'is, and Kurds battled it out for control of land and resources, with Turkey and Iran pulling and pushing their proxies according to their own national interests. The Shi'a political elite in Baghdad had also fallen in on itself by mid-2017, leading to the emergence of the former hardline Shi'i prime minister Nouri al-Maliki to return to his old job in the elections of 2018. His opponents in the Sadrist Movement loyal to Muqtada al-Sadr took to the streets to challenge the security forces dominated by the newly returned prime minister.

Meanwhile, North African countries had continued to unravel following the heady days of the Arab Spring. From being the starting point of the Arab Spring revolutions, Tunisia had struggled to further consolidate its democratic aspirations, or, more accurately, had struggled to accommodate the Islamist manifestations of popular democratic processes in action. The result was predictable. By 2017, Islamist movements became more prominent, and significant swathes of the country fell under the authority of localised Islamist groups that would begin to build their own links with the more global, and still strong, networks of the Islamic State and al-Qaeda in a way that would be replicated to devastating effect some months later in Egypt.

Viewed as concerning, but warranting no direct intervention, the future of Tunisia was sealed as much by Western complacency as it was by jihadist determination. Throughout 2017, the Western-backed state, with its military and security forces, held at bay waves of pro-Islamist demonstrations, often through the use of intense violence. Over a short period, these demonstrations began to fly the feared black banner of Islamic State, before the presidential and governmental compounds were overrun and a new Caliphate was declared.

But Tunisia, while worrying, was a sideshow compared to what had been unfolding in Libya. Having ceased to exist in anything like a unified form, several different fiefdoms, even city states, had emerged from the wreckage of Ghaddafi's *Jamahiriyah*, or socialist people's republic.

Tripoli existed as the home to a new government formed from various Islamist groupings deemed to be more or less acceptable to Western tastes. But the reach of Tripoli quickly evaporated outside the city limits. Misrata, with its powerful militias, continued to exercise its influence across the central coastal area of the country, including Sirte, from where it had expelled the remaining Islamic State presence in 2016. Meanwhile, General Khalifa Haftar was in full control of the Benghazi–Tobruk region, and his forces also held the hugely important oil facilities and the port areas from which Libya's oil would find its way to market.

The Islamic State presence still existed in Libya, but had been pushed further south, into Fezzan and the desert areas, where they operated with the impunity given to those brave enough to embrace the harsh and vast desert environment. Indeed, there were claims that new groups had grown in the aftermath of Islamic State's defeat in Iraq and Syria in 2018, and that some of them moved quickly and quietly between various remote camps, displaying high levels of evasive techniques. But few took notice of these wild rumours. Instead, the Western powers seemed to be reasonably comfortable in working directly with General Haftar to bring Libya's oil to market, while also recognising the close relationship between Haftar and his Egyptian sponsor, General Sisi.

Neither were particularly palatable figures for Western diplomatic tastes, but more importantly, the two of them together provided a bulwark against any further spread of radical Islam, in the form of a resurgent Islamic State, across Libya and into Egypt. If buying Libyan oil meant that the Haftar–Sisi alliance would be stronger, then this seemed a small price to pay for stability in North Africa and the limiting of the debilitating refugee flows that had already brought the European Union project to the point of collapse.

The problem was, however, that others had designs on the North African space, and coveted the oil reserves controlled so effectively by Haftar. These others also had time to reorganise, regroup, and plan their resurrection as the new incarnation the *dawla Islamiyya*, or the Islamic State. But, this time, they would learn lessons from the failure in Iraq and in Syria, not only from their own actions but from the strategies and tactics pursued by the international community against them. Far from going quietly into the night, the Islamic State would plan to go even better than they had done in Iraq and Syria. Mosul and Raqqa were, after all, provincial outposts compared to what they now planned to have as their new capital – Cairo. But, to achieve this, they would have to overcome many of their structural problems, and not least the massive internal factionalisation that existed within the Sunni jihadist camp itself.

The al-Qaeda–Islamic State Alliance

The period following the rise of President Sisi in Egypt had proved to be a tortuous one for Egypt's Islamists. Commonly associated with the Muslim Brotherhood, Egypt's political Islamist community was in fact heavily divided, with Salafis of varying persuasions and allegiances existing alongside hardline jihadists, some of whom maintained strong links with the al-Qaeda leadership that remained holed up in the tribal lands of Pakistan. Their leader, the ailing Ayman al-Zawahiri, longed for a regrouping of al-Qaeda with his Egyptian homeland.

It made sense. Egypt, with its history of being the birthplace of political Islam and with a large and increasingly restless and religiously minded population, would make an ideal place from which to resurrect the al-Qaeda organisation. And it would not be difficult. True, since the killing of the emir Bin Laden by American forces some years before, al-Qaeda had struggled to present itself in the same romanticised way that it had done under his charismatic leadership. But, while Zawahiri did not have the appeal of Osama, he did have a strategically adept mind and understood the changing nature of world politics, Islamist movements, and al-Qaeda's place within them.

For many outside observers, al-Qaeda had been challenged and even damaged by the rise of the Islamic State. Seemingly with greater courage of conviction, Islamic State had achieved a stunning coup by capturing so much territory in Iraq and Syria from 2014 onwards. Yet its heavily *takfiri* doctrine, and its brutal targeting of Shi'is, was too much even for al-Qaeda to bear. Believing it was too early to declare the Caliphate, a schism occurred between the two organisations, with the division being driven as much by the personal animosity between Caliph Ibrahim and Emir Zawahiri as any other reason.

Zawahiri had seen it all before, though, and realised that the Islamic State message could give new impetus to the far greater global organisation that was al-Qaeda. All he needed was to find a way to reach out to the Islamic State leadership, now that it had been expelled from its stronghold in the Maghreb and found itself in the Sub-Saharan vastness of the Libyan–Egyptian border region.

Unfortunately, well-meaning and highly informed Western analysts were blinded by their own knowledge, rather than empowered by it. Conditioned as they were to believe in the absolute fact that al-Qaeda and Islamic State had so many deeply riven theological and doctrinal differences – and that so much blood had been spilled between al-Qaeda affiliates, such as *jabhat al-nusra*, and Islamic State in Syria – the notion that there could be any coming together of rival jihadist groups, especially including Islamic State, was rarely, if ever, entertained. Rather than see the many similarities that existed between the groups, in terms of background, outlook, vision, and aims, they focused on the fewer issues that divided them, out of the deceptively wishful view that the jihadist political and military space was forever destined to be dominated by vicious infighting between several core entities.

Analysts, academics and advisers would talk about the impending jihadist civil war, between different groups of Sunnis all competing for the mantle of leadership of the Sunni jihadist worldview, with them all relying upon various constellations of sponsors – both state and non-state – to allow them to prosecute their dangerous game. Islamic State, in this scenario, was finished. The world now belonged to the patient, guarded, calculating, and highly dangerous al-Qaeda organisation of Zawahiri.

But Zawahiri and his lieutenants had different ideas. No longer did they wish to be holed up in caves in the North-West Frontier; they wanted to return home, to Cairo, and they realised that they needed the experience, skills, and appeal of their once-arch rivals in Islamic State to achieve this. After all, Islamic State knew how to take control of urban environments, how to defeat armies, and how to implement the crusaders' own tactics of 'clear, hold, and build', and the winning of 'hearts and minds', while also building immensely capable intelligence and security structures as befitting an organisation that could trace its lineage to Saddam's highly effective regime. And Islamic State needed Zawahiri.

Capable though they were, they had been defeated, and heavily. The location of the Caliph was unknown, and Islamic State could no longer operate in its home territory of Iraq. Instead, they found themselves in *terra incognita*, in the harsh deserts of North Africa. True, Cairo was an opportunity, and many times larger than Mosul that they had left behind. But Cairo was Egyptian, and not Iraqi, and even the tactically efficient military planners of Islamic State could not overcome the basic sociological problem of outsiders taking over a city of Cairo's character and proportions.

To succeed in Cairo, and to re-establish the *dawla islamiyya* as a territory rather than merely an idea, Islamic State needed to form a partnership with entities that could appeal to the banal nationalism of the Libyans, the Tunisians, and most importantly the Egyptians, to then build a new Caliphate across the southern Mediterranean, the likes of which would make the Caliphate of Syria and Iraq seem inconsequential. But, to do this, Cairo, and al-Qaeda, were key.

The Build-Up

In 2018, Egypt was in a ruinous state. Economically, the country was rarely ever more than a few weeks away from bankruptcy. This economic stagnation had begun much earlier. In the early days after the coup in 2013, which removed the elected Muslim Brotherhood from office in Cairo, the military regime of President Sisi had been reliant upon aid from the US and Saudi Arabia. Both saw stability in Egypt as being critical for their own vital interests. From the perspective of the US, Egypt was a geopolitically critical state, and one that was important to keep within its own patronage structure, lest the older alliance between Egypt and Russia became reinvigorated.

The US also understood fully the opportunity Egypt gave to radical Islamist causes, and the election of the Muslim Brotherhood government of Mohamed Morsi in 2012 had been met with considerable angst in the Washington DC beltway. Democracy was all well and good, if it brought forward those deemed acceptable to US interests. Morsi did not satisfy this particular expectation, and so few tears were shed, and even fewer words were said, when General Abdel Fattah el-Sisi led an army coup to remove the Brotherhood from power, setting himself up as the new President, and secular strongman, of Egypt in June 2013.

The US agreed to allocate Egypt up to $1.5 billion in annual military aid, along with assistance funding that ran into hundreds of millions per year – funding that the Egyptian state would become heavily reliant upon to survive from one week to the next.

Saudi Arabia, too, also supported the military regime of President Sisi. Contrary perhaps to Western understanding, the one development the Kingdom of Saudi Arabia seemed to fear and oppose more than any other – notwithstanding the rise of Shi'i political actors across the region – was the rise of Muslim Brotherhood regimes. For the traditional and conservative Wahhabi establishment of Saudi Arabia, the Muslim Brotherhood presented a different way forward for Sunni political Islam – and a way that would be deemed alarming to Saudi state and religious leaders. The Brotherhood was certainly religious in its outlook, but also modern in its approach, seeking to embrace democratic principles to gain access to power, and to promote educational, charitable, and social initiatives globally, in a forward-looking way that would see the Brotherhood build a vast network across the world.

For the Saudi regime, there could be only one country that claimed to be ruled by Sharia, to be the protector of Islam, and the leading Muslim state. To have this monopoly challenged by an organisation that was also embracing democracy, thus disproving the belief that Islam and democratic norms were incompatible, constituted not only a slap to Saudi Arabia's pride, but a direct threat to the integrity and cohesion of Saudi Arabia itself. After all, if Egypt was ruled by a Muslim regime, and had full representative elections and transparent government, then why should the same not be the case for Saudi Arabia?

As Mohamed Morsi and the Muslim Brotherhood became

closer to the Saudis' aggravating smaller neighbour, Qatar, it was no surprise that Riyadh hoped for a change in Egypt that would bring back the traditional power-holders. More so than in any other Middle Eastern state, save perhaps Turkey up to the 1990s, the military remained the leading political force in Egypt. Successive leaders, from Nasser through to Mubarak, had derived their authority and legitimacy from their military background, with the military establishment viewing itself as the guardian of Egypt against all enemies – external, and especially internal.

Following the military coup in 2013, the prominent observer of Saudi Arabian politics, Madawi Al-Rasheed, noted that it was 'a moment of joy for the Saudi regime', and Riyadh moved quickly to express its support for President Sisi by organising a $12 billion aid package – which dwarfed the $1.5 billion and $1.3 billion from the US and EU respectively. Discounted oil also began to flow from Saudi Arabia – a lifeline for the economy of the country – and Riyadh promised to compensate Egypt for any loss of funds from the US and EU, which were both struggling to accept the removal of the democratically elected Morsi by what was, in effect, a military junta.

But Saudi Arabia's largesse was not mere charity. Riyadh saw in Sisi an opportunity to end the Arab Spring and to stop the steamroller that seemed to be inexorably heading towards the Kingdom. Preventing democracy, and especially democracy that would empower Muslims, was deemed crucial. But the Saudi government also seemed to have a greater plan in mind – for Egypt, with its sizeable and capable military forces, to be a partner with Saudi Arabia in the regional struggle against what was seen, with good reason, as an expansionist Iran.

With Iranian influence becoming overwhelmingly strong

in Iraq, and with the Damascus–Tehran axis beginning to show itself from 2013 onwards, Saudi Arabia's threat perception of Iran was at an all-time high. True, they had concerns about Iranian WMD. But by far the bigger concern was to do with the propagation of the ideology of the Islamic Revolution – which from Saudi Arabia's perspective was a Shi'i Islamic Revolution, as far removed from the Wahhabi-dictated worldview of Riyadh as could be.

But Cairo did not play this particular role.

Indeed, as the Syrian War progressed, Egypt was notable not only by its quietness, but even by what could be viewed as a show of support for the Assad regime. Perhaps seeing Assad as leading a military-dominated republic in partnership with Egypt – and the Egyptian and Syrian Arab Republics had enjoyed extremely close relationships in the past – Egypt even supported a Russian UN draft resolution in October 2016 that would allow Syria and Russia to continue to attack rebel-held areas of the decimated city of Aleppo.

This diplomatic snub to Riyadh was but the latest in a series of developments suggesting that President Sisi, far from being loyal to Riyadh, was instead showing more interest in becoming closer to Russia and Vladimir Putin.

With the Sisi regime moving to diversify its sources of arms and be less dependent on the US – while also benefiting from more economic support from Russia – the US and Saudi Arabia responded in kind. The Kingdom halted its oil supplies indefinitely to Egypt, and the US started to reallocate its economic aid to other North African countries, and especially Tunisia.

By mid-2017, the Egyptian economy was already broken and the regime bust. *The Economist* placed Egypt's budget and current-account deficits at a staggering twelve per cent and seven per cent respectively, leaving Sisi little option but to seek a $12 billion bail-out from the IMF. Youth unemployment rocketed to over forty per cent and, with the private sector sclerotic, the levels of unemployment across Egypt's youth, educated and uneducated alike, became biblically high. The situation only worsened over the next year, leaving Egypt now teetering on the edge of bankruptcy.

The Scenario

President Sisi, aware of what the economic stresses and strains can do to a society with a prodigious youth bulge and with post-Arab Spring aspirations, responds as Middle Eastern dictators have always done before – by strengthening the security organisations of the state and giving them even greater powers to snuff out dissent before it arrives at the gates of the presidential palace. The military, too, will be supported to the hilt, with the US keeping in place its military aid programme, in the vain hope of preventing Sisi from becoming ever closer to Moscow.

The result sees the enhanced securitisation of the state, and Egypt becomes a country divided. However, unlike in Iraq, Syria, or Yemen, this division is not ethnic or sectarian, and it is also not geographic, like in Sudan, or in Iraq with the Kurds. This is an even more volatile division that is being played out in the mega-urban environments of Egypt's cities, and especially Cairo. Egypt remains for the most part an ethnically and religiously homogenous place, with the majority of people being Arabs and Sunni Muslims.

While there is a significant Christian Coptic population, numbering some ten per cent of the near 90 million population and a smaller number of Berber and Nubian communities along the Nile, Egypt simply does not display the same level of immense social complexity seen in other Middle-Eastern states. And this, arguably, makes the growing conflict even more intense. The division that emerges is basically between the military regime and state on the one hand, and those who oppose it on the other. With a variety of different trends coming together among those who oppose the military regime, there is little organisational coherence amongst the initial protestors who appear on the streets. Gone are the abilities of the Arab Spring demonstrators to use social media to crowd public areas, at least in the early days of 2017. And the security forces find it easy enough to put down brutally those who are brave enough to be standing against them.

By 2018, Egypt has become a militarised state. The government, while ostensibly technocratic, is wholly shadowed, or even controlled by the military establishment. From the Ministry of Interior to the civilian security services, through to the security, intelligence, and counter-terrorism organisations, the blending of responsibilities, staff, and reporting lines between these state institutions and their military controllers has become total. Sitting at the top of this military-state complex remains President Sisi, but gone is the pretence of being a civilian president. Increasingly, his title will interchange with that of Field Marshal, and his attire of choice will be that of the commander-in-chief of the military, rather than the urbane Italian-cut suits for which he had previously developed a penchant.

Military parades are also increasingly common. Replete with their incongruous assemblages of the latest US-supplied equipment being paraded side by side with their Russian and Chinese counterparts, the Egyptian military look well-prepared for any eventuality. But Sisi remains true to his word of four years before – of keeping the Egyptian military prepared for matters of importance to Egypt – and not to be used as the foot-soldiers for the Gulf states, or against Iran in a sectarian conflict that, for Sisi, is as irrelevant as it is nonsensical.

Strong though Sisi and the military regime are, 2019 brings a new challenge to the attention of the world – the return of political Islam. Following the execution of former President Morsi, after a wave of bomb attacks against government targets, the Islamist parties of Egypt begin to show more determination in their opposition to Sisi. They have little choice but to show themselves more. For some years, since 2017 if not before, several districts of Cairo have begun to see the black flag of Islamic State fluttering. While there are reports of Islamic State camps existing in Libya, however, few in Egypt have ever considered that Islamic State could venture over the border – the distances are too great, and the Egyptians, Islamists or not, would not find the message of these Iraqi and Syrian fundamentalists at all appealing.

But this is a serious strategic miscalculation. The Islamic State leadership, the remains of which have managed to evacuate themselves to the depths of the Libyan desert, have had much time to reflect upon the reasons for their defeat in the *mashrek*, on the state of their network in North Africa, and on the approach that has been made to them by none other than Ayman al-Zawahiri himself.

With Osama bin Laden now no more, Zawahiri has found himself the leader of an organisation that needs to revitalise its mission, and to inject new blood into the organisation. An urbane, intellectual figure, he misses the exciting environment of his homeland, particularly of Cairo – a city in which he enjoyed many years as a medical student before serving in the army. He also remembers clearly his time in the Muslim Brotherhood, following the charismatic Sayyid Qutb, almost to the gallows alongside him. Unknown to many, his connections with his Brotherhood friends from those days when they planned to overthrow the government and form an Islamist state – and to put their mentor Qutb's plans into action – have never ceased. Indeed, there are many in Egypt who long for the return of the deeply thoughtful, logical, calm and highly effective Zawahiri, and to bring the Brotherhood back to its rightful place of leadership.

The task of building a unified jihadist front is not straight-forward. Over the years, thousands have died in the often-unseen internal conflicts that rage between myriad Sunni Islamist groups across the Middle East, and especially in Iraq and Syria. In Libya, too, Islamists are probably more adept at killing each other than killing their secular enemies. The reason is straightforward, and entirely in keeping with the history of religious warfare in Europe several hundred years earlier. While the fight against the external enemy is the stuff of history and is what mobilises thousands to join their causes, the internal rifts, personality slights, and often banal contestations that exist between groups of broadly the same complexion can result in far greater and more brutal levels of bloodletting than that inflicted upon their 'real' opponents.

The Islamic State leadership has learned this over many years. Since almost destroying their 'own' offshoot *jabhat al-nusra*, over its refusal to accept the leadership of Caliph Ibrahim, Islamic State has found itself on the receiving end of a ferocious counter-assault from *nusra* and a range of other groups. Whoever is now calling the shots in the Islamic State bolthole in Libya – and it is unclear whether it is Caliph Ibrahim, as 'The Ghost' remains as mysterious as ever, or whether it is the strategically aware, and highly skilled figures who hailed from Saddam Hussein's former Special Security

Organisation, the *jihaz al-amn al-khas* – a new way of looking at the world is also evident. Far from opposing Zawahiri's overture to combine their efforts in North Africa, the Islamic State leadership embraces it.

Envisioning a new Caliphate in North Africa, Zawahiri and the Islamic State leadership see two principal objectives. The first is to turn Cairo into the new Mosul and to return the city to being the seat of the Caliphate, as it was under the Abbasids from the thirteenth to the sixteenth centuries. From the City of a Thousand Minarets, the Caliphate would not only endure, it would learn from the lessons of Abu Bakr's Islamic State in Iraq and Syria and move against its weaker and shocked enemies quickly. Already, Islamic State is beginning to make inroads into the Palestinian population and has begun to assassinate uncooperative HAMAS leaders. Moving into Jordan will be straightforward. The fragility of the Hashemite Kingdom, with its huge Palestinian presence matched now by Sunni Arabs from Iraq and Syria, makes it an easy target of opportunity – exceptionally low-hanging fruit – and that will then lead the Caliphate to the borders of the Hijaz and, from there, to Medina and Mecca.

Abu Bakr al-Baghdadi has been praised by his followers for his swiftness and clarity of action. But, for Zawahiri and for al-Baghdadi's military advisers from Saddam's days, he is not brave nor clear enough. Upon the fall of Mosul, they consider that he should have moved quickly and with immense aggression to Baghdad, rather than picking a fight with the stubborn Kurds, whom no one apart from the Turks cares about in any case. By failing to take Baghdad immediately after Mosul, the fate of the Islamic State in Iraq was then sealed. Zawahiri and his companions will learn from this mistake following the collapse of Cairo.

The second objective is economic, but also strategically

important. Oil will be important for the new Caliphate, as
will the removal of strong neighbours. While the Iraqi and
Syrian initiative has succeeded in gaining control of some
decent oil reserves, they are not huge, and, this time, the
population of Cairo and the other cities of Egypt will require
supplies at vastly greater levels than did Mosul and Raqqa.
These supplies will be found in Libya. Since 2016, General
Haftar's Libyan National Army has succeeded in taking over
the crescent oil ports of Libya, Ras Lanuf, Es Sider, and
Zueitina. Haftar has also succeeded in removing the presence
of Tripoli's forces from the al-Hilal oil fields.

The al-Qaeda–Islamic State (AQIS) initiative desperately
needs not only to capture the oil fields, but also to destroy
Haftar and his army. Remembering all too well the damage
that was inflicted upon Islamic State by having the Kurds to
their north, in Syria and in Iraq, and how easy it was for
Western powers to support a group that had been largely
ostracised in the past, it will pose a dangerous strategic weakness to allow Haftar, Sisi's ally, to exist to their west as they
attempt to consolidate their hold on Cairo. Haftar will also
have to go, and to do this AQIS will provide further support,
and manpower, to the Benghazi Revolutionary Shura Council
(BRSC).

Throughout the end of 2019 and into 2020, AQIS reaches
into its key target areas. In Cairo, AQIS finds its message
falling on fertile ground, not least because of the belief that
Zawahiri himself will return. The ability of two previously
implacable enemies – al-Qaeda and Islamic State – to find
common cause, also makes other Islamist groups consider
their own position. While they could previously make a name
for themselves by moving between the two groups, the opportunity to do this does not now exist, and to oppose such a
powerful and influential bloc would be idiocy.

And so, over the remaining months of 2019, Western intelligence services begin to see what many believed would be an impossibility barely a few years before – a common political and military platform emerging among Islamist groups across the region, with the tantalising names of Zawahiri and Baghdadi being mentioned, but with these figures never being seen. Emulating what they have done previously in Iraq, in 2013 and 2014, AQIS begin to take over the administration of some of Cairo's remoter parts, enforcing taxes and expelling local law enforcement officers. They also begin to undertake bolder military attacks into outlying towns, targeting military officers for assassination, and, increasingly, detonating spectacularly large VBIEDs – vehicle-borne improvised explosive devices – in the heart of Cairo and Alexandria.

Meanwhile, in Sinai, the AQIS unit there, previously known as *Ansar Bayt al-Maqdis*, opens up a full military assault against Egyptian forces, culminating in the capture of the Egyptian army headquarters and the execution of every soldier. While it is tempting for the insurgents to move against the weakly defended, multi-national peacekeeping base at El Gora, they leave them time to evacuate. No one wants to give the US an opportunity to engage AQIS at this moment in time. Not least while President Sisi is still alive.

Cairo Falls, Benghazi Defeated

The 29th of June is an important date for Islamic State – it is the anniversary of the proclamation in 2014 of the worldwide Caliphate from the Grand Mosque of Mosul. But, by 2020, this fact seems to have been lost on the security services of the Egyptian government. Columns of AQIS fighters begin moving across the Libyan desert, with local support. The southern column moves quickly to Aswan, to take control of the dam and control the headwaters of the Nile. Word has already been given to loyal forces in Luxor and Al-Minya to rise against the military, while three columns make their way quietly through the desert roads to the outskirts of Cairo, much as the columns that moved on Mosul those many years ago had done.

From there, the heavily weighed-down lorries meander toward the president's Abdin Palace, to the General Intelligence Directorate, and to the Military Intelligence Services and Reconnaissance Department. Other vehicles also pick their way towards Army bases and the most prominent police departments in the city – with the complicity of many who have come to despise the heavy-handed security services of the state.

The explosions rock the city. By the end of the day, Sisi and his closest advisers have been obliterated by successive VBIED attacks, with SBIED (suicide-bomber improvised explosive device) attacks moving in to the ensuing carnage to finish off their bloody work. With Special Forces units being held down in the Sinai, there are few if any options to mount a counter-attack, even if there were any leaders in place to order this. The speed and ferocity of the attacks take Western embassies by surprise. None of them had prior warning to leave, and their countries watch with fear as they expect their diplomats to be hunted down and executed. Again, the AQIS leadership balance their aggression with caution when needed. Instead of slaughtering the West's diplomats in front of the world's media, they merely allow them to leave on the aircraft that were trapped on the tarmac at Cairo's airport.

Meanwhile, in Libya, Benghazi erupts in a frenzy of violence on the evening of 29 June. The BRSC appear in great numbers and find it easy to retake the city, with most of Haftar's troops still consolidating their hold on the oil fields and ports. Meanwhile, further AQIS support columns, and tribal irregulars, move against Haftar's forces in a series of moves that can have only one outcome. By the end of three days, Haftar is isolated in Ajdabiya, trying to return from the oil ports to lead the fight in Benghazi, but surrounded by AQIS and BRSC. Unfortunately for Haftar and his army, neither the AQIS nor the BRSC forces are minded to show them the same degree of benevolence as granted to the Western diplomats fleeing Cairo. Instead, the world's media is flooded with an orgy of violence and executions from Ajdabiya over the course of the next week, culminating with the public beheading of Haftar and his officers by the victorious jihadist forces.

Cairo has fallen to the forces of AQIS, and Benghazi and the eastern region of Libya to the joint forces of AQIS and BRSC, with the latter duly merging into the rapidly growing AQIS initiative. These two cities, together with Alexandria, now form a new axis across the coast of the Mediterranean – covering a territory that is far closer to Europe than the Caliphate of Mosul–Raqqa had been, but also has control of the vast oil reserves of Libya, can threaten and attack Israel at will, and can trade, smuggle, and engage with states across Sub-Saharan Africa. The potential capability of this newly emerging entity is apparent for all to see. The question that stalks the halls of Whitehall and the Beltway is one of future intent. Who will emerge to lead Egypt and Libya in the chaotic and bloody aftermath of one of the most spectacular, and unforeseen military and political takeovers of the last century?

The answer is as astonishing in its simplicity as it is in its audacity. On 29 June, exactly six years to the day that Abu Bakr al-Baghdadi proclaimed the Islamic Caliphate from the

Grand Mosque in Mosul, a convoy of black, heavily armoured Land Cruisers, previously owned by the obliterated President Sisi, winds its way through Cairo's streets. It is heading for the hill known locally as *Jabal Yashkur*, or the Hill of Thanksgiving, on which stood the Mosque of Ahmad Ibn Tulun – the oldest mosque in the city, hailing from the Abbasid period. Inside the convoy is none other than Abu Bakr himself.

From where he has come, no one knows, which adds further to his almost ethereal reputation as being a shadowy, ghost-like figure. The mosque is decorated with the customary banner of the Islamic State once again, but also bears the scars from a significant amount of crass sledge-hammer work by Islamic State fanatics, destroying the twelfth-century restorations commissioned by a Fatimid wazir, who had ordered Shi'a inscriptions to be included in the fabric of the old mosque.

The subsequent show is reminiscent of Abu Bakr's appearance in Mosul three years earlier. The symbolism, rhetoric, and messaging remain focused upon the consolidation and expansion of the Caliphate, and now, also, the return of the Caliph's homeland of Iraq to the dar al-Islam, after its retaking by the Shi'a heretics and Kurdish apostates. But this time, he has another message – one which addresses Europe, and particularly 'Rome', as the seat presumably of Christendom. He will not ignore the threat from across the sea, and will not wait for his opponents to come to the *Maghreb* to challenge the Caliphate, as they did in the *Mashreq*.

This time the Caliphate, the Islamic State, from Cairo and its North African base, will not rest until Andalusia is restored, the West defeated, and the Russians destroyed. Waiting in the wings behind him, as he delivers his impassioned speech, is a figure in the shadows, but one whose profile is familiar to the analysts who have spent thousands of hours interpreting his language, gestures, and posture on the many video tapes released from al-Qaeda-linked outlets in Pakistan and Afghanistan. Emphasising the union between the Islamic State and al-Qaeda, the Egyptian-born leader of al-Qaeda, Ayman al-Zawahiri, steps forward to the accolade of the assembled crowd.

Proclaimed *sahabi*, or companion, to Abu Bakr al-Baghdadi, in an attempt to mirror the relationship between the Prophet Mohammed and his most senior aide Abu Bakr al-Siddiq, Zawahiri's quiet, nasal tones carry far over the courtyard of the mosque. He outlines a new vision – one that al-Qaeda itself has always shied away from, but one which he now embraces – of the new Caliphate, under a Caliph from the line of the Prophet Mohammed, with the global networks of al-Qaeda and the Islamic State to bring the black banners of the Caliphate to every corner of the world. Abu Bakr may have been Caliph, but power and the strategic vision will rest with the careful, cautious, and calculating Zawahiri, who will now ride a wave of popularity in his native Egypt.

The West Reacts

The speed with which events have happened in Egypt and Libya leaves the Western capitals flatfooted. They have been aware for years of the structural weaknesses that exist in Egypt, and of the dangerous division that has opened in Egyptian society between the military establishment and everyone else. They have known of the collapse of Libya into a complicated map of fiefdoms, and about Islamic State having strong links with the BRSC and other Islamist groups all the way over to

Tripoli. There have also been reports of high-level meetings between various Islamic State and al-Qaeda intermediaries, but the Western powers have chosen to ignore something that is so beyond the realm of usual explanations.

But, by the beginning of August 2020, a new Caliphate has emerged – one that stretches from Cairo to Benghazi, and which is spreading across what had been Egypt and Libya. Foreign fighters are flocking to the new Caliphate, responding to the call of the Caliph. Meanwhile, Zawahiri is imposing his authority on the Islamist movements of Egypt, forcing them to unify under his leadership on behalf of the Caliph, or to be handed over to the uncompromisingly brutal *hisbah* – religious police – of the Islamic State to face trial and almost certain execution.

Jihadists across the world suddenly feel empowered, and to an even greater degree than they had been by the Mosul declaration. In Afghanistan, Pakistan, Bangladesh, the Philippines, Indonesia, Central Asia, and even in Europe, jihadists seek to emulate the success of the spectacular developments in Cairo and Benghazi, and are supported to do so by the new patronage structures centred on the Caliphate, financed by the lucrative proceeds of the Libyan oil fields.

Even when faced with such tumultuous changes and challenges, the UN Security Council cannot reach agreement upon the crisis constituting a UN Charter Chapter 7 threat to international peace and security. Perhaps shocked by the scale of what is unfolding, Security Council members hope that the new Caliphate will simply unravel as quickly as it has appeared, thus mitigating against a Chapter 7 vote. This suits most members – even under the Trump presidency, there is little appetite for committing vast numbers of US troops to peacekeeping missions in such an extremely dangerous setting, and the new, inexperienced president still needs to make good on his promises to enhance the US military, rather than see it further degraded in another debilitating conflict.

Britain and France, too, are torn between action and inaction, desperate to show that they are facing up seriously to the threat of the new Caliphate, but not so much that they will have to commit military forces they simply do not have. China remains watchful, as ever, wary of the impact the new developments will have on their African investments, but also wary of the impact a military engagement with the new Caliphate will have on their own Muslim problem with the Uiygurs in Xinjiang. Only Russia demands immediate action, and reserves the right to take it unilaterally if needed.

Somewhat meekly, the Security Council does at least manage to make a Chapter 6 resolution, allowing for the pacific settlement of disputes in a non-legally binding framework. As such, the UK, along with other Western powers, is called upon to assist in alleviating the immense humanitarian crisis that is now enveloping North Africa. Vast refugee movements have already begun, as Egyptians move across the Sinai Peninsula, only to be held at the Israeli border by extremely tense soldiers of the IDF. They have also begun to move south, into Sudan – which is clearly far more accepting of the new Caliphate than many Western countries appreciate.

Libyans also begin to move, to escape what is believed to be an unstoppable Islamic conquest emanating from the east. Not only do they venture west, to Algeria and to Morocco; they also take to their small boats, with hundreds of thousands of people making the perilous crossing to southern Europe. Western TV screens become filled with daily footage of drowned corpses washing up on the beaches of Greece, Italy, and France.

The UK government is called upon to contribute specifically to urban policing, and to help in relieving what is now a humanitarian crisis of massive proportions unfolding in the ramshackle refugee camps that are appearing across the region. At first, the intention is to deploy UK personnel to Cairo and Alexandria, but this is quickly realised to be impossible, such is the hold of AQIS across Egypt and Libya. Instead, the UK moves to further strengthen its key ally in the region – Jordan – and also to deploy advisers to Tunisia, in the hope of maintaining law and order in these key states, and also preventing the spread of the Islamic State message, or even personnel, to these countries.

This is easier said than done. Ma'an, in the south of Jordan, along with Zarqa and Irbid in the north, were all strongholds of Islamic State support even before the fall of Mosul, while Islamic State sympathies among those Tunisians who are not tied to the patronage networks of the government – and that is the vast majority – have also become strong, especially in the south of the country. Morocco, too, has considerable problems to contend with, especially in Casablanca and in Meknes, where an Islamist insurgency breaks out that is impossible to quash.

The UK is thus already massively overcommitted, simply by the task of stabilising states that have not, as yet, been overrun by the Caliphate. The Royal Navy, too, finds itself required to secure the Mediterranean and to police the never-ending flow of refugees choosing to risk all in making the crossing to Europe. Ironically, the new HMS *Queen Elizabeth* comes into her own. While not having any aircraft on board an aircraft carrier was derided by observers before the Second Caliphate Crisis began. Having such a huge facility available to act as a floating refugee camp in the middle of the

Mediterranean gives the initiative to manage the refugee crisis a much-needed hostel facility.

But the problem of the refugees is even more intense than before. The numbers are now of such magnitude that the refugee camps of Europe are as big, if not bigger, than those in North Africa, and AQIS has learned the lessons of infiltrating their fighters with refugees very well indeed. The UK now needs to bring to the fore its intelligence capabilities and refugee-camp management, in the form of urban policing, counter-terror operations, and urban warfare, as the refugee camps become some of the most dangerous environments to have existed on the European continent since the dark days of the Balkan Wars.

The UK can also not escape the formal deployment of military forces, in a bid to contain the expansion of the Caliphate. But this is not as easy as it was in Iraq and Syria.

There, the UK and her allies could rely on local partners, or proxies, to do the lion's share of the fighting. Under Operation SHADER, the UK trained and equipped thousands of Kurdish *peshmerga* forces, while the US and other European allies did the same, and with the Iraqi Security Forces (ISF) as well. Over to the west, in Syria, the UK and US had worked closely with Syrian Kurdish forces of the YPG and SDF. While critical of Russia further strengthening the Assad regime, the US and UK did little to stop them attacking the YPG and SDF. Complicated though this world was, there were local friends and allies to work with, and enemies of enemies would become friends.

In North Africa, and into the Levant, following the emergence of the Second Caliphate Crisis, as it becomes known, this is simply not the case. There are no local allies with which to fight AQIS forces. The remnants of General Haftar's Libyan Army have been routed and are being hunted down with ruthless efficiency by the *hisbah* of the Islamic State and the notorious *Bin Laden* Brigade, tasked by Zawahiri to destroy any vestige of internal opposition. Instead, Western powers are having to mount a city-by-city defence, deploying military units – usually those from the massively overstretched units of the UK Special Forces (UKSF) – into cities at risk, and at best assisting in the organisation of their defences or, more commonly, managing the evacuation of their population centres, which only add further to the refugee burden now unfolding.

As 2020 wears on, there is little to suggest the UK has managed to achieve 'success', or at least 'success' as determined by some pre-agreed definition of outcomes. The situation has simply unfolded too quickly, and too surprisingly, for the UK or any other Western power to put adequate responses into place. Instead, the UK mission is one of rapid firefighting, moving to deal with immediate problems quickly, but without a coordinated response that allows for further ramifications to be factored in.

Meanwhile, the leadership of the Caliphate has learned its lessons well from Iraq and Syria. They have learned when to pick fights, and when not to; they have learned how they can be undermined, and what they need to do to remain cohesive; and they have realised that, if they have the opportunity to expand, then they have to take it. If Abu Bakr has any regrets from 2014, it is not advancing on Baghdad following the collapse of Mosul. In failing to do this, and in attacking the Kurds instead, he allowed his Iranian, US, and Western opponents to regroup, while also making a dangerous local enemy in the form of the Kurds – and this would spell the end of the First Caliphate.

Now, however, and with Zawahiri alongside him, he is wise to this weakness. As 2020 draws to an end, the skirmishes in

Misrata are lessening, and Tripoli has more or less fallen. Tunis is now isolated and black banners are flying in Algiers. His own advisers are now planning the re-establishment of the Ummayid Caliphate – Muslim Spain – within a few years and, this time, his opponents will struggle to stop him.

CHAPTER 6

THE PASSENGER IN SEAT 7B
Crime, Terror and the Darknet

Great Britain, 2020

In the UK, Prime Minister Theresa May's attempts to secure a viable post-EU trading future seem to have taken on a life of their own, morphing from second-guessing into gamesmanship and then into a phase of nervous brinkmanship, but by January 2020 the British exit – or 'Brexit' – from the European Union is nearly complete. Yet while the negotiations might well be almost over, as yet little of real substance has been resolved, leaving a fog of uncertainty to linger over vital areas of UK–EU cooperation.

After the Prime Minister triggered Article 50 in March 2017, the UK, hoping to retain tariff-free access to the European Single Market, attempted, at least in the EU's perception, to 'cherry pick' three of the four sacrosanct 'freedoms' – the movement of goods, services and capital – while rejecting the free movement of peoples. The UK negotiators were encouraged to 'think again' by its former trading partners – some out of spite, others merely *pour encourager les autres* – who pointed out in no uncertain terms that it was 'all or nothing' and tariff-free trade was only available to members of the trading bloc. Her attempt to persuade the EU into adopting a more flexible stance came in the form of her Lancaster House speech on 17 January 2017:

We want to buy your goods and services, sell you ours, trade with you as freely as possible, and work with one another to make sure we are all safer, more secure and more prosperous through continued friendship . . . At a time when together we face a serious threat from our enemies, Britain's unique intelligence capabilities will continue to help to keep people in Europe safe from terrorism. And at a time when there is growing concern about European security, Britain's servicemen and women, based in European countries including Estonia, Poland and Romania, will continue to do their duty.

No matter how persuasive, at first the Prime Minister's overtures fell on deaf ears and the seemingly never-ending talks ground on through 2019. But come the closing months of that year, the thorny issue of UK–EU inter-agency defence and security collaboration was finally front and centre of the debate, a prime example of the various issues being given too little attention in the run-up to the June 2016 referendum.

Now, in 2020, the topic has come to dominate both the faltering negotiations and the headlines and, somewhat ironically, after decades of the UK being dismissive of EU defence and security efforts, the UK negotiators find that it is one of our strongest levers in the Brexit negotiations and finally, after their initial rejection, Prime Minister May's overtures in her Lancaster House speech are gaining traction.

A major consequence of the drastic reduction in overall government expenditure is that UK infrastructure has become brittle: ageing transportation networks are falling into disrepair at the same time as the private rail companies implement still more price-hikes. This has the effect of pushing increasing numbers of commuters onto an already congested road system, across crumbling bridges and through poorly maintained tunnels. City ring roads are in semi-permanent gridlock and the leitmotif across all media is to lay the blame for it all squarely in the government's lap, citing years of slashed funding. By way of an example, the M25, often jokingly referred to as a 'six-lane car-park', is now often precisely that.

The crisis deepens still further as commuters search out alternative routes – 'rat-runs' – in a bid to avoid the clogged arterial routes originally intended to keep congestion off the A roads, B roads, and especially the streets choked during peak hours by parents on the school run. Accidents involving cyclists and pedestrians, a high proportion involving children, have risen by twenty-three per cent since 2015.

All this plays badly and in a concerted bid to divert the headlines onto more government-friendly topics, the Prime Minister decides to invest heavily in a series of fashionable but high-risk solutions, such as self-driving cars and drone delivery systems. The ideas receive a mixed reception, elements of the media detecting the ruse immediately and questioning the government's intentions. The response from specialists in the field is slower to emerge, but more damaging when it does: why, they ask, pursue such risky solutions when there are better, longer-term, more rounded solutions on the horizon?

Worse news is to come: while the safety concerns posed by deployment of automata on a faltering civilian infrastructure have not gone unnoticed by risk consultants, they seem to have entirely bypassed the nation's mechanical and digital engineers. While undoubtedly appealing at first look, these high-tech solutions are also presenting unforeseen problems. Despite the manufacturers emphasising 'security by design', their measures are largely nullified by the lack of maintenance. But the point of no return has already passed: the manufacturers need a return on years of punitively expensive research and development and the government now finds itself in the invidious position of publicly supporting an industry, whilst wilfully ignoring the degraded infrastructure upon which its products will have to operate.

As for the public, there's no choice but to continue using the failing road network to get to and from work, hospital appointments, schools and the rest, except that they are now obliged to share the worn-out roads with driverless vehicles widely believed to cause more accidents than they prevent. Not only that, but 2019 sees the first major aircraft–drone collision, which costs thirty-six lives in the air and sixteen on the ground, when a hobbyist flies his machine into the path of a Russian Volga-Dnepr An-124 cargo aircraft as it prepares to land at Stansted Airport. The wayward drone is simply sucked into a jet engine and the effect is catastrophic.

The world in 2020 is indeed a complex place; interconnected and heavily inter-reliant. For example, the pre-existing stress fractures in the EU are now firmly linked in the public mind to the existential crisis enveloping the North Atlantic Treaty Organisation (NATO). Since Montenegro joined NATO in mid-2017, the expanded Alliance of twenty-nine nations has remained resolute, but as yet untested. The organisation repeatedly states its commitment to Article 5 of its founding treaty: the principle of collective defence. It is a credo intended to bind its members tightly together, committing each one to the defence of its fellows in a spirit of unshakeable solidarity. But times are changing and it seems nothing is now above scrutiny.

The perennial and cyclical debate surrounding the UK's independent nuclear deterrent comes to the fore: is it untested and therefore irrelevant, or relevant because it is untested? Depending on the chosen standpoint, NATO remaining 'untested' is either proof positive of its effectiveness, or a signal that it is now peripheral.

NATO in 2020

It seems that NATO can do no right. In 2014, in an attempt to face down a resurgent Russia and simultaneously reassure the world of its readiness to act decisively, NATO committed to limited forward deployments in the Baltic States. Despite being intended to serve simply as a 'tripwire', which in the event of serious military contact would precipitate other, more sizeable deployments, to many analysts the battlegroup deployments looked more like political symbolism than a serious attempt to deter an increasingly belligerent Russia.

NATO's crisis has been a long time in the making. By the end of 2016, Estonia, Greece, Poland, the United Kingdom and the United States were the only members complying with the NATO guidance regarding the annual proportion of GDP each member nation should allocate to defence spending. The situation had prompted US President-elect Donald Trump to publicly muse as to whether NATO 'may be obsolete' and to hint that perhaps the United States would no longer deign to protect any ally who chose not to 'pay their bills'. As the Republican Presidential candidate, Mr Trump's comments could be readily dismissed; as President-elect, his tweets provoked consternation; after he was inaugurated as the 45th President of the United States on 20 January 2017, NATO's future abruptly became a matter of serious debate.

President Trump's doubts as to NATO's utility spread throughout his administration and a bruised and demoralised US intelligence community had little to say. The US leadership of NATO and its strategic engagement with its European allies began to reflect US frustration and impatience at the same time as the relationship between NATO and the EU continued to fall short of all hopes and expectations, and the latter began to actively consider establishing a pan-EU rapid reaction force of some description.

By 2018, President Trump's repeated instruction to the European members of the Alliance to increase their annual contributions to the stipulated two per cent of GDP per annum, or face the consequences, precipitated a fracturing of NATOs traditional solidarity. President Trump, increasingly confident of returning to Presidential office in 2020, re-energised the debate and re-tweeted his views. This was met with fresh consternation and renewed debate among the USA's NATO partners. 'Exactly what,' the US President asked, 'is NATO's purpose?' Other testing questions were posed, always in less than 140 characters.

The Alliance members on the Baltic coast began to question whether Article 5 of the Alliance's founding Washington Treaty would actually be invoked and honoured by their NATO allies in the event of a Russian land grab. Or would a Russian challenge to their territorial integrity be contested instead under the terms of Article 4 of the Washington Treaty – widely interpreted as a commitment to 'consult' rather than fight?

Once a thoroughbred racehorse, in 2020, the NATO Alliance now resembles something more akin to a nervous filly.

'Brexit' 2020

In parallel with the issues absorbing NATO, it is now abundantly clear that Brexit is having wide-ranging effects on aspects of international cooperation. The defence and security sectors are being increasingly challenged as access to European defence export markets calcifies and, after a brief period in excess of two per cent, UK military expenditure adopts a downward trajectory past, and then below, that critical two per cent of GDP. With defence procurement reducing year on year, the UK government is also facing increasing pressure from its domestic defence manufacturing sector, as the latter lobbies for either an increase in UK defence procurement, or a suspension of the restrictions that currently prevent them securing lucrative contracts overseas. In fact, they campaign actively for complete *laissez-faire*.

Facing mounting pressure from within the ranks of her own party and an electoral threat from the UK Independence Party (UKIP), Theresa May remains confident in public (less so in private) that a swing to the political right on the issue of the free movement of peoples will clinch victory for her in the coming 2020 General Election. Meanwhile, the national mood becomes increasingly soured by the persistent rancour surrounding the Brexit negotiations. Despite receiving unequivocal instructions to achieve quick results, coordination and discipline between the UK and Brussels diplomatic teams remains 'more honor'd in the breach than the observance' and this provokes a spate of embarrassing headlines. In fairness, the long-suffering, seasoned diplomats express their customary professional determination and poise, but are set against a frequently hostile EU27, many of whom see little reason to make the process any less painful for the UK than it must be. Their hope is this: by giving the UK the roughest possible ride, perhaps it will act as a disincentive to other malcontent EU states toying with their own version of 'exit'.

The Security of the Realm

Government tax revenue is falling at the same time as demands on the public purse surge. But the rigorous austerity policies sustained by Theresa May's government as an article of faith since the passing of the Cameron/Osborne regime are nevertheless ratcheted up yet another notch. Theresa May now finds herself in another quandary: obliged to champion the uniformed services – Police, Army, Royal Air Force, Royal Navy and the UK Border Force – while at the same time implementing a programme of punitive cuts to their funding. The UK Border Force, having endured budget reductions between 2015–2020, is now demoralised, under-equipped and under-staffed. Staff retention rates are at such an all-time low that some officers resort to taking bribes to subsidise their wages. As the Border Force struggles to maintain effectiveness, corruption within their ranks is on the rise.

The uniformed services are not alone in having to contest budget allocations every year. Established as an extension of GCHQ, the National Cyber Security Centre (NCSC) has been placed under constant budgetary pressure, despite an impressive record in countering a wide variety of national security threats.

Likewise financially challenged, the organisation intended to control the spread of corruption, the UK National Crime Agency (NCA), is also suffering from sharply reducing levels of funding while engaged in a bid to tackle rising serious and organised crime, principally modern slavery, human trafficking, the distribution of illegal firearms, cybercrime and money-laundering. Organised crime economies benefit from the development of anonymous cryptocurrencies and the problem now looms so large that only by raiding other budgets can the NCA create a taskforce specifically to assess the scope and scale of the use of these cryptocurrencies and then attempt to counter them.

Unfortunately, details of the NCA's activities are leaked and this has the 'Streisand Effect': their concerted effort to conceal the cryptocurrencies from the public has the unintended consequence of publicising the information more widely than would otherwise be the case. Somewhat ironically, the Internet is the principal means by which that information is disseminated.

By 2020, the practice of 'tumbling' digital currencies to ensure the anonymity of a payment's origins is now commonplace and a relatively simple process even for the non-specialist user. After its launch in April 2014, the 'secure, private and untraceable' digital currency Monero enjoys widespread popularity among criminal groups and attracts huge amounts of investment from speculators, many of them Chinese and Russian, hoping to see the new 'currency' skyrocket, perhaps as far as Bitcoin's high of over $1,100 per unit in November 2014. They will be disappointed: by 2020 the Monero's reputation for fuelling the activities of criminal groups and despotic state actors severely hampers its mainstream uptake.

The UK is pushed and pulled into an increasingly isolated position in world politics and it is not alone: after the 2016 US election, the Trump administration, held to its campaign promises by its far-right elements, instigates a programme intended to progressively tighten the regulations governing the entry of Muslims into the US. Australia ratchets up its rhetoric to match, initiating draconian immigration laws under the renewed leadership of Tony Abbot, in office once again after yet another leadership change – the fourth in as many years.

This isolation dramatically interrupts the flow of capital, people and information in and out of the UK. The operational gaps between one national law-enforcement organisation and the next now begin to widen, exacerbated further still as the NCA walks away from its reciprocal inter-agency partnership with the European Cyber Crime Centre (EC3), and then from what it believes to be 'one-way' information exchanges with Europol and the Club de Berne intelligence-sharing forum.

Fortunately, the UK's intelligence and security malaise isn't universal: on the other side of the Atlantic, the United Nations Office on Drugs and Crime (UNODC) bears the global responsibility for tackling the criminal and terrorist activities that the NCA is briefed to confront in the UK. By contrast, blessed with impressive resources and funding, its investigations are beginning to bear fruit.

The faith traditionally invested in the United Nations and multilateral diplomatic fora remains relatively high, despite the UN delivering precious little real-world change or even manifesting much in the way of concerted political drive. The tendency towards 'post-truth' politics, coupled with a distrust of 'experts' and other enlightened elites, creates a climate in which even the idea of evidence-based research is ejected into the long grass.

The History

AQIM

In the late 1990s, the smuggling of Moroccan cannabis resin, cocaine, and then kidnapping for ransom, sowed the seed of a spate of military coups and the creation of a string of newly minted terrorist and trafficking organisations in West Africa. In 2003, the abduction of thirty-two European tourists in southern Algeria showed the ruthlessness and ambition of one such recently formed group. They were not heard of again until another daring attack on a Mauritanian border post in 2005, after which they achieved the notoriety they desired and adopted the title 'al-Qaeda in the Islamic Maghreb' (AQIM).

AQIM then embarked on a series of kidnappings intended to provide much-needed funds for their operations. In December 2007 four French tourists were murdered in Mauritania and over the following four and a half years, forty-two foreign nationals were kidnapped and ransomed. Of these, over half were eventually released, five were murdered and the remaining hostages were either held as captives or remain unaccounted for today. Failed rescue attempts, or refusals to pay, led to televised hostage executions. This proved to be a significant success for AQIM, both in terms of publicity and fundraising: during that five-year period, estimates as to AQIM's proceeds vary from 40 to 60 million Euros, each hostage attracting a price tag of between euros 1.5 and 4 million euros.

Meanwhile in late 2011, an AQIM off-shoot had sensed a significant opportunity and captured several northern cities from the Tuareg tribes, who were looking the other way at the time; in the southern regions a bloody insurgency was raging and journalists, politicians and pro-government forces were being targeted. The Tuareg tribes were in open rebellion, their stated aim being complete independence for the northern region of Mali known as Azawad. They succeeded in ousting President Amadou Toumani Touré in the *coup d'état* of March 2012 and proceeded to overrun city after city – Kidal, Gao and Timbuktu – in a mere three days.

It took a French military offensive to bring all this to an end – history repeating itself. In 2015 a UN-backed Mali peace deal, the Algiers Accord, was struck between the Tuareg rebels and the Mali government in Bamako, the country's southern capital. This heralded almost two years of relative peace in northern Mali until the truce was shattered in 2017 and the region plunged into bloody conflict once again. Glimmers of hope re-emerged as the French-sponsored negotiations reconvened, but it all counted for nought as the negotiations collapsed in 2019, their failure attributed largely to the depredations of a nationalist anti-Muslim terror group known as 'Danbe'.

The emergence of Danbe

The Bambara, 'the people who refused to be ruled', are the largest Mandé ethnic group in the West-African state of Mali, where they comprise about thirty-five per cent of the population, but their history is glorious relative to their present-day situation. In the 1700s the Bambara ruled over much of West Africa, until in the mid-1800s, the Muslim warlord al-Hajj Umar ibn Sa'id al-Futi Tal turned a covetous eye in their direction. Frustrated by a sequence of defeats at the hands of the French, he marched his 'Army of Jihad' towards the Bambara kingdoms of Kaarta and Ségou – modern-day Mali – comprehensively destroyed them, and burned their fetishes (objects believed to inculcate supernatural powers). Umar installed his son as the chief imam in Ségou and imposed Islamic rule for the next forty years, until the French arrived to eject him. Nevertheless, the Muslim invasion left a permanent legacy, as did their French successors: today, the Bambara are seventy per cent Muslim and French is the official language. That said, even though they might claim to be Muslim, many Bambarans still adhere to ancestor worship, while others among the remaining thirty per cent are fiercely anti-Muslim.

Most Bambara are farmers, growing millet, sorghum, groundnuts, maize, cassava and tobacco, but in these times of recurrent drought, the Bambara are being forced to diversify as best they can. While Muslim villages can usually boast a school, for the non-Muslims the option of an education simply does not exist. Consequently, for many Bambarans, the only way of interrupting the cycle of poverty, even simply to subsist, is to become either a gun-for-hire, or a drug runner. Resentment of their Muslim neighbours, once kept firmly out of sight, is beginning to surface. A manifestation of this is 'Danbe', meaning 'honour' in Bambara, a pan-Sahel-Sahara nationalist terror-group based in Mali. The Sahel-Sahara is a geographic subsection encompassing Saharan Morocco, Mauritania, Mali and Niger to the centre, and Algeria and Libya to the north.

Danbe's fierce anti-Muslim sentiments date as far back as the Muslim incursions of 1861 and now, 158 years later, they are intent on waging unholy war to avenge their historic humiliations and drive all Muslims and their legacy from their country forever.

In order to finance their operations, they have established a network of gun-running and people-trafficking routes. A geographical success, they are now set on gaining political credentials, and to achieve this they are intent on carrying out a 'spectacular' terrorist strike. They already have the financial means and a range of methods at their disposal, but lack a suitable opportunity.

A more modern grievance has also attracted Danbe's attention. Of great geo-political importance, the Sahel region extends across the breadth of North Africa, a band of greenery bordering the Sahara Desert to the north, the Atlantic Ocean to the west, and the Red Sea to the east. It touches on the sovereign territory of fourteen African states, covering an area so vast, contested by so many competing militias, ethnicities and beliefs, that the region has become a melting-pot of lawlessness, corruption, trafficking and extremism.

There are also huge profits to be made from legitimate activities, and over recent years external interests, for example Chinese extractive industries, have begun to arrive in significant numbers, accompanied by well-armed, highly trained security teams. Danbe are determined that the native population, themselves at the top of the list, should reap a share of the proceeds of this latter-day 'gold rush'. As a result, the region has become the focus of intense security activity and with organised crime on the rise, the Sahel-Sahara region has become synonymous with instability, corruption, the kidnapping of Western nationals and terrorism.

～

While the Economic Community of West African States (ECOWAS) attempts to establish legitimate trading opportunities, the criminal economy continues to boom, shielded by government officials in receipt of generous bribes. Come 2019, the northern Malian authorities are so complicit that the whole area is fertile ground in which terrorist organisations like AQIM are able to flourish. The effect on the native population is catastrophic: the tourism industry implodes and there is little or no opportunity for aid work.

Voices pleading for the re-establishment of the rule of law grow louder. In an attempt to deflect attention away from their own lack of commitment, the international community look to ECOWAS to plug the security gap, but it is not to be: ECOWAS are logistically and militarily stretched thin, already deploying significant numbers of men and matériel in Burkina Faso, Cote d'Ivoire, the Gambia and Sierra Leone, and cannot coordinate and sustain an effective military response.

Fearful that AQIM will take advantage of the power vacuum, the West responds as best it can, seeking to build up the capacity of legal institutions in the hope that the rule of law might be re-established by these means alone. The UN's response is similarly perfunctory and the defence community now look to NATO for a solution, citing the Alliance's 2016 Warsaw summit communiqué, in which it agreed a Readiness Action Plan and established a Very High Readiness Joint Task Force (VJTF) – at the same time as noting that the turbulence in the Middle East and North Africa presented an 'arc of instability along NATO's periphery and beyond' that could have 'direct implications for the security of NATO'.

The conflagration in the Sahel-Sahara appears to be a perfect opportunity to redeploy elements of this much-vaunted VJTF, enabling it to both demonstrate its effectiveness and also earn its keep. Was it not, after all, intended as a 'spearhead force'? But once again NATO appears flat-footed; the 'spearhead' does not appear to be attached to a spear and NATO finds itself facing still more existential questions. Further discouraging noises emanate from the USA, suggesting that they no longer regard the conflict in West Africa as their problem. Faced with a demonstrably serious international security issue, the USA blinks and other NATO members follow their lead, and what little impetus existed promptly evaporates.

So, instead of a decisive intervention, the UN dispatches a palliative aid package to assist with the developing humanitarian crisis and an advisory team intended to bolster the security and policing functions. Both responses collapse in short order; much of the aid is misappropriated by corrupt officials and it soon becomes clear that the police and security services are enjoying the proceeds of corruption far too much to countenance change.

The extent and durability of the network of corrupt officials and criminal organisations has been catastrophically misjudged and little or no success is achieved in interdicting, still less preventing, ransom payments reaching AQIM. But their resurgence has been closely observed by their declared enemies, Danbe. Angered at AQIM's growing influence, envious of their wealth and irked by their very existence – an eloquent reminder of the Bambaran people's historic oppression – Danbe vow to drive out AQIM wherever they are found.

The region is now effectively divided up into a patchwork of organised crime fiefdoms and terrorist factions. The government forces resemble more a loose confederation of heavily armed militias rather than a coordinated, state-run military, and operate outside any state-sanctioned legitimacy. The state army has ceased to exist and Mali is officially declared a 'failed state' and power devolves to any organisation capable of generating sufficient money to pay its men, in other words criminal networks committed to people-smuggling, drug- and gun-running. Danbe and AQIM now lock horns in a bitter turf war, most notably in a bloody contest for domination of the city of Goa's black economy.

Having infiltrated both the pro-government forces and militia groups nominally loyal to the remnants of government, Danbe is ultimately triumphant and gains significant traction among the non-Muslim communities in the north of the country, where they are cast in the role of liberators waging war against their oppressors. This is exactly the profile Danbe craves and creates a perfect opportunity for them to exert a brutal retribution upon their Muslim fellow countrymen. They are zealous in its prosecution.

By 2019 Algeria is a significant regional power. Alarmed by the brutality being inflicted on its fellow Muslims, and fearing the consequences of criminal and terrorist organisations embedding themselves along its southern border, Algeria prepares to intervene to deter Danbe and other groups from further advances, but its Air Force's target selection abilities are poor and civilian casualties correspondingly high. Algeria's belligerent stance is viewed with alarm by ECOWAS, but once again there is no consensus for a response beyond the usual diplomatic handwringing.

The Build-up

International condemnation of Algeria's 'indiscriminate use of aerial ordnance' is not slow in coming. Algeria's hope is that the UN will be prompted to intervene by establishing a buffer zone along the Algerian/Mali border, but it is not to be. Worse still, the provision of aid continues to be patchy in the extreme, fomenting even more local unrest and criminal activity. Once again, it is the local militias and warlords rather than the unarmed population that are the principal beneficiaries. Danbe step up their activities to ensure they receive their share of the proceeds and push further north. In desperation, Algeria responds by creating its own buffer zone and its ground troops are deployed on foreign soil.

As the situation continues to deteriorate, calls for an international peace-making intervention, followed by a sustained peace-keeping operation, increase in volume. However, with their early twenty-first-century military adventures still very much in the minds of military planners and a critical media, the major Western powers are reluctant to embroil themselves in another foreign war. Major Western democracies – the USA, the UK, Germany, Italy and Canada – all abstain, citing a plethora of compelling reasons for their restraint. France alone responds, reminding the world of their historic interests in the region, but even their contribution falls short of a decisive intervention. Their previous mediation by force, while undoubtedly successful, appears to have exhausted what little public appetite remained for foreign military adventuring.

The major Western powers have grown progressively more isolationist and now focus almost exclusively on internal issues. Without the USA as cheerleader, national governments and multi-national institutions are reluctant to engage. Russia is ambivalent, concentrating its attentions further north in Syria, Iraq and Iran. The USA, hamstrung by introspection and protectionism, continues to sit on the fence, and even in the presence of such a dangerous power vacuum, Germany and the UK are similarly reluctant to act. There is no hope of a cogent, coherent Sahel-Sahara anti-terror policy and China alone appears to favour determined intervention; while the Security Council averts its gaze, China acts in its national interest and steps into the gap, asserting its interests in North Africa's industrial facilities, funding large-scale infrastructure projects in road, rail, telecommunications and energy production, and developing mineral extraction operations in the area.

France, stirred into action and bristling at the prospect of losing out to Chinese influence in an area once seen as its demesne, points an accusatory finger at the United Nations, criticising its apparent inability to either intelligently assess the region's security and political challenges, or commit meaningful numbers of blue berets to the West African hotspot. Raising the temperature still further, the substantial Malian diaspora in France and a collection of human-rights bodies ramp up their campaigns to exert pressure on the French government to intervene. In response, the French Foreign Legion are dispatched to Bamako, ostensibly on an 'assistance and training' mission to the pro-government forces.

At the same time as supplying the pro-government militias with French-made, military-grade equipment and training in modern combat techniques, they also find ways to provide the state-controlled militias with a decisive military edge by ensuring they're supplied with sophisticated military hardware, occasionally even matériel proscribed by international law. Self-evidently illegal and in contravention of France's agreements with Algeria, this is carried out very much at arm's length to ensure complete deniability. They allocate a significant budget and instruct the Mali Defence Force (MDF) to obtain the necessary equipment for themselves. In short, they bankroll elements of a patchwork of militias, while denying others. Predictably, once financial control is handed over, any influence as to where the money is spent is lost. Fortunately for Danbe, they have infiltrated the fledgling MDF so comprehensively that they now share its access to a range of weaponry previously beyond their wildest dreams.

Now in the ascendancy, the French-backed, pro-government MDF flush AQIM out of the north regions. Danbe, aware of the risk of being eclipsed by the MDF, look to pull off a 'spectacular' to garner publicity, revenue and fresh recruits. They must act fast, realising that with AQIM largely out of the picture and French influence growing, their drug-smuggling and human-trafficking operations will soon become the subject of increasing international scrutiny. They have a good deal at stake: for several years, Danbe have been generating funds for their operations by trafficking 'human cargo' into the UK and elsewhere, and the proceeds of these activities alone are significant. They have also gained both an impressive 'reach' and a place, albeit low down, on the National Crime Agency's target list.

That said, many of Danbe's activities are 'off-piste', carried out beyond even the peripheral view of the Western intelligence agencies who, in any case, still continue to suffer severe budget cuts and paralysing understaffing. But there is another reason they are allowed to go about their business relatively unhindered: while people-trafficking might be political anathema, Danbe's anti-Muslim agenda and the financial support they receive from an unwitting French government mean they are almost entirely left to their own devices.

But Danbe has a still darker side: their human-trafficking activities have produced a number of well-established 'runs' out of the Sahel-Sahara and into the UK. Their 'human cargo', their victims, are convinced they are destined for a chance to claim asylum in the UK and so begin a new, safe and peaceful life. Instead, they find themselves occupied as either sex workers in the case of the younger women, girls and boys, or modern slave labour for the men and older women. This generates significant amounts of foreign currency that Danbe then applies to its wider operations. Add into this mix the military hardware being funnelled into the region courtesy of French funding, then the lack of attention from the security organisations, and it is easy to see how Danbe has developed its current structure and reach.

The Scenario

Until now, Danbe has concentrated on Muslim targets across the Sahel-Sahara region, while under strict instructions from Bamako to avoid attacks on innocent civilians in the northern Malian cities, for fear of losing favour with the French and, by extension, the other Western powers. Then, in late 2019, Danbe are contacted by Daouda, a Malian exile and former key member of the group, wanting to re-establish contact with its current leadership. Daouda was once a respected member of Danbe, having infiltrated an MDF unit on active deployment during the 2012 coup until, realising the presidency was doomed and that government forces would soon be rounded up and more than likely 'disappeared', he fled to Spain via one of Danbe's people-trafficking routes. His instincts were proved right, as reports surfaced of a mass grave containing thirty bodies just outside Bamako, all bearing clear indications of extra-judicial execution.

More interesting still, Daouda claims to have formulated a plan to put Danbe firmly back on the geo-political map and at the same time score a significant blow against their bitterest enemy, AQIM. An imam linked to AQIM and near the top of Danbe's hit list is preparing to visit the UK on a clandestine fundraising 'tour'. After that, he intends to travel to the USA for the same purpose and is booked on board the British Intercontinental Airlines flight BIA762 out of Heathrow on Thursday, 20 February 2020, approximately three months prior to the UK General Election.

His overtures are received warmly and, thus encouraged, Daouda outlines his plan to take down the aircraft on which the imam is to fly. He goes into detail, even to the extent of specifying the weapon ideally suited to the task. As far as Danbe are concerned, their old friend has provided them with a remarkable opportunity: obtaining the weapon will not prove overly difficult and Danbe have the perfect means at hand to smuggle it into the UK.

The deal is simple: Danbe will pay the asking price for six of the weapons and ensure they arrive in the UK on schedule. One of the weapons will be used in the attack and the remaining five sold on to another interested party. The proceeds of this onward sale will easily outweigh the costs of the entire project, so Danbe stand to make a handsome profit, as well as deliver a devastating blow to their bitterest enemy. AQIM's ambition to re-energise its activities in the Sahel-Sahara will be forestalled and Danbe will then assume its rightful place on the geo-political map.

As unofficial 'friends of the West', Danbe can operate relatively unhindered, but somewhat less helpful is the growing perception in their sphere of influence that they are, in fact, 'proxies of the West'. In danger of losing traction within the communities currently supporting them, a terrorist spectacular on foreign soil will also serve to restore their credentials. Observing the decline in Western influence and its lack of appetite for foreign intervention, Danbe are ready to cast off the last vestiges of Western sponsorship.

Daouda's plan will enable them to nail their colours very firmly to the mast of independence and at the same time polish their anti-Muslim credentials. Daouda's proposal is ideal on several levels. With the imam's flight mere weeks away, and having had the green light, Daouda refines the detail of his 'spectacular' terror attack and receives an advance of $500,000 from Danbe to fund the operation.

Meanwhile, in the Darkest Corner of the Internet . . .

Daouda's next move is to cultivate his contacts involved in the supply of drugs and small arms via the Internet. He has a choice of several groups located in southern Spain, but one in particular appears ideally suited to the task in hand; as entrepreneurial as any Silicon Valley start-up and with all the skills and technical panache required to gain access to, and then negotiate, the 'darknet', where weapons, drugs and information can be secretly bought and sold. It employs the brightest, most talented computer experts it can recruit from among the forty-four per cent of unemployed Spanish youth.

They are not only overjoyed to be working, applying their hard-won skills at last, but are now earning undreamed-of amounts of money.

Daouda's new friends employ a combination of bespoke and commercial computer hardware together with pre-programmed software packages to access the darknet and its cryptomarkets. They have also learned valuable lessons from their rival organisations regarding the 'how to' and the 'how not to' of their chosen field and their teams of hackers apply the latest OPSEC, 'operations security', techniques to keep their hardware and procedures one step ahead of both law enforcement and rival operators. In short, they are the very best at their work and accomplished at covering their footprints.

All this is perfectly suited to Daouda's purpose: an environment in which the crime-terror-cyber nexus is practised on a day-to-day basis; refined, improved and maintained at the cutting edge of technique and technology. The principal motivation of the hackers is financial, although they also relish the sense of 'belonging' that the group gives them and the sophisticated challenges they face. The youthful operators could be making over €45,000 annually were they to follow the 'white hat' route, applying their skills and knowledge in the defence of legitimate networks, but the major financial institutions are simply not hiring. While the wider digital economy is booming, the wider world awash with emerging 'tech' jobs, none of this is happening in Spain; after the EU controversially ended its 'free movement of peoples' treaty principle, any young Spaniard with talent has only one way to turn.

The obvious benefits aside, this is no business for the faint-hearted: computer crime carries an element of risk, not least a spell of fifteen years or more in a federal prison if caught and convicted. But it can also be highly lucrative: the money to be made as a 'black hat' operator can be over ten times the amount to be earned working for a legitimate firm. Daouda's new friends are each making in excess of €500,000, almost entirely the proceeds of extortion and data ransom using cryptolocker malware. Their usual targets are Western hospitals and law firms that will usually pay a reasonable fee if their back-ups are compromised and the solution is held to ransom.

That is not to imply that everything always goes their way. The illicit marketplace Silk Road's well-documented demise in 2013 led to the arrest and conviction of a mastermind system administrator, Ross Ulbricht, and precipitated a string of arrests that rippled throughout the darknet, temporarily gripping its acolytes in fear and paranoia. More disruptive still, in 2016 the cryptomarkets were exposed as elaborate frauds, hoaxes or breeding grounds for law-enforcement undercover operations. The effects were magnified as other sysadmins ('system administrators') were turned from the 'dark side' and persuaded to surrender detailed chat logs that exposed their partners in crime. Paedophiles, human traffickers and cybercriminals all rely on the same underlying technology to keep their digital fingerprints hidden, but their activities and contacts were suddenly in real danger of being exposed to the world of law enforcement.

Worse was to come: in late 2014 Armory, the biggest single vendor for small-arms on the darknet, was revealed to be a law-enforcement sting operation and this took down a long list of buyers. The operation's success had a lasting impact on the trafficking of arms on the darknet, shattering trust in the fragile ecosystem of weapons-dealing single-vendor sites. Nobody dared to purchase from the weapons dealers – Guns4UK, Weapons Stock, Balkan Store, or any of the other dozen-or-so outlets. In 2015 two sysadmins, Verto and Kimble of Evolution Marketplace, were scammed and all the escrowed cryptocoins of their users impounded: approximately $12 million-worth of the Bitcoins allocated to pending transactions. Enraged users vented their anger on Reddit's message boards, talking of revenge and of hiring hit men to murder Verto and Kimble.

Without a steady stream of Monero filling their digital coffers, the likes of our Spanish hackers were starved of the working capital necessary to support their activities and in 2015 they were even forced to shut down their single-vendor site after it was compromised. In any case, the site had performed badly of late, only generating a few dubious leads to paranoid users unable to establish that essential degree of trust by leaving verifiable feedback. To reinvigorate their cash flow, they aggressively advertised their weapons on cryptocurrency markets like Alphabay, Outlaw and Valhalla, making sales throughout Europe posing as US vendors. The small team left in place kept a tight digital ship, surfacing only to reply to encrypted messages during US Eastern Time business hours. They are among the few survivors, but all the more effective for it.

An established cryptomarket can provide the user with almost any manner of offensive weapon ranging from knives and knuckledusters to Tasers and pistols, from rifles and machineguns to crew-served weaponry, and then all manner of ammunition and accessories. They operate in much the same way as legitimate online marketplace vendors, placing advertisements in reply to which verified buyers leave feedback. But there is a key difference: cryptomarkets limit the amount of personally identifiable information they collect and typical OPSEC techniques include falsifying the shipping source and delivery destinations, increasing the stealth-value of sending parcels through the post (such as by concealing weapons in printers), and using espionage-style dead drops, aliases and untraceable digital currencies with zero transaction fees.

Confidence, the essential darknet commodity, has been slowly re-established and then maintained via verified transaction histories and comprehensive feedback. With Evolution Marketplace taken down, another black-market vacuum ensues until, hydra-like, other marketplaces emerge to fill the gap, market demand seldom remaining unserviced for long. Dozens more cryptomarkets emerge to fill the void left by the likes of Silk Road and the black market soon recovers its former reach. Between 2016 and 2017, out of perhaps forty remaining cryptocurrency sites, the majority of weapons deals take place on Alphabay and together with the smaller Outlaw Market and Valhalla, the darknet is re-established as a conduit for an ever-increasing number of black-market sales.

~

In 2019, Daouda learns from the Spanish gang that an unusual consignment of weaponry has come onto the market via a proven darknet source in the Ukraine. The seller's credentials are good: the gang has worked with them before, providing them with heavy weapons during the November 2013 'Euromaidan' or 'Revolution of Dignity' uprising. Since then the Ukrainians have stayed in sporadic contact with the gang, most recently buying two crew-served heavy machineguns and an M40 sniper rifle. The weapons left Spain, were driven to the Balkans and then dead-dropped at a warehouse with instructions for a local smuggling ring to transport the guns north and into Ukraine.

For the gang, this transaction of $300,000 (BTC 401.6064) is their largest single weapons deal to date, but it is about to be superseded. Of great importance to Daouda is that a new business relationship has been established and then secured when all communications are moved off the darknet onto encrypted communication channels, so as to leave the smallest possible digital footprint.

Resolute in the face of the international community's condemnation of its annexation of the Crimea and incursion into the Donbass region of Ukraine, Russia then applied pressure by all means at its disposal, including cyberattacks and direct military intervention. The deconstruction, then reoccupation, of the Ukraine in 2018–19 then resulted in a surge of military-grade weaponry appearing for sale on the dark web and this time the flow is in the opposite direction. What Daouda has learned is that the same Ukrainian rebels have acquired six PULSE2 state-of-the-art, shoulder-launched, surface-to-air missiles (SAMs) and are keen to unload them for the right price via the darknet. This has come at the right time; having so successfully penetrated the MDF, Danbe are ready to use their untraceable, unaccountable funding to pay the asking price. There is a crucial difference with this transaction: unlike the various other batches of weaponry acquired by the MDF, the missiles will never arrive in Mali.

The SAMs are hardly Danbe's preferred choice of weapon: manufactured by US Defence Systems (USDS), PULSE2 is a highly sophisticated technological incarnation of 'CHAMP' (Counter-electronics High-powered Microwave Advanced Missile Project). Everything about them is state of the art, even the so-called 'quantum dot' markings: unforgeable and unalterable nanoparticles spin-coated onto the weapon's components by which a missile's provenance can be easily proven. Given their $250,000 unit cost, the Ukrainians' asking price of only $600,000 for all six is tempting and the deal is struck. The next step for Danbe is to smuggle the weapons into the UK, but this will not be a significant problem given their proven smuggling expertise.

All is now set fair for the attack; however, what Danbe does not know is that Daouda has been 'turned' . . . but not by the Western intelligence services. In fact, Daouda is now working via an intermediary for Vulcan Avionics, a major UK-based military avionics manufacturer engaged in the manufacture and sale of sophisticated aerospace systems and associated weaponry. What will not be discovered from their impressive website is that Vulcan Avionics, Daouda's new employer, also sells weapons on the darknet.

Vulcan's most recent legitimate success has been the design of the new command, control, communication, computers, intelligence, surveillance and reconnaissance (C4ISR) systems for the Royal Air Force; the Brexit schism with Europe having precipitated a political impetus to reject the air-defences systems designed and serviced by NATO, regarding them as 'chiefly European'. Now, the UK MoD commits innovative capacity and funding to bring the Air Defence of Great Britain (ADGB) up to scratch. With it having been reliant upon allies and allied AD systems for decades, the new feeling is that the UK should be more self-reliant in defence of its airspace, cyberspace, waters and coasts. This will prove to be Vulcan's first and last boon to emerge from the EU.

In response, and somewhat more controversially, Vulcan has designed and manufactured its own suite of indigenous missiles and other weapons systems intended for unmanned aerial vehicles (UAVs) otherwise known as drones. Vulcan now has its own platform, 'Harvester', similar to the General Atomics MQ-9 'Reaper' in size and capability, but now rated as the largest military-grade drone in service capable of autonomous flight operations in remote locations. It has an impressive maximum flight time of eighteen hours when carrying a full complement of munitions and can remain aloft in excess of fifty hours when optimised for endurance and ISR missions.

But 'Harvester' is in dire need of customers. With many defence and security markets locked down and European deals drowning in red tape, additional taxes and a swathe of new business regulations, UK defence exports have suffered greatly since Prime Minister May's 'Hard Brexit'. In response, Vulcan have been diligent in targeting overseas business opportunities in the Gulf States, doggedly pursuing contracts with Oman and Saudi Arabia, who have agreed in principle to purchase two ground stations and four Harvesters each, costing £400 million in total over a five-year period. But even these successes will not be enough to keep Vulcan's accounts in the black and, subject to a more liberal import/export regime, General Atomics' 'Reaper' platform is in danger of scooping up too many clients before Vulcan can even cut its way through all that red tape, and find a way to pacify EU hostilities.

The Terrorist 'Spectacular'

The six PULSE2 missiles are acquired by Danbe from their Ukrainian suppliers and only one major task still remains, to transport them quietly into the UK in time to strike the intended target. The traffickers arrive at a simple solution: exploiting their infiltration of the UK Border Force and using their adapted trucks, one of their human 'cargoes' is about to share their concealed fibreglass box with six mysterious crates.

The hard work of setting up the smuggling routes is complete, the product of several years of painstaking preparation. Danbe's first move had been to acquire a legitimate international removals company registered in Spain: TR (*Trasladar Rápidamente*). The second had been to seed TR with Danbe recruits from the Sahel-Sahara. They decided to operate two routes intended for their illicit cargoes and four others to run legitimately, thus creating the illusion of a company carrying out its work entirely within the law.

The 'distractor' routes were Calais–Dover, Caen–Portsmouth, Zeebrugge–Le Havre and Ostend–Ramsgate. The two remaining routes, Bilbao–Portsmouth and Cherbourg–Poole saw a high level of lorry traffic and this suited Danbe's purposes perfectly. They also operated these routes entirely within the law until they were satisfied that the over-stretched UK Border Force, after at first searching a number of their vehicles, had become so used to seeing TR's bold livery that they had begun to turn their attentions elsewhere. The drivers and crews, three or four men to a truck, while not being precisely on first-name terms with the Border Force staff, were at least known to them and were now routinely waved through with little more than a second glance.

The TR removals trucks working the Bilbao–Portsmouth and Cherbourg–Poole routes were then adapted, inserting a concealed compartment behind the cab and protecting it from sniffer dogs by encasing it in fibreglass. To defeat any CO_2 emissions sensors, the concealed compartment's air circulation system could be switched off while passing through security and only switched on again once the vehicle was a safe distance beyond. Danbe also incorporated a vital fail-safe measure to cut in should an unforeseen delay occur and the truck be immobile within earshot of Border Force officers and within range of their sniffer dogs' acute sense of smell: each occupant was to be provided with a scuba re-breather tank system, sufficient to provide roughly sixty minutes of compressed air.

This overheated, stinking box was where the truck's illicit cargo of 'clandestines' and anything else they cared to transport would be concealed. Then, 'dry runs' were carried out until the converted TR trucks were passing through European and UK ports up to eighteen times a week. Inside the concealed fibreglass box men, women and children were forced to endure the journey of about forty-eight hours tightly packed, with barely enough room to move their limbs and, periodically, even without fresh air.

The UK public is under the impression that its Border Force is fully funded, efficient and with all manner of sophisticated detection equipment ready at hand. In fact, it has very few heat-sensing lorry scanners at its disposal, despite repeated requests for more and improved scanners. What little equipment they do have has been superseded by several generations of more effective and reliable hardware. 'Passive Millimetre Wave Imaging' (PMWI) devices are able to scan vehicles for the presence of 'clandestines', but each scanner not only costs £800,000 to buy, it also costs a small fortune to run for any significant length of time.

Budgets have been tightly squeezed year on year, by twenty per cent in 2012–13 alone, and this pattern has been repeated until, come 2020, the number of machines available to the UK Border Force is a paltry twelve, three of which are out of commission awaiting repairs and/or spare parts. Not only that, the same run of budget cuts has limited the use of the remaining nine machines to a maximum of six hours in any twenty-four-hour period. Danbe not only know this, but thanks to an informant inside the Border Force, they also know weeks ahead of time should either of the two ports through which they run illicit 'deliveries' have a PMWI scanner deployed and, crucially, exactly when they are scheduled to be actually switched on. In this way Danbe is given anything from one to six weeks' notice to avoid the better policed routes and wait for any scanner in place to be moved on, before sending out the next shipment of human cargo.

On the other side of the Channel, Vulcan now have an additional problem on their hands. Their US rival, USDS, has prompted an investigation via the UNODC, the United Nations Office on Drugs and Crime, into Vulcan's darknet dealings. The UNODC are now of the opinion that USDS's allegations may indeed have substance and have dispatched one of their staff to investigate. This is potentially disastrous for Vulcan, the selling of unlicensed systems being very definitely in contravention of UK export-control regulations and also international law.

The allegation is, in fact, very well founded: Vulcan have been covertly selling unlicensed, unbadged and untraceable weapons systems for several years to a particularly belligerent Gulf state as it fights a protracted war-by-proxy against an al-Qaeda presence in a neighbouring state. Its 'client' now benefits from various types of modern weaponry from bullets to bombs and all manner of matériel in between. The present problem for Vulcan is that rumours have begun to circulate and then gather credence that massacres of the civilian population have been carried out within the war zone. It is also possible that a good proportion of the munitions dropped on those market places, hospitals and schools were supplied by Vulcan.

All that follows might well appear logical in business terms, if also morally perverse. Vulcan intends to deflect the unwelcome attention away from themselves while at the same time finding a way to boost their ailing stock value. In the event, both objectives prove easily achievable. The six USDC-manufactured PULSE2 missiles are shipped first to Spain and then into a TR warehouse to await onward shipment to the UK. TR are then contracted to remove the belongings of Mr and Mrs Harcourt from Catalunya back to their home town of Windsor. The Harcourts are entirely fictitious, their belongings contrived, and their new home in Windsor owned, albeit at a safe distance, by Vulcan. What is very real indeed are the six PULSE2 shoulder-launched SAM missiles concealed in the TR removals truck soon to be on its way to Bilbao and then to Portsmouth.

In early February 2020, an apparently unremarkable delivery of house contents is made to a modest-looking house in Windsor, some even displaying a distinctly Spanish flavour (a nice touch). One of the six PULSE2 SAM missiles is set aside and the remaining five are carefully disarmed and deconstructed to the point at which the constituent parts are rendered completely anonymous and untraceable, to the extent of removing the nanoparticles spin-coated onto the components. This is crucial to Vulcan's plans; while only one missile remains ready for active use, traceable nanoparticles included, the other five must be completely decommissioned and their destruction kept secret.

While Danbe has been paid for the 'missing' five missiles and they now constitute no active threat, the mere possibility of their presence on UK soil will be enough to set hares running. And this will be Vulcan's first move once the single surviving missile has fulfilled its purpose; they will ensure that credible intelligence is made public that a total of six PULSE2 missiles have found their way onto European soil. By then the UK threat level will already be set at 'CRITICAL', but this additional piece of news will send JTAC, the Joint Terrorism Analysis Centre, into overdrive.

Thursday, 20 February 2020

British Intercontinental Airlines Flight BIA762 to New York leaves on time. Sitting in First Class, seat 7b, is a nervous flyer: Oscar Andersson. He is *en route* to make a confidential report to UNODC at the UN Headquarters building that will unequivocally state that Vulcan are guilty as charged of supplying prohibited arms. As BIA762's wheels leave the tarmac of Heathrow's third runway and the aircraft begins to rapidly gain height, from the garden of the 'Harcourts' home in Windsor a PULSE2 missile arcs gracefully up into the air and directly into the path of the state-of-the-art 'FutureBoeing' plane. It does not even need to get close: as soon as it is within range, it emits a devastating electromagnetic pulse (EMP) that knocks out the aircraft's control systems. The effect is immediate and catastrophic: despite its sophistication, the fly-by-wire FutureBoeing looks like it has been struck by a huge fist. It loses all power and control and after turning steeply first to the left, then to the right, completely inverts, drops like a stone and ploughs into an industrial park. Casualties on the ground can only be estimated at seventy-five, any human remains having been completely incinerated, while all 407 passengers and crew of the FutureBoeing are killed instantly, including the UNODC investigator sitting in seat 7b: Oscar Andersson. He will never make his report damning Vulcan in person, but not that this will matter; the delay is all that Vulcan needs.

It is win-win all round: Danbe receive their US dollars, but will forever puzzle at how their intended target, the fundraising imam, not only survived the attack but appears never to have even been on UK soil at the time. For Vulcan it is a triple win:

1. The scandal of their supplying illicit arms is completely overshadowed by the hysteria that follows the terrorist attack on BIA762. The persistent rumours that five more such devastating weapons are in circulation only serves to heighten the tension.

2. The company enjoys an upward surge in their stock value when UK government defence expenditure is increased by a massive four per cent, much of the extra money destined for airport perimeter defences, anti-missile detection and interdiction technologies. Better still, the crisis induces a Europe-wide relaxation in arms exports from the UK.

3. More significant still, tracing the nanoparticle 'fingerprint' on the missile fragments reveals the SAM to have been manufactured by none other than USDS, US Defence Systems, and their shares plummet as rapidly as Vulcan's soar.

The Assessment

Once the United Kingdom made its decision to extract itself from the European Union, the majority of the British population imagined that the country would be free to choose for itself from a *smörgåsbord* of overseas trade opportunities, but they have now discovered the world to be a highly interdependent place. They also imagined that politics would become more accountable and the country wealthier, but instead of this, an increasingly isolationist Britain has found itself confronted by a profusion of foreign dangers, compounded by a sustained period of economic downturn that shows no immediate signs of reversing.

The United Kingdom is not alone. In 2020 the world is

contending with a range of unprecedented political complexities. For the public, these are realised in fearful, ill-informed
speculation, but among those in authority an all-pervading
sense of fragility is now paramount. Two main issues have
come to the fore: firstly, the much-vaunted benefits of globalisation have not been realised and the disparity between rich
and poor has never been so much in plain sight; secondly,
post-truth politics is now in direct conflict with fact-based
journalism.

The terror attack leaves the British public in a state of
deep shock. As the country enters a period of mourning the
threat level is raised, and then remains at the highest level
– 'CRITICAL' – indicating that an attack is imminently
expected. International condemnation of the tragedy is swift,
the loudest voices emanating from the United States, their
nationals having comprised the majority of the victims.
Outraged by the loss of life on UK soil, the public demands
answers from the intelligence services tasked to protect them.
After all, has not the UK seen this before over Lockerbie?
Have lessons not been learned?

Questions are raised as to the competence of the UK
intelligence agencies. MI5, who have the lead on domestic
counter-terrorism, is vilified, but other organisations are not
spared – JTAC, the organisation responsible for setting the
threat level from international terrorist attack, had set it at
'SEVERE', or one level below 'CRITICAL'. Both MI5 and
JTAC are roundly accused of 'being asleep at the wheel' and
even the Home Secretary finds herself in the firing-line and
scrambles to defend the government's sustained budget cuts
to the intelligence and security services over the preceding
four years.

Print, broadcast and social media press for answers to the
questions posed by the 'Twenty-Two-Twenty' attack. Who is

responsible? From whom were the missiles procured? And then comes the most significant question of all: who was the target – US citizens? UK citizens? Or could it have been a specific passenger? No convincing answers are found, despite a twenty-four-hour news cycle of non-stop repetition of speculation and horrific images on television, Internet, newspapers and radio. The theory gaining most traction is that extremists returning from Syria after fighting for ISIS have turned their expertise and fury on the innocent civilians of Flight BIA762. No organisation claims responsibility for the attack until, after a telling silence, a lengthy queue forms of terrorist groups all seeking to garner enough credit and infamy to bring them funds and fresh recruits.

Media representations of the attacks draw parallels between 20/2/20 and the 7/7 London bombings. President Trump follows their lead by tweeting, in his inimitable style: 'All free people are the victims of this attack. America's heart go [sic] out to the British as they did with 9/11. Never forget.'

The UK leadership is at first commendably measured, even reflective, before finally drawing its conclusions. Caution is well advised as Prime Minister Theresa May is very much aware that with the UK General Election mere months away, and her party lagging in the polls, how she conducts herself over the coming days may easily decide the leadership of the country over the coming years.

While rumours have been in circulation for a while, the leaked intelligence now surfaces. Vulcan have given it sufficient credibility to convince the intelligence community by ensuring that it emerges from three separate, equally reliable sources. Now JTAC states, with a high level of confidence, that more SAMs, possibly as many as five, may be on UK soil. The 'may be' is of importance: they know that six missiles had left Ukraine for Europe and one was used in the 20/2/20 attack, but the whereabouts of the remaining five is uncertain. The nation is gripped, white-knuckled with terror that more attacks are imminent, and the alarm spreads throughout Europe.

In the UK, with the threat level already at 'CRITICAL', not much more can be said without increasing public consternation still further. Nevertheless, heavily armed security teams are dispatched to reinforce the UK Border Force and at key transport hubs across the UK, perhaps intended more to reassure anxious passengers and aircrew that every effort is being taken to ensure their safety than to act as a credible deterrent to the next determined terrorist assault.

Once the leak concerning the presence of the PULSE2 missiles somewhere in Europe is common knowledge, it becomes obvious to pundits following the events that at least one SAM must have been trafficked into the UK. More incriminating still is that the missile's quantum dot 'fingerprint', together with the distinctive characteristics of the EMP pulse it emitted, indicate that it was a USDS missile and not that of a British manufacturer. The media spotlight is pulled away from a grateful intelligence community and shone unforgivingly in the direction of the UK Border Force and NCA. So it is that the lion's share of the blame for the 20/2/20 atrocity is laid firmly at the door of the country's overstretched policing services and one element of the country's intelligence community.

A damning narrative gradually unfolds concerning the NCA's withdrawal from those vital reciprocal information-sharing arrangements with its European counterparts. More incriminating still, the bribe economy that has compromised certain Border Force personnel is exposed and the links between well-financed criminal networks, traffickers and terrorists become clearer by the day. The NCA confirms there is a 'cyber' angle to the trafficking of people through

UK borders with a strong suspicion of involvement by foreign nationals living in the Sahel-Sahara region.

Danbe keeps a low profile until the full list of casualties on board the plane is made public. Realising their target was not aboard flight BAI762, they realise they have been manipulated by Daouda. They bide their time, waiting patiently for him to resurface, but Daouda appears to have simply disappeared from the face of the earth.

Prime Minister May attempts to take control of the news feed and over the days following the attack releases a string of press statements hoping to simultaneously stifle speculation and secure any political capital to be extracted from the disaster. She takes an increasingly hard line regarding the failings of the nation's security apparatus, mainly to deflect attention from the effects of four years of budgetary attrition, repeatedly and determinedly rebuffing the merest suggestion that her government's budget cuts were the *causa causans* of the attacks. Instead, she consciously presents an unassailable image: imbued with gravitas, repeatedly emphasising her expertise and experience in dealing with the Home Office, Foreign and Commonwealth Office, Ministry of Defence and the UK security and intelligence agencies. The Foreign Office also springs into action and, via their diplomatic networks of Embassies and High Commissions in Commonwealth countries, urges them to share any intelligence of possible interest to the British government and promising to return the favour.

In the wake of the attacks, highly sensitive and valuable intelligence floods into UK hands from Europe, first as a sign of goodwill and then in a concerted effort to prevent further attacks on either side of the Channel. It is the French intelligence agencies that pass on the decisive intelligence 'card' to the NCA; their involvement with the MDF and darknet monitoring operations by the EC3 have enabled them to assemble crucial strands of evidence into a partial image. In the UK, links are forged between undercover MI5 officers and the Border Force officers who have been taking bribes from people smugglers in the form of untraceable cryptocurrency. In return for MI5 turning a blind eye to their activities, the officers reveal the first indications of operations about which MI5 have been previously unaware, thus highlighting glaring gaps in their Middle-Eastern and North-African coverage. In their turn, the Whitehall policymakers realise the importance of this intelligence and move decisively to formalise these new intelligence-gathering relationships.

Seizing another opportunity to spin the story in her favour, and fearful of a swing to UKIP, who have been roundly criticising the level of UK defence expenditure for several years, Prime Minister May's administration adopts a unified party line that turns the public perception of the damaging security debacle into a battle in the war on terrorism. This is rather more than a simple lapse in border security, for which the government would otherwise have been obliged to take responsibility. The Conservative Party takes its cues from the US and Australia, toughening up an already stringent immigration policy and passing draconian legislation against 'economic refugees' through both Houses of Parliament. This proves resoundingly popular in the polls.

Only two months away from the UK General Election, Prime Minister May decides to adopt a new campaign slogan – 'Britain for the British' – and then announces a further bill aimed at strengthening Britain's porous borders. On the floor of the House of Commons, she echoes former Australian Prime Minister John Howard, saying, 'We will decide who comes to this country and the manner in which they come.'

The bill passes, to be read into law as the 'Fighting the Origins of Radical Terrorism and Reinforcing Electronic Surveillance for Security' Act of 2020, better known by its acronym 'FORTRESS'.

Later the same year, Theresa May is returned to office with an increased majority, thereby turning a national security failure into a political victory.

CHAPTER 7

DARK CODE
The Cybersecurity Challenge

The Build-Up

The overcast sky in central London during winter washes the city's buildings steel-grey. Whitehall is no exception as its outline seems to blur into the low clouds above. From street level, the buildings of Whitehall have not changed significantly in the past one hundred years, but unknown to the casual observer, it now houses the most important node in a network of international intelligence and political decision-making, much like the synapses in the human nervous system.

Even at this early hour, tourists on the street below are busy taking photographs of the only things in vivid royal red: the buses, postboxes, telephone booths and the mounted troopers of the Life Guards. These tourists would be surprised to learn that many of the Londoners hurrying past them are actually MI5 and MI6 staff and civil servants on their way to a morning briefing.

It is December 2020 and in recent years the evolution of London's digital architecture has continued at an exponential rate. The 'Internet of Things' has permeated everyday life: power-hungry 5G phones demand more and more screen time from their owners, who are enthralled by the digital objects, tokens and landmarks that overlay the physical world; watches, phones, keys and jewellery are already being linked to the Internet for always-on connectivity; and consumers eagerly await the next phase in this digital revolution, when electric cars, buses, trucks and taxis will be self-driving, autonomous vehicles ferrying people to and from work, home, and nightclubs. Autonomy has already reached for the sky, with drones delivering products to houses and between businesses, and now there is talk of office buildings with rooftops running networks of people-carrying drones between meetings, hotels and railway stations.

The technological promises of the future have not, however, resulted in greater time for self-indulgence: there is no additional free time to spend and relax with loved ones this holiday season. Rather, London is a bustling metropolis where no taxi seat is left vacant, no bed unslept in, no gym class empty, or spare moment unoccupied by advertising or data-generating exercise. It is full-on consumption, both virtual and physical.

The digitisation of life and the growth of the Internet of Things have been enabled by the step-change in computer science. Inexpensive, 'near quantum' supercomputers are expected to enter the consumer market within a matter of years. Incremental advances in nano-scale manufacturing techniques are bringing consumer electronics ever-closer to true quantum capabilities. Even now, small companies can crunch vast datasets that were once the exclusive province of multi-national banks, tech-industry giants and governments.

Deep-learning algorithms can be designed by young coders and engineers to manage anything from shipping inventories, to car-pooling and ride-sharing, to reducing traffic jams and real-time visual analytics of CCTV footage.

These services have come to change the world by providing easy access to the digital architecture of cities and the way people interact, consume and live. Some of the brightest technological minds are still preoccupied with advertising and marketing, while others have no less an ambition than to bring innovation and new technologies into every corner and crevice of human life.

The winter chill seems to have accompanied the men and women entering the Cabinet Office in Whitehall. The men and women who were scurrying moments earlier along the London street now file into Cabinet Office 'Briefing Room A', or COBRA. It is a Friday morning in early December in a week that seems to have been dragging on forever. The atmosphere in the room is tense. The surprise rescheduling of the briefing meeting, and the inclusion of some senior American officials, has not gone unnoticed.

The Scenario

Going Dark

The spooks and suits gathered around the large table in COBRA share expressions of concern, reflecting the topic of this morning's briefing. The Cabinet Office has throughout the week played host to a revolving door of intelligence agencies, with a highly unusual cadre of directors, chiefs and assistant secretaries from the Government Communications Headquarters (GCHQ), the Security Service (MI5), the Secret Intelligence Service (SIS or MI6), the National Cyber Security Centre (NCSC) and the Ministry of Defence (MoD), all of whom sit around the briefing-room table, screens churning out data feeds, a BBC news broadcast echoing in the background.

At the opposite end of the room, the US Four-Star Generals in charge of the US Cyber Command and the National Security Agency are featured on video-link from the Situation Room in Washington, DC. One of the British officers launches a Powerpoint presentation, with a panoply of logos on the first slide, and the heading: 'Going Dark: Chinese Quantum Satellites Reach Full Operational Capability'.

Quantum cryptography using satellite communication is the cyber age's equivalent of the 1940s Enigma machine. Except in 2020, it is the Chinese leading the quantum space race with their Quantum Experiments at Space Scale (QUESS) programme. Governments have kept a keen eye on the incremental developments of quantum cryptography for many years, mindful that it poses a 'game changer' to the practice of intelligence.

It is the confluence of a number of discoveries and break-throughs that is needed to enable truly un-hackable communications technologies. Experts have previously classified the emergence of quantum cryptography as a 'low probability / high impact' risk, which, like quantum computing, but for different reasons, was thought to be at least ten years away from implementation. The faulty analysis and underestimation of the prospect of quantum cryptography has been mostly due to its fantastically technical complexity.

The ripples of the QUESS programme are being felt throughout the Western world – broadly Europe, the US, UK, Canada, Australia and New Zealand – because of what the Chinese have achieved; a sequence of breakthroughs of astounding ingenuity. It is a Black Swan event; so unlikely as to be unbelievable, and an outlier compared to all other kinds of systems that behave in a similar way.

No other state has come close to achieving a proof of

concept (POC) for actual quantum communication, let alone reaching full operational capability. The Chinese have managed to overcome the prohibitively high barriers to space travel by adopting lean business models, akin to those of Silicon Valley tech start-ups, to reduce the cost of sending satellites into orbit. Chinese universities have pooled together their collective resources in an open-robust system, which enables both free-thinking and open criticism of others for the betterment of the project at hand.

The political and social triumph cannot be overstated, the pursuit of scientific knowledge has trumped the uncomfortable tension of the political context and the single-party system. Western governments are stunned that they were not the first to achieve it, and it feels remarkably similar to the shock when Russia launched Sputnik, the first satellite, beating the US into space. The Chinese have gone quantum and the Western intelligence network has gone dark. Fear is rising amongst members of the Five Eyes (FVEY) intelligence-sharing network, comprising the UK, Australia, Canada, New Zealand and the United States.

It was standard end-to-end encryption, used to secure phone-texting messaging platforms like WhatsApp and iMessage, that made governments, police and intelligence agencies in the West start to take notice. Then quantum encryption captured the attention of intelligence agencies, making defence ministers deeply concerned at the thought of asymmetric capability in the hands of a hostile rival. Particularly after the NSA, who were Five Eye's best shot at breaking the quantum-encryption challenge, warned them in technical language that it was essentially un-hackable, with the information assurance certificate signed by no lesser authority than 'fundamental physics'. It would take an act of God to break quantum encryption.

Since the first Monday in December 2020, only a trickle of highly classified information has entered the Five Eyes global intelligence-sharing network. There has been an ever-shrinking list of intercepted messages and signals intelligence (SIGINT) from both the Politburo in Beijing and the Kremlin in Moscow. Fifty years of information supremacy since the advent of computing has meant that SIGINT has become the staple diet for policymakers in Whitehall and FVEY. Running down human intelligence (HUMINT) capability has been a Western phenomenon, unlike Russia and China, who retained many of their HUMINT assets. All the FVEY countries have now lost much of their ability to run field agents, instead chasing digital signals over wires, airwaves and electrical circuits.

As soon as the meeting starts, it becomes apparent that there are deep rifts among the attendants; everyone views the challenge ahead through their particular institutional lens. The intelligence agencies of MI5, MI6 and GCHQ are in the firing line, since they are the ones going dark. The Prime Minister and the other ministers are concerned with heavy scrutiny from the press and risks to their electoral support. The military strategists at MoD have never been more concerned about protecting the sovereignty of the nation and are more desperate than ever to know the intentions of their adversaries.

The head of GCHQ is first in the line of fire to 'hack up a solution'. The other agencies look on with thinly veiled contempt, as if GCHQ needs only to be shut down while their computers are restarted for the problem to be fixed. MI5 are fearful they will not be able to secure London from a terrorist attack, or secure their counter-intelligence missions to track and thwart espionage operations on British soil. But it is MI6 that has the US and the broader FVEY alliance insisting that it break into Moscow to steal the encryption keys to the quantum encryption network. The US has assigned itself the task of getting into Beijing to break the Chinese quantum encryption. While the Prime Minister has been fielding questions from the media circus surrounding the ordeal, the pressure has been mounting on Secretaries of State from the Home Office, Defence, Justice, and International Trade simply to 'do something' about the problem.

Outside on the busy streets of central London, more tourists gather to take photos and videos of the iconic places dotted around the city. The tourist groups are armed with the latest smartphones – most of Chinese origin – and collect moments of time, impressions of places and large group gatherings with crystal-clear, 4K definition. The ability to discern faces in a crowd, track them over time and see who they interact with, has been within the realms of possibility for some time.

The challenge for counter-intelligence operatives has been to use these surveillance technologies to dismantle the mesh networks, and even run disinformation campaigns to render the analysis useless. The seemingly innocent tour groups, like the ones hanging around Whitehall taking endless videos of grey skies, grey buildings and grey faces, may in fact be collecting intelligence like grains of sand; one tiny piece at a time. The vast amount of data, that to all appearances looks benign, is in reality being sent back to the collective hive-mind of foreign surveillance agencies for mass analysis.

Back inside COBRA, the room has emptied to leave only a select few key players, all from the premier intelligence agencies. At its core, QUESS is an intelligence problem that requires an intelligence solution. It is not a policing problem, nor a military or diplomatic issue, although it does affect each of these arms of government, if only secondarily. MI6 is briefing the remaining intelligence agencies and the Prime Minister, presenting four key pieces of information that inform their mission to crack QUESS.

Cosmic Top Secret//FVEY//SIS

//Breaking QUESS through mission LOSTKEYS

The main objective: find the encryption keys in Moscow central intelligence to decode QUESS.

Key intelligence assessments:

1. An increased presence of Chinese intelligence operatives has been detected in Washington and London.

2. Russian and Chinese capabilities have grown in recent months, not only with the advent of QUESS.

3. Russia has launched a new pro-Kremlin campaign of 'patriot hackers' and calls for a digital militia to mobilise.

4. Chinese and Russian intentions are unknown at this stage.//

But before the MI6 chief can finish his briefing, the lights in the room begin ever so slightly to pulse. Over a few seconds, the dimming and brightening of the lights occur with the mathematical curve of a sine-wave. It lasts a few long moments. Nothing is said, and this new normal of peculiar pulsing becomes part of the energy of the room, long enough for those present to begin to question their own perceptions: is it just me, or are the lights really pulsing? Then, as this thought is finished, all the lights go out. The electricity has been cut. The room is plunged into complete darkness.

Blackout

The room waits a beat – two beats – for the back-up power generators to kick back in. Except it does not happen. Some groan and mutter expletives under their breath. In the dark room, there is no telling who said what. Someone turns on their smartphone torch, dazzling everyone else in the room in the process. There are still red, green and yellow LED standby lights dotted about the room on screens, projectors and laptop chargers. Is there still power?

The thought is interrupted by an oncoming rumble, like a passenger jet flying overhead, causing a boom to resound throughout the room. The smartphone light pops off and the power surges, killing the little beady electronic eyes around the room. As all signs of electronic life fade away, the room descends into total darkness and silence reigns. The lack of stimulus starts to fill the space in the room, and ears are left ringing.

The initial silence and darkness pervading the room gives way to adrenalin-fuelled panic. What was that rumbling? Did whatever happened to the power also affect all the electronic devices? It seems more than a power surge, since the unconnected smartphones were fried, too. Someone exclaims that a powerful electromagnetic pulse – EMP for short – must have been generated. Panic washes over those in COBRA as they scramble over desks and out of the room. Is this the beginning of a terrorist attack? One of many orchestrated attacks about to occur throughout London, perhaps even the Western world?

'Where's the PM?' someone yells into the darkness. 'Everyone get themselves to the secure room downstairs!' The yelling and panic endures as the heads of GCHQ, MI5 and MI6 huddle together in the darkness like a rugby scrum, feeling their way around chairs and holding onto each other's suit-jackets, while they attempt to reach the door and the outside world.

Once back in the natural light of the Cabinet Office hallway, one of the young policy aides caught up in the scrum breaks free, as the PM is rushed downstairs in a rolling maul of suits. She navigates to the nearest room with daylight flooding in through the window panes, which are opened to let street noise fill the room.

Sound is a primitive form of information, but information nonetheless. The noise coming from the streets is unmistakably chaotic. The digital playground of London is turned into a hostile urban jungle. The power surge was also accompanied by an abrupt, intense energy pulse that produced a transient boost of thousands of volts, killing all semiconductor devices inside its blast radius. Central London, around the streets of Whitehall, as far as those inside can tell, has been plunged back into the analogue era.

The most immediate and horrific effects are felt at the individual level, where the attack claims the lives of its first victims. The tiny microprocessors inside pacemakers are especially vulnerable to this type of assault. The sudden increase of power sends a jolt of electricity to the device, which instantaneously short-circuits and passes on the surge to the patient's heart. The fault claims the lives of two civil servants in Whitehall, and another two parliamentarians in Westminster Palace. In the days that follow the attack, the reporting of the deaths will occupy the media headlines, in place of more shocking images containing carnage, gore and horror. Instead, psychological trauma, the fragility of human life, and 'over-reliance' on technology will occupy the national media's narrative of the event.

Smartphones begin to act decidedly dumb. The way people connect and communicate with one another – and now the inability to do so – is the major source of chaos in the city. The overriding sense of isolation is keenly felt, as nobody can reach out to loved ones and tell them all is well. After the power is cut, there is an equal and opposite sense of freedom that spreads like wildfire. Looting breaks out in various pockets of London, many of which are unaffected by the blackout. The overwhelming feeling of anonymity, and reports of London's CCTV network going dark, are the momentary lapse that some were looking for.

The attack places a great amount of strain onto the social fabric of society. The gridlock of the city cannot be overstated. Autonomous electric vehicles have ground to a complete halt, blocking the path of the older generation of buses and taxis, whose diesel motors are still running. The iconic 'Boris Bikes' are inaccessible to rent or return, with their user-interface terminals and touchscreen stations offline. Mercifully, the London underground is unaffected and able to survive an EMP blast wave, thanks to its hardened computer infrastructure and back-up electricity generators. But it takes only a matter of minutes for the trains to become overcrowded and for severe disruptions to break out over the Tube network. As the only form of functioning transportation in London, the Tube does not cope, and normal service is not restored until much later into the evening of the attack.

At the macro-level, life in London has slowed to the point of almost total standstill. All the major flows that are essential for any city to function – electricity, transport, communication, capital and information, as well as the basic human requirements like fresh food, water and air – are largely absent on the afternoon of the attack. From high above, London looks dark, cold and still – none of which were attributes ever intended by the designers of a future 'smart city'.

Returning downstairs, inside the buildings of Whitehall, there is a shielded secure communications room with electromagnetic compatible devices that have survived the blast wave. A heavily protected underground room, originally designed to survive a nuclear attack, now houses the PM and the agency heads of MI5, MI6 and GCHQ. There are no flat-screen LED TVs down in the secure bunker, no complex phone systems or fancy computers. Instead, there are rudimentary vacuum-tube technologies connected to an uninterrupted power supply, as well as manual, petrol back-up generators, better equipped to survive an e-bomb attack.

More vital still is access to the dedicated fibre-optic network for means of entry to the secret SIPR-net, the clandestine US communications network available to the UK MoD and intelligence community. The system is accessed through a hardened military-grade computer terminal, that looks more like an arcade machine than it does a piece of indispensable twenty-first century communications equipment.

The first update on the information-sharing platform is

an intelligence brief flagged 'urgent' by GCHQ analysts in Cheltenham.

Top Secret//NOFORN//GCHQ

//Malicious hack on UK power grid.

The Control Centre staff at the National Grid report they are probably suffering from a persistent cyberattack, as they are unable to connect remotely to the local distribution substations experiencing blackouts.

Blackouts are confined to central London where six distribution substations have been taken offline.

The power stations are unable to switch to manual management mode using emergency operating procedures.

Early estimates suggest power has been disrupted to approximately 3.5 million customers, many of whom are businesses and government offices.

National Grid currently working with National Cyber Security Centre and GCHQ Information Assurance teams to restore systems. No root access can be gained over substations in Cheltenham area.//

Without more specific information following the blast, the heads of agencies begin trying to answer urgent questions. What about the EMP? Surely, the EMP must have occurred from the oscillating power. Who are the hackers? Going through the list of usual suspects, it quickly becomes apparent it could have been anyone. But is the leadership faced with a disgruntled teenager hiding away in a London basement, or an organised nation-state attack?

The sole person with explicit cyber expertise, the head of GCHQ, points out that infrastructure attacks like this have previously only been conducted by nation-state actors or rogue actors backed by nation states. But if there is a nation state behind these events, who are they and what do they want? The motivations may be even more in doubt than the attribution. It is plain that there was an intent to cut power in Central London and Cheltenham, but was that the end goal, and if so, for what purpose? Is there a larger plot that remains to be played out? In the absence of clear communication channels, the fog of war is near complete and the room remains shrouded in uncertainty.

Civil Dusk

A full day has passed since the initial blackout and power surge struck central London. Vast portions of the city still wait to be reconnected. The sun has disappeared below the horizon and dusk starts to fall. A colourless Whitehall is going into its second night of technological darkness, only to find its citizenry beginning to realise what is happening around them.

Two of the major substations around Whitehall and Westminster that suffered the EMP blast have been unable to re-image their servers successfully from back-ups. The localised blast and shockwave affecting the few miles' radius surrounding Parliament has meant the persistence of the dead zone for at least another day or two at the earliest, until the systems can be fully restored to operational status.

News channels have been speculating all day about the

motivation of those behind the attacks, why nobody has claimed responsibility, and whether the government will make an announcement about what it knows on the issue. Although some are constantly reiterating the 'facts', the situation remains ambiguous. Taking to Twitter, the same conversation continues non-stop for everyone to follow publicly. There were no reported deaths from the first-order effects of the power cut. The effect of the EMP blast, on the other hand, did cause loss of life. Four deaths occurred immediately after the EMP shockwave, with unfortunate victims suffering from complications with their heart pace-makers. Fortunately, no hospitals were in the relatively small blast radius. As a result the news media are unable to roll out the fearful narrative of a bloody terrorist attack. The sentiment has been that the incident has the look and feel of a state-sponsored 'cloak and dagger' act of subversion, but nobody is bold enough to implicate any foreign state at this stage.

In the aftermath of the blackout, many of the 3.5 million affected are jammed only temporarily by the EMP shockwave, without their electronic devices turning permanently into 'bricks'. Whilst only temporary, without power coming back onto the local relay towers broadcasting mobile-phone signals, or the ability to connect to the Internet at home, many hundreds of thousands now search for the next best thing: free open Wi-Fi.

Shortly after the blackout, a public wireless network starts to appear in urban centres affected by the power cuts in an apparent attempt by local authorities to restore communications. 'FreeCityOfLondon_SECURE' is the camel-case name of the Wi-Fi network now available. Before loading their website of choice, as with many other open Wi-Fi networks, users are prompted to log in through a standard-looking landing site offering Terms and Conditions of service, a Privacy Policy, and a log-in form asking for a name and email address.

But looks can be deceiving. There is nothing 'secure' about the network, nor is it truly 'free'. Unaware users are lured into a well-concealed dragnet that siphons off their personal data, costing them their browsing habits and private information, and infecting their devices with malware to log every keystroke they make. Desperate for Internet access, users look past the obvious fact that the Wi-Fi hotspots would need a secondary source of power, since the mains are still dead. Powered by both lithium-ion battery packs found in smartphones, and tiny solar panels, next-generation micro-routers and access points are the perfect tools to set up a low-cost, but widely distributed mesh surveillance network in London.

The vast majority of less computer-literate users freely click 'accept', whilst the more sceptical hesitate before acceding to the same request. Only a small contingent of highly knowledgeable IT security experts and computer science researchers, who possess the advantages of expertise, time available and a healthy amount of hacker ethos, manage to investigate further the mysterious origins of the supposed free, secure London Wi-Fi. These members of the community self-identify as Anonymous London, or @AnonLDN as they become known through their Twitter handle.

The hackers collectively self-organise underneath the Wi-Fi network, taking it apart from within and initially sharing their knowledge on open-source blogs and forums. After pulling apart the local Wi-Fi-devices, leading hardware hackers voice strong suspicions that the information is being siphoned off to who knows where, to be analysed by intelligence bots, deep-learning algorithms, and AI computers. In light of the severity of these revelations, AnonLDN selectively take their activities off the clear web and onto 'hidden services' and darknets to further collaborate with other non-conformist Internet denizens.

Organised into a leaderless group of like-minded individuals, AnonLDN are quick and agile enough to reveal to the public that the mesh network must be run and organised by China. A bold and brazen claim, coming out of the dark web and hitting the clear web for everyone to see, based primarily on the fact that the hardware was made, designed and owned by Huawei, the Chinese telecommunications giant. The finger-pointing is also supported by the information that much of the web traffic is being routed through Chinese DNS – domain name servers, the Internet's address book – which is abnormal for UK Internet traffic.

The media draw a stark distinction between AnonLDN's action and Whitehall's relative passivity. It has been forty-eight hours since the blackout and there is still no official acknowledgement or government position on the security of the Wi-Fi network that has mysteriously popped up in London. The government and its eminent security establishment has failed in the eyes of the public, the private sector, and the financial industry to keep them collectively safe and secure from foreign threats, whoever they might be. One of the main reasons for the paralysis in Whitehall is the fact that there is no lead on cybersecurity issues facing government. In much the same way that every successful company has become a technology company, every one of HMG's ministries is now a technology ministry.

The political elites of Whitehall, those senior politicians and civil servants from the Cabinet Office, Home Office and Foreign and Commonwealth Office, accuse the intelligence agencies of not keeping their finger on the pulse. The Cabinet

Office, responsible for the UK's National Cyber Security Strategy, speaks publicly about the Intelligence Community's (IC) inability to see the 'red flashing lights', similar to the events of 9/11.

This pressure to admonish the IC is coming from the National Security Council, where the Prime Minister and her National Security Adviser simply want to avoid a 'cyber-Pearl Harbor' scenario, where the UK would be forced to consider full armed response to a 'non-kinetic' attack conducted with nothing more than computer code. The PM also wants to name and blame those responsible, promise better performance in the future, and move past the crisis as quickly as possible. Others caution against hasty over-reaction, arguing instead for patience, perseverance and level-headedness, until the IC has had time to do its job properly.

More time is exactly what GCHQ needs. They are already anxious about not meeting the demands of their partner organisation, the National Security Agency (NSA) in the US, as well as fearful of being left behind technologically by the Chinese and Russian success of quantum communication. After the hacking of the power plants, GCHQ is particularly concerned. With a workforce twice the size of MI5 and MI6 combined, they are having difficulty squeezing additional capacity from their Information Assurance branch, who report that they have no capacity to deal with any further communications problems.

GCHQ's internal social-networking platform – known endearingly as 'SpySpace' – has also revealed they are understaffed for the number of simultaneous projects that they are being tasked to manage. They are already preoccupied with trying to crack QUESS, designing their own rival quantum channels, and now they have to investigate allegations of supposed Chinese state-sanctioned sabotage against critical national infrastructure. The climate inside 'the doughnut' at Cheltenham is close to breakdown. The agency is simultaneously being browbeaten for 'allowing' the hacking to take place and encouraged to negotiate additional funding and resources to meet the demands of their growing list of customers. The only net-negative is the continuing number of headlines about the agency.

MI5 are working in tight coordination with the National Crime Agency (NCA), the Counter Terrorism Command of the Metropolitan Police (Scotland Yard), and explosives experts from the MoD, to fill in the blanks about the EMP blast wave that accompanied the power surge. They have found clues and details lying on the rooftops of two of the substations, including blast patterns suggesting that a foreign object had exploded to produce a powerful EMP.

The physical security of both sites had been compromised some twelve months earlier, when it was suspected that Russian intelligence operatives tried to gain access to the substations, for unknown reasons. Whether or not these events are connected still remains to be seen. Territorial disputes break out when access to the site is precluded by MI5, because of the highly probable links with foreign espionage. However, the police are under mounting pressure to hold a press conference and present what they know about the issue to the public, and to reassure them that everything is being done to bring those responsible to justice.

MI6 see the hack and power outage as their opportunity to pursue their own agenda for increased resources. They have been closely observing the failings of both the GCHQ efforts to crack QUESS and MI5's inability to track foreign operatives or do much about the mass-surveillance techniques used by foreign governments. MI6 present themselves as the only organisation that can be reasonably confident of ascertaining the encryption keys used by QUESS, in order to break their one-time pad communication method. They also have a clear vision for the survival of their agency, after their budgets were cut when the Cold War ended and the days of James Bond were put decidedly behind them. Their vision is to combine human intelligence (HUMINT), the bread and butter of the agency, with cyber expertise, into a new discipline of CYBINT, with which they would become responsible for cracking cyber-physical systems and thereby dominate an emergent strategic problem. These are missions that 'techies' can crack, and as yet no machine-learning algorithm can match human creativity and genius.

After seventy-two hours, a GCHQ intelligence cable appears on the SIPR-net:

High probability malicious hacking of UK energy grid carried out by known Chinese malware. High probability Chinese Politburo actively considered and condoned sabotage of UK power grid.

At the same time, the work of MI5, NCA and Scotland Yard solves another piece of the puzzle. Initial findings show that the shockwave and subsequent EMP was far more powerful than initially assumed. Since the servers had been wiped, there are no logs at the distribution channels to describe the voltage of the surge. Cautious estimates put the EMP effect down to a few hundred yards and maximum distances not in excess of one mile. It is now widely believed that either an EMP enhancer or an additional weapon was used in conjunction with the power surge. This kind of weapon and style of subversion is not consistent with recent Chinese tradecraft, and has the hallmarks of a Russian sabotage mission.

For the PM, even against the counsel of the National Security Adviser, there is enough evidence to link the Chinese government to the malware used to attack the power grid. Keen to 'name and shame' those culpable, the PM orders a press conference to be organised and the Chinese Ambassador to be summoned to Downing Street. Feeding off the newly won confidence in the attribution of the attacks, it is hoped that the press statement will put an end to the chaos and uncertainty surrounding the hack.

Whitehall's proposed response to the crisis is to commit more people and more money; the kind of predictable, linear response many have come to expect from a political establishment in denial as to the significance of civilian-empowered networks. During the events of December 2020, the agile structures of a flat-decentralised and leaderless group of hackers proves vastly superior to the traditional hierarchical-centralised and top-heavy organisations, which also require the conventional on-costs. By enabling the hive-mind of ingenious hackers, the government could have invited the members of AnonLDN to make an acknowledged contribution, but chose not to.

In the public statement on the issue, the government points the finger directly at China as the perpetrators of the 'criminal acts'. By using the language of security and law enforcement, and having the PM flanked by Scotland Yard and MI5, the tone is an acknowledgement of the US approach to dealing with foreign hackers, especially those who are state-sponsored. In an attempt to defuse the situation, the government reasons that calling the hackers out as criminals and threatening prosecution, while implicating the criminality and corruption of a government that supports and condones such criminal acts, will send a strong message without risking further retaliation on an already damaged Britain.

The political sleight of hand to treat foreign threats as a criminal issue will prove to be a precarious position for the government to occupy in the coming weeks. The government has also pledged to increase the analytical strength of the intelligence community with additional staff who are to be on the payroll of the MoD, whilst working in tandem with GCHQ. There are no mentions of the supposed links between the blackout and the Wi-Fi networks, nor any acknowledgement of AnonLDN's role in solving the attribution problems.

Astronomical Twilight

The buildings of Whitehall are silhouetted against the clear, cloudless sky above. Some street lights in London are still not working after the power outage, and there are no clouds reflecting the light pollution of the city. In the dead of night, a sneak attack is launched by a huge network of computers in a distributed denial of service (DDoS) attack. It is launched from central London, directed at the friendly and allied Baltic states of Estonia, Latvia and Lithuania.

The DDoS attack seems to come out of nowhere. The vast majority of the junk network traffic comes from devices connected to the Wi-Fi dragnet in central London. An enslaved conglomerate of devices consisting of IoT technologies are redirected from their usual job to pound the servers of the most-used consumer websites in the Baltic states. Banks are hit, along with online-shopping websites, social media websites and local news authorities. Cleverly, the devices back in the UK are still performing normally as far as the public are concerned, but on the technical level, each home that has reconnected their computers to the phoney free WiFi network that popped up around London has been tricked into being part of a large botnet of slave devices, to do the bidding of its creator.

The proliferation of Internet-connected devices means that any one person in central London has upwards of four devices connected to their home router, typically a laptop, tablet, smartphone and TV. It is the newer, luxury-apartment complexes, boasting the fully digital lifestyle, where the highest number and most vulnerable devices are hijacked, including Internet-connected security cameras, connected light bulbs, smart locks, washing machines and self-monitoring fridges, as well as toasters and coffee-makers. The truly shocking fact is the timing of the attack, on Christmas Eve. Many Londoners are preoccupied with the holiday season and are simply unaware that their apartments and offices have been turned into a twenty-first-century battleground. And even once they are made aware of the misuse of their networks, most are technically inept and unable to regain control over their devices and prevent the data attacks.

In the Baltic capitals of Tallin, Riga and Vilnius, the Internet has ground to a halt, and anyone attempting to access it is left staring at a spinning beach-ball or a ceaselessly turning hourglass. The Internet is broken and offline, with junk packets of data from the 25-million-strong UK botnet pummelling the DNS of Baltic countries.

Events are about to turn even more grim. EMP bombs are detonated on the tops of subway stations, much like the attacks in London some three weeks earlier, causing widespread blackouts and technology dead zones. Worryingly, the power is cut extensively across all three Baltic capitals to such an extent that their city hospitals are caught in the blast radius and immediately go dark, causing essential life-support systems to be switched off, while others on the periphery of the blast zones are forced to rely on back-up generators.

The Five Eyes intelligence network is still receiving only a trickle of information as QUESS quantum satellites reach full operational capability. Open-source threat-data reports posted by antivirus and cybersecurity firms throughout Europe place the blame squarely at the feet of a joint Russian and Chinese hacking ring called 'Cold Panda'. The assessment agencies believe that the state-sponsored hacking group are working in close coordination with the Kremlin and Beijing to pursue their strategic agendas. Predictions by the same assessment agencies are that Russian state media will cover the attacks as a sign of chaos in the NATO alliance, as well as evidence of Russian ethnic minorities in the Baltic republics needing their protection.

In time, it will be revealed that the Russian cyberspace operation called холодно Ботнет ('Cold Botnet') is only part of the wider campaign to distort, disrupt and degrade the information environment of the Baltic states. 'Cold Panda' is the public scapegoat for the offensive, which implicates China in the attacks despite their having no direct involvement in the execution of the botnet. Operation Cold Botnet is an attempt to confuse the NATO alliance, drawing the UK into a strategic quagmire and all of this to drive a wedge between Whitehall and Washington. The Russians believe that NATO cannot function without the leadership of the UK, the central node in the alliance network, given their role in bridging the divide between continental Europe and the Anglosphere of the United States and Canada. The ambiguity surrounding the cyber event and its origins is a deliberate ploy to prevent the Western allies from attributing blame for the attacks.

The operation is joined by the CyberBerkut, a group of pro-Russian hacktivists who emerged during the civil war in the Ukraine in 2014. Modelling themselves on Anonymous, with the same defiant, vigilante slogan of 'We will not forget! We will not forgive!', the group of hackers take it upon themselves to target NATO assets and personnel, going after the personal email accounts of senior generals in search of material with which to blackmail them. By unleashing the CyberBerkut on the NATO Cooperative Cyber Defence Centre of Excellence, the Russians' intentions are clear.

At the time, it is not evident who is the master of the IoT botnet in central London, nor are reports getting to news media through reliable and verifiable channels. The British news media hold back from breaking the IoT story, since all the initial evidence points to those responsible being ordinary Londoners. The hunch is continually espoused by AnonLDN on Twitter, urging the populace to disconnect their routers, restore their systems to factory setting and select a new username and password. Self-help guides and discussion boards are rife with tips and tricks for everyday users to improve their security. The lack of social media traction is in part a move by the UK government following the power cut and EMP blast.

Adwords are placed against AnonLDN and biases into social media platforms on Facebook and Twitter to suppress the news articles from trending. By containing AnonLDN, the government has placed itself back at the centre of power and taken responsibility for cyber issues out of the hands of an active citizenry. Now the people wait for the government to step in.

Russia does not claim responsibility for the events, insisting instead that its involvement cannot be proven and rejecting all media insinuations as bullying on the part of Western governments. The robust political rhetoric coming from the Russian government and news sources indicates they are prepared to undertake humanitarian intervention in order to restore stability and protect the rights of ethnic Russians within the Baltic republics. Russian armed forces have already begun to gather in all three border areas, to the knowledge of military intelligence of the US and the broader NATO Alliance.

Not wanting to add to the ambiguity over the facts and details of the power-station attacks, many news agencies now wait for the government to take a lead on the situation before reaching any conclusions. Instead, anonymously uploaded videos are being published on YouTube through Tor-encrypted channels, documenting the power outage and bricked electronic devices in the Baltic countries. It cannot be ascertained whether this is part of a state-led disinformation campaign, or simply uploads from journalists, human-rights activists or concerned citizens.

Trust is breaking down between the UK and its allies, since scepticism and deception are the product of reliance upon solely digital sources of information. Dual- or multi-factor verification is necessary to guarantee the classification of digital objects as trustworthy, and the knowledge they contain as reliable.

Back in Whitehall on Boxing Day, an urgent meeting of COBRA is called to determine the kind of response the government will make – either 'traditional' or 'modern', or some combination of the two. The cadre of agency heads are once again assembled around the long, narrow table in a meeting room newly equipped with projectors, flat screens and emergency lighting designed to withstand a repeat EMP attack.

It has now become clear to many that Russia's doctrine of 'new generation warfare' is being exercised, and this time it is directed at the UK and the NATO Alliance. Large-scale cyberattacks have clearly become a form of strategic warfare on another level entirely from the 2007 cyberattack on Estonia. Russia's decision to invade Georgia in 2008, at the time when the world was preoccupied with the Olympic Games, was another example of a new form of aggression, where cyberattacks were carried out in tandem with troops, tanks and armoured personnel carriers rolling across the border.

Since then, Russian doctrine has matured into a full branch of 'sub-war' activities, on display for the first time in Ukraine in 2014. Trained and equipped soldiers had crossed the border bearing no identifying insignia or patches on their uniforms, no markings on their vehicles and their faces obscured by balaclavas, allowing the Kremlin to maintain a level of plausible deniability and claim 'separatist' fighters were to blame. These tactics evolved during the Syrian crisis of 2016, where they came uncomfortably close to crossing the 'red line' set by the Western allies.

There is a broad consensus that events have now escalated into a major strategic crisis, pushing the National Security Council into 'strategic response' mode, configured loosely yet characteristically along Cold War lines. There is a shifting belief that it has ceased to be an intelligence issue and has evolved into a strategic crisis, compromising the sovereignty of the nation, the security of its people and the ability of the state to govern free from foreign intervention.

The National Security Council is wise to the fact that the UK is being drawn unwillingly into some form of confrontation. Commentary is leaked from the Cabinet, Foreign and Home Offices that many of the failings had been caused by other foreign actors and the events were therefore beyond their control. Industry is pressured to bring long-awaited secure IoT devices to market and regulators are required to ensure such security standards are met. Individual irresponsibility and the lack of a work ethic are claimed to explain technological incompetence and apathy towards the botnet threat being run by every unsecured private computer, Internet-linked device and business network.

The media are also castigated for publicising baseless speculations as to the root causes of the cyberattacks certainty on the basis of incomplete information. Civil society, think-tanks and academics do not escape either, since they have a role to play in the security ecosystem; they are accused of a lack of leadership, an inability or unwillingness to inform the public, and a failure to generate the sophisticated level of debate essential to a healthy democracy.

Admittedly, the government is aware it has become over-whelmed by the multi-layered, ambiguous and intelligence-centric problems that have strained limited resources. In their own way, the National Security Council reason they have done the best that they can do, given the problem-set and the tools they have.

Simultaneously, a meeting is being held at NATO Headquarters in Brussels. All twenty-eight participating member states are represented at the ambassadorial meeting of the North Atlantic Council. The meeting has been called by some of the newest members of the Alliance, the Baltic countries who joined in 2004. Estonia, Latvia and Lithuania are requesting that the crisis be recognised as an Article 4 matter, obliging NATO members to consult together when-ever the territorial integrity, political independence or security of any of the Parties is threatened.

NATO, being consensus driven, cannot technically meet under the guise of Article 4 since one of its own members, the UK, seems to be the source of the botnet attack, and the UK is unwilling to agree that they are threatening other member states. Pressing on, the senior delegates from each country pore over the definition of Article 5, the mutual self-defence clause, that an armed attack against one country will be considered as an armed attack against all of them. Knowing that the debate has remained unresolved for many years over the application of the term 'armed attack' in cyberspace, the meeting stalls.

As the disappointed representatives of the Baltic states prepare to leave Brussels their mobile phones ring simultaneously, and their respective defence ministers explain, in hushed tones, a call they have just received from the British Defence Secretary. An offer has come through to provide assistance, training and support to protect their countries against future cyberattacks and IoT shutdowns. The irony of the situation is not lost on the three men: they exchange raised eyebrows and question the motivation of the country they deem responsible for the recent attack on their transport and information systems. Nevertheless, they agree that the resources and expertise of a country with such relevant knowledge and expertise should not be refused.

In a matter of hours, a delegation is formed by the three countries to meet the British contingent in Geneva, Switzerland – a neutral location where officials can meet without arousing the suspicion of their colleagues or the media. This meeting is firmly off the books, as none of the four countries involved wants this exchange of cyber expertise to be recorded. Sharing intelligence of this confidential nature will make them all a target, and once cyberattackers have cracked the code of one country, it will make them all vulnerable.

Emissaries from the MoD, MI6 and the FCO sit in the meeting room, watching the city's famous *Jet d'Eau* outside the window. Will they be treated to a lecture from their Baltic counterparts on the state of their own IoT security and self-preservation before they accept their help? Will they throw the offer of assistance back into the face of the UK?

Fortunately, once the Estonian, Latvian and Lithuanian security experts have arrived it becomes immediately clear that all in the room recognise their common aims and decide to move forward together. Over the next few hours, codes are exchanged, tactics revealed and examples played out on a secured micro-network.

The four parties leave the building via different exits, stepping out into the bright Swiss sunlight exhausted, but satisfied. The next steps are agreed: experienced agents, well versed in cybersecurity and protection, will be seconded from MoD, MI6 and FCO and deployed to the Baltic states to assist in building effective defences, both physical and digital. A six-month programme is arranged for cooperation and security information sharing, with the Baltic states agreeing to forward any intelligence they uncover on security threats that extend beyond their own borders.

All four have gained something from the meeting: the three Baltic states with their secretly obtained security intelligence, and the British team satisfied at having wiped the ledger clean and cancelled out the damage done by the recent UK-based cyberattacks.

However, one reservation remains in the mind of the delegate from MI6: these three countries are under constant threat from their neighbour, the Russian Federation, with tanks frequently driving across their borders on 'training exercises'. What happens if these apparently discreet emissaries inadvertently convey their new-found knowledge and skills to Russia, revealing everything and leaving not only the UK, but the NATO Alliance under threat of an attack.

Dawn is breaking on Latvia's border with Russia. A border guard, looking hard in an easterly direction, sees the unmistakeable shape of a soldier silhouetted against the horizon, then the outline of a T-14 Armata Main Battle Tank. Soon, the sounds of entire armoured divisions on the move fill the air.

CHAPTER 8

A DISUNITED KINGDOM
UK Domestic Security

The History

In 1978, when General Sir John Hackett was writing *The Third World War*, the challenges faced by the UK were very different from those that we must contemplate in 2020. Relatively speaking, the world was a simpler place in terms of the conflicts that guided and shaped foreign and domestic policy. The complexity and sophistication of the military campaigns of the early twenty-first century were not envisaged. The Internet, mobile phones, mass digitisation and 24-hour news coverage were the stuff of futuristic fiction novels and scientists' wilder dreams.

The Cold War had arguably passed its peak by this point, though there were considerable tensions felt along the fracture lines in Europe where East met West. The 'arms race' was still being run and vast sums of money were being spent on nuclear weapons and on developing the kind of technology that might produce a significant advantage on the battlefield. For Western military powers, a principal focus was on producing the kind of hardware that was sufficiently advanced in terms of its lethality that it would make up for the woeful disparity in manpower numbers that they could field in comparison to the seemingly endless supply of conscripts for the Soviet forces. The wisdom and prescience of the old

Russian military maxim 'quantity has a quality all of its own'
was, and remains, hard to ignore.

This could not be better illustrated than when considering
the fate of 7th Armoured Brigade, who had the unenviable
task of fighting a so-called delaying battle centred around
Vahlberg, just a few miles from the inner German Border.
They were equipped with about one hundred tanks, some
armoured infantry with mortars and machine guns. Their task
was holding up Soviet armoured columns, many times their
size and strength for about twenty-four hours, safe in the
knowledge that a glorious death awaited them. A Cold War
equivalent of the Thin Red Line. Most of them would have
exercised in the area several times, almost certainly would
have positioned, and quite possibly dug the trenches that they
were expected to occupy when the war came. They would
have drawn out their range cards indicating critical road
junctions, bridges, buildings and choke points for tanks, and
known the distance from their trench to those target locations.

There was certainty over which Soviet armoured formation
they were facing, quite possibly they had the names of some
of the senior commanders leading it, and they could certainly
identify all the principal vehicle types of the formation from
the Corps recce, the vanguard, the main body and all the
classic hallmarks of the enemy they were to face. All this
information could be found in the infamous 'pink pillow':
the British Army intelligence field manual. It took its nickname
from the fact that the material was printed on pink paper,
denoting the sensitivity of the information it contained, and
was so crammed full of maps, diagrams, technology briefs,
tactics, techniques and procedures of the enemy that it would
often double-up as a pillow for the bespectacled, gnomish
intelligence staff officer, who was expected to know its
contents by heart and to never let it out of his sight.

The point is very simple: this was a military task that had absolutely certainty in every element of it. The only doubts that existed around this plan related to which particular unappetising menu from the Quartermaster's rations store would be issued to the soldiers on deployment.

In the late 1970s, Hackett was writing from a position of near certainty. The enemy was well known. His ideology and political beliefs; where he lived and how he lived; what he read, how he thought and behaved; what he would do on the battlefield; where he would attack and what he would attack with; how long he could run without refuelling, how far his planes could fly, what bombs they would drop. All these were 'known knowns' and all were adequately planned for and rehearsed. A regular military exercise carried out in Germany in the 1970s and 1980s was one where troops were crashed out from their barracks to the operational positions from which they were to fight in the event the Soviets invaded. It was a well-known routine, usually called in the early hours of the morning after a boozy night, and almost always to spoil a weekend of leave.

At home, the Royal Observer Corps waited patiently to take up their posts and watch the skies for the anticipated invasion and doubtless the oft-talked-about nuclear armageddon. Tens of thousands of military reservists were ready to deploy forward to Germany. The secret intelligence services, particularly MI6, were well placed with spies serving in every one of our embassies, futuristic and secretive listening stations perched on remote Yorkshire hillsides, and a network of agents across the Soviet empire passing vital information daily. Civilians were encouraged to stockpile tins of beans and other sundries that would help them survive a nuclear winter. Government-sponsored information films were aired on TV reminding us what to do in the event of a nuclear strike. It was simply a question of not if, but when the Soviets would start the war.

In 2020, such certainty as this will only exist in the memories of Cold War veterans gathering for old comrades' reunions in Royal British Legion halls across the country.

The so-called 'Troubles' in Northern Ireland were the only other major distraction for the British military in 1980. At its height, Operation Banner, as it was known, required the deployment of upwards of 20,000 British military personnel at any one time. Of the Regular military component, some of these were on two-year tours in well-established barracks, others were on 'emergency deployments' of six months, usually operating from inner-city fortresses or border outposts. These were supplemented by a locally recruited militia that numbered over 10,000 troops in a mixture of full-time and part-time roles.

The primary task of the military force was to support the local police constabulary in maintaining law and order and containing the various insurgent groups from both Republican and Loyalist communities. The vast bulk of the contingent were conventional troops drawn either from British Forces Germany for six-month tours or rotated through Northern Ireland as part of troop rotations. There were also small elements of military intelligence and special forces operating alongside these troops. There was some air force support to provide helicopters, and naval ships were deployed to monitor the sea frontiers at either end of the border and to interdict arms smugglers bringing in weapons by sea.

Apart from a few thousand lucky service personnel enjoying the sun of Cyprus or the humidity in Hong Kong, as well as a small contingent of Royal Marines stationed on islands in the South Atlantic, the British military were living a very predictable and manageable garrison lifestyle; a very ordered and relatively comfortable existence at the end of the 1970s.

Margaret Thatcher was leader of the Conservative Party in 1978, which was in opposition to a Labour Party government that was imploding as a result of a faltering economy, ballooning public-sector costs and mass industrial action. She and her colleagues would go on to win the 1979 General Election, coming to power on a commitment to smash the trade unions, reduce public spending and revitalise the economy. The Ministry of Defence, a bloated bureaucracy with separate ministries for each of the three Services, and with well over half a million civil servants and service personnel on its payroll, was one of the early targets for the Conservative Party to cut. The huge equipment bill that came with the Navy, Army and Air Force was serviced by a lethargic defence industrial sector, which knew that so long as there was the prospect of a Third World War, they were on to a good thing.

This was the perfect target for savings and downsizing. An exercise that would be repeated by each government thereafter, whether Conservative, Labour or a Coalition. Cuts to manpower and material carried out in the face of the consequences of real-world events and intelligence, bolstered by an inflated sense of confidence based on a rapidly diminishing reputation, wilful ignorance of military advice by senior political leaders, and a policy of supine acquiescence by civil-service officials.

The Build-Up

The result of the June 2016 referendum on Britain's membership of the European Union is a strategic game-changer. The narrow vote that sees fifty-three per cent support for withdrawal has more unintended consequences than anyone ever imagined. Very few people predicted that the UK would vote to leave the EU, not least those who were leading the various Leave campaigns. That the UK would vote to Remain was a foregone conclusion. No one, neither the parties in the UK, the regions in the UK nor the EU, has made plans based on a 'leave' result and the country is thrown into chaos.

The Prime Minister subsequently resigns the morning after the vote and this ushers in a short and ugly leadership election. The Labour Party are likewise rocked and most of their senior members resign from the Shadow Cabinet, triggering a nasty leadership contest there, too. Britain goes into political meltdown, just at the time it needs to remain steady and calm.

This moment is the highpoint of nearly forty years of British strategic complacency, in which 'speaking truth to power' has become hopelessly unfashionable. Instead, winning the battle of the narratives is the dominant activity, where short-term expedient and catchy sound-bites rule the day. Contingency planning, horizon scanning and worst-case scenarios have been consigned to the shredder by the all-knowing staffers and so-called 'SPADs', or Special Advisers, in Number 10 and the Cabinet Office.

In the two years following the Brexit vote, the most significant impact is the strategic shock to the economy; much worse than modelled, the fiscal cost to the UK economy sees GDP down by five per cent by the end of 2018, with the pound dropping to record lows. This forces the government into an unplanned additional round of austerity cuts in the autumn of 2018, removing a further ten per cent from the budget of several government departments, including Defence. Unemployment rises by over 250,000 during this period with the impacts felt most acutely in the regions.

Both Scotland and Northern Ireland, where ironically the majority voted to remain in the EU, see major international companies close down their operations, leading to job losses in the crucial middle-income sectors. National credit ratings are written down and critical national infrastructure programmes, such as the HS2 rail link and the construction of the new nuclear power plants, have to be delayed. There is a period of prolonged negative inflation that precipitates a correction in the property market. However, the government chooses not to delay or downscale the Trident successor programme.

Politically, the years 2017 and 2018 are tumultuous. Article 50 is triggered by the UK Prime Minister in March 2017 and Brexit negotiations begin in earnest in Brussels. They do not proceed well. The EU negotiators, emboldened by a number of senior states bitterly angered by the UK's decision to leave, make the two-year exit period as difficult as possible for the UK team. Negotiations, conducted in French not English, are lengthy and major agreement is not made until autumn 2018. In London, the Supreme Court once again intervenes to insist that any Brexit deal has to be approved by a vote in Parliament.

The Scottish Nationalists take advantage of the political uncertainty caused by Brexit and the First Minister of Scotland calls for a referendum on Scottish independence, so-called Sexit. This is against the advice of senior Nationalists whose long-term strategy has been to extract the maximum political freedom from London without losing the economic advantage of remaining within the Union. It is clear to them, at least, that Scotland cannot support itself financially, but the younger leadership hold a different view.

Reluctantly, late in 2017 the Prime Minister and her Cabinet agree to this demand, based on advice that the outcome of such a vote is too tight to predict, but that in any case, the prime focus for the long-term strategic future of the UK has to be on Brexit negotiations. The referendum campaign is dirty, long on rhetoric and short on detail. The principal point of choice is centred on the Scottish Nationalist position 'to be a Nation again' and bring to an end the 400-year-old Union between Scotland and England. Those leading the campaign for the Scots to remain in the Union focus on the benefits of remaining within the UK, including access to the sterling currency, the benefit of collective defence and the offer of enhanced devolution powers, including the right of Scotland to conduct its own trade relationships with EU countries separate from a UK position.

Meanwhile, the Republic of Ireland, the EU country that is most dependent on the UK in terms of trade and relations, takes a considerable time to come to terms with the result of the UK decision to leave the EU. The decision has major implications on the island of Ireland, both economically and politically.

Ireland is a country of two parts with an international land border separating them. The so-called 'Troubles' in Northern Ireland were brought to an end in the 1990s through a series of ceasefires and peace agreements, which guaranteed the citizens of both countries free movement across the island, a near-invisible border and the opportunity to enjoy dual citizenship if so desired. These considerations were unique across the EU and ensured a period of calm and prosperity on the island with free trade and free movement. The security situation settled down, the British Army was withdrawn from the streets of Northern Ireland and the police underwent a radical transformation from a force dominated by the battle against terrorism to one that focused on community policing.

In early 2016, relations on the island of Ireland, and between the UK and RoI, are at the best they have been in the ninety years since the island was partitioned. Then the Irish general election in February sees Fine Gael narrowly returned to power for a second term, although their much-reduced vote means that they will be governing in a minority. The new government has barely been in post when the UK votes to 'leave' the EU. The shock of the result hits the Irish hard and they wobble. The major economic consequences of the vote are matched by concerns about what this will mean for the border in Ireland, which will now become an EU land frontier. The government fails to recover from this and in autumn 2017 the Fine Gael government collapses after a vote of no confidence in its leader.

A bitter round of elections follow with no single party gaining a majority. Both the larger parties court Sinn Fein, until eventually Fianna Fail and Sinn Fein conclude an electoral deal and enter power in a coalition. This is the first time since partition that the political forces most passionately aligned to an all-island Republic have come together. Both parties are electorally and constitutionally committed to ending the partition of Ireland. Sinn Fein, the only party represented electorally on both sides of the border, make a border poll the principal precondition for their entering a coalition. This poll is one of the mechanisms included in the Good Friday Agreement of 1998 that allowed for the people of Ireland to vote on partition. In sum, it requires a majority of the citizens on both sides of the border to vote in favour of unifying the island.

The new Irish government lobbies the UK government to authorise the poll on the basis that as they have given in to the demand of Scottish Nationalists for an independence referendum, then Irish Nationalists and Republicans ought to be allowed the same facility; crucially, it is also made clear that the granting of the poll is a requirement for Irish support to the UK Brexit negotiation position.

The UK government is of course pro-Union and this initial demand is turned down. The ten pro-Union MPs from Northern Ireland are a critical number in maintaining the government's majority in Parliament and enjoy dispropor-tionate influence as a result. However, it becomes clear to Conservative Party strategists by the end of 2017 that they will have sufficient Labour votes to carry any Brexit vote in Parliament. The PM, like all her recent predecessors, takes a decision that the strategic relationship with Ireland is more important than continuing to meet Unionist demands.

In the simple hope of securing Irish support for the Brexit deal, the UK government agrees to a border poll and the date of elections is set for October 2018; the same date is also agreed for the Scottish referendum. Unionists in Northern Ireland, who had supported the Leave campaign and aligned themselves with the Conservative Party in government, are horrified by this decision and now withdraw their support, helping to defeat the Government in a number of crucial votes in Parliament.

The Government's high-wire strategy is simple enough; to secure an attractive Brexit deal by September 2018 that will tip the balance of the referenda in favour of remaining in the UK.

The leaking of the draft deal by a French newspaper, claiming that the UK will have to pay £35 billion in 'exit fees', coincides with a state visit to London of the US President Donald Trump in August 2018. Millions of protes-tors descend on London to express their anger at the visit of President Trump and in a last-gasp effort to reverse Brexit. The Labour Party leader, having overseen his sixth cabinet reshuffle, refuses the Queen's invitation to attend the state banquet at Windsor Castle. The leader of the Scottish Nationalists also declines the invitation, as does the Sinn Fein Deputy First Minister of Northern Ireland.

President Trump visits Blenheim Palace with the PM, paying a visit to the grave of Sir Winston Churchill. Then he addresses both Houses of Parliament, recalled from the long summer recess, in the Great Hall at Westminster. Standing at the top of the steps, with the First World War memorial behind him, Trump speaks passionately about the US decision to enter the Great War and how approaching the centenary of the Armistice has brought him to reflect on the special relationship. He remarks on the UK holding out against the Germans in the Second World War, the stoicism shown during the Blitz, and how the US and the UK fought together at D-Day and throughout Europe to end that conflict. Moving off-script, perhaps emboldened by the moment, he promises a no-holds-barred trade deal, stating that the UK will be the US's global trade partner and their primary broker in Europe, secured with a currency deal between the US dollar and sterling.

The Scenario

The Irish and Scottish referendums take place in October 2018 and the result is much closer than the polls have predicted. The Scottish Nationalists win their referendum with fifty-three per cent of the electorate voting in favour of Sexit. This is not a surprise; at no point in the campaign did the polls show anything other than a vote of that nature. In Ireland, ninety-two per cent of voters in the Republic vote for a united Ireland; in Northern Ireland, a majority of sixty per cent vote in favour of remaining in the UK. So, Scotland is to leave the UK and Northern Ireland to stay.

Scotland is to become an independent country on 6 April 2020, exactly seven hundred years to the day from the signing of the Declaration of Arbroath, where the Scots submitted a petition to Pope John XXII declaring their independence from England and their right to defend themselves militarily. The general elections for the UK Parliament planned for 7 May 2020 will not be fought in Scotland and the Union will no longer exist in its current form.

The first major policy decision made by the Scottish Nationalist government is to request membership of the EU and an agreement to sign up to the twin EU principles of free movement and free trade. In keeping with their consistent anti-nuclear policy, they demand that the submarine-borne Trident nuclear missile system is removed from Scotland and the naval bases at Faslane and Coulport handed over to the newly formed Scottish Defence Forces.

So, at the beginning of May 2020 we find a 96-mile-long international border separating England and Wales from Scotland. The Scottish Defence Forces are responsible for the defence of over 30,000 square miles of land mass and also the seas around Scotland, now re-designated as non-UK territorial waters. The monitoring and defence of the Scottish airspace is still the responsibility of the UK air force as part of a transitional security deal signed between Edinburgh and London. The UK Trident submarine fleet has relocated to an interim base at King's Bay, Georgia, on the US East Coast, where they sit alongside their American naval counterparts. New facilities to replace those at Faslane and Coulport will be built at Devonport and Falmouth at a cost in excess of £10 billion and will only be ready in time for the successor submarines entering service no earlier than 2030. At over £40 billion and rising, Trident replacement will cost more than the whole UK defence budget for a year.

The Scottish navy has inherited a small fleet of minesweepers and coastal protection vessels from the UK, which they are using to patrol the 6,200 miles of Scottish coastline and nearly 800 islands in their waters. The small stretch of sea known as the North Channel, separating Scotland from Northern Ireland, only thirteen miles wide at its narrowest point, has become the focus of increased submarine activity. Russian and US submarines regularly pass through on their way in and out of the Atlantic Ocean, causing concerns not only to the Royal Navy, but also to fishermen and commercial cargo ships who are frequent users of this busy stretch of water.

The Royal Air Force have had to station a newly acquired maritime patrol aircraft at their base in Aldergrove, in Northern Ireland, to keep watch on these movements. Its regular flights are routinely monitored and shadowed by Russian aircraft, who are able to exploit the now unclear regulations that govern the skies above the Irish Sea. On a number of occasions, Irish fishing boats have had their nets snared by the subs and several of them have been sunk. As a reaction to this, the British have had to place an anti-submarine frigate on constant patrol in the Irish Sea.

UK and US naval commanders have reported various incidents in which their submarines were targeted by Russians in mock underwater attacks. The UK frigate has intervened and on one occasion attempted to force a Russian sub to the surface, only to watch it disappear off their radar screens as it escaped northwards past the Mull of Kintyre into Scottish territorial waters. They are unable to pursue it, as the Scottish have declared their coastal waters a defence exclusion zone. Something that the Russians wilfully ignore, but the British painstakingly observe.

On the east coast of Scotland, human trafficking has become a major cause of concern. Scotland's policy to maintain free travel in order to access free trade from mainland Europe has made it the destination of choice for illegal immigrants who want to get to England. The major cargo routes from Holland and the Baltics are one of the entry points that immigrants use most regularly. Passenger ferries running from Zeebrugge on the coast of Belgium to Rosyth port, on the other side of the Firth of Forth from Edinburgh, are also considered a hot ticket for gang masters that want to move women into England for the burgeoning sex trade.

These routes have become a key part of the international people-smuggling network, making it much easier to slip in unnoticed to Scotland and board a train to London, crossing the border into England at Berwick, where only irregular passport checks are carried out. A much safer and more secure route than attempting to cross from Calais, where the British Borders Agency and French counterparts have a much more sophisticated and robust operation. The infamous 'Calais camps' were closed in 2017 and regular passport checks and screening operations remain in place on the French coast at the ferry ports and entrance to the Channel Tunnel.

The Royal Navy and HM Coastguard continue patrolling the English Channel to deter migrants from trying to reach England in small craft. However, the Scottish navy and customs organisation simply cannot monitor the North Sea on a similar basis. Their meagre resources are stretched to breaking point on the north-east coast providing security to the oil industry installations and supporting the economically vital fishing fleet. The rich Scottish fishing grounds and shellfish are regularly plundered by illegal foreign fishermen. The Scottish Fisheries Protection Agency remains resolutely independent of the navy and its ageing fleet of three unarmed small vessels and two light aircraft cannot be everywhere all the time.

The Royal Navy has had to reduce its overseas operational rotation so as to provide an additional ship to monitor either end of the Irish border, with a small minesweeper regularly shuttling around the coast between Carlingford Lough and Lough Foyle, performing partner patrols with similar vessels from the Scottish and Irish navies. This new tri-partite force is a direct result of the newly negotiated defence treaties that Britain has been forced to agree with Ireland and Scotland to try and cover the numerous gaps in national defence. As well as watching for drug- and people-smugglers, they are also now on the look-out for illegal arms shipments that dissident Republican terrorists are trying to bring into Ireland to boost their renewed terror campaign in Northern Ireland.

The almost impossible task of securing the coastline has made Scotland a favourite target of illegal smugglers. However, these are not the romantic clandestine activities on the Galloway coast of the eighteenth century made famous by the Scottish poet Robert Burns, himself an exciseman for a time. Whisky and brandy are no longer fashionable for modern smugglers; in 2020, people and class A drugs are the favoured contraband. Ships carrying cocaine make their way across the Atlantic from South and Central America; one of the unintended consequences of the much-heralded peace deal in Colombia in 2016, where President Santos and the FARC rebels finally made their peace.

By 2020, the former Colombian rebel leaders have established a highly lucrative cocaine-smuggling network on either side of the Atlantic. Stripped of their powers under the peace deal, the rebel leaders have diversified into the narcotics business on an industrial scale, while the Colombian authorities, in order to maintain the peace, turn a blind eye. A longstanding relationship with Irish Republicans has been turned to commercial benefit with a partnership that sees the Colombians producing the drugs and the Irish overseeing their transport across the Atlantic and their onward distribution into criminal networks spanning Europe. Meanwhile Cuba forms a useful staging and trading post, where both these groups are allowed to live and trade without harassment.

Evading detection in 2020 is relatively easy for these transatlantic smugglers. A depleted Royal Navy has little capacity or capability to interdict drugs boats once they have gone beyond the Caribbean. The US and EU maritime forces are focused on the Pacific and Mediterranean respectively, making an Atlantic crossing a fairly straightforward affair.

Sitting within sight of Ireland, the smugglers transfer their cargo to much smaller boats, which then make the short but hazardous journeys to the west coasts of Ireland and Scotland, where their booty is brought ashore at remote harbours, well beyond the watch of police, coastguard and revenue agencies. The drugs can be on the streets of Glasgow, Dublin or Belfast within days and the money laundered through a network of hotels, restaurants and taxi companies. A well-run operation that has survived the Troubles in Ireland much better than most legitimate institutions.

The remote western Scottish coastline is an ideal location for smuggling. The Organised Crime Command that oversees the joint-agency approach to drugs smuggling in the remainder of the UK has no remit in an independent Scotland. Drug cartels from Eastern Europe, operating out of Glasgow, have a relatively easy task of distributing the drugs into other Scottish cities and across the border into the north of England.

The Scots had chosen to have a soft unmanned border as they simply did not have the financial resources to fund such a task. Soldiers from the new Defence Forces conducted some exercises on the border to confirm that they could man it in the event of an escalation in security, but otherwise it was open.

The numerous minor roads that criss-cross the scarcely patrolled border make an excellent network for the smugglers, who can have hundreds of kilos of cocaine in Liverpool and Manchester within two hours of crossing the border. It is not only drugs that are on the move. The Colombians also do a very good line in explosives and weapons, neither of which they have any use for now that they have abandoned their jungle camps.

In these northern English cities, a new breed of dealers, led by a network of recently returned jihadists, is using their drug monies to raise funds for a future terror campaign in Britain. This highly sophisticated and disciplined group, brought together fighting for Islamic State in Syria and Iraq, is spread out along the M62 corridor. In Hull, they regularly receive shipments of heroin from former Islamic State counterparts running routes out of Afghanistan and Pakistan, via Yemen and the Horn of Africa and on to England by sea. This group, linked to the Islamic Jihad Union, is using secure online 'dark' Internet sites to manage their finance operation and develop links to other like-minded former jihadi terror groups across Europe.

Their battles in Syria may be over, but the war is being carried on in a new and much more threatening way. British intelligence chiefs' assessments shared with COBRA estimate that the numbers and logistics of this new movement are larger than anything seen since the days of the Provisional IRA. As a result, the outgoing Home Secretary raised the national threat state to CRITICAL in England and Wales ahead of the first post-Brexit and Sexit general election in May 2020. In simple terms, this recognises that an attack is expected imminently.

~

Across the Irish Sea, in Northern Ireland, the threat level has already been at CRITICAL for the previous twelve months. Dissident Irish Republican groups, dismayed and angry at the result of the border poll in 2018, have returned to violence. Several of the splinter groups were formed in the wake of the peace process in the late 1990s, unhappy with the Provisional IRA ceasefire in 1997. Others sprang up after 2007 with the formal end of Operation Banner, the British military campaign in Northern Ireland. Some have already been active in the early half of the decade before the border poll, killing policemen on both sides of the Irish border and a prison officer, setting off a number of explosions in Belfast and attacking police stations.

The early calm following the poll is attributed largely to Nationalist and Republican politicians across the island of Ireland reiterating that the only way to secure a united Ireland is through a peaceful democratic process. Key to the sense of unity on the island is the focus on maintaining the open border, which allows easy movement throughout the island, and the specific arrangements that enable Northern Ireland residents to have Irish citizenship.

However, the outcome of the Brexit negotiations in 2019 has a considerable impact on the open, so-called 'soft' border.

The EU insist that in the Brexit treaty the Irish border is regarded as a formally recognised customs boundary between the EU and the UK, with signage stating that there are separate jurisdictions in Ireland. This requires an increase in monitoring of cross-border trade and tourist traffic, alongside regular security checks of motor vehicles. The Belfast–Dublin rail link also has to undergo new identity checks at stations along its length. Points of entry across Northern Ireland, both airports and ferry terminals, have to introduce rigorous new passport-control checks.

The Irish border is considerably longer than that in Scotland, running to over 300 miles from Warrenpoint to Derry City. It is criss-crossed by hundreds of roads and lanes, farm tracks, and numerous bridges across rivers. It is impossible to police across its length. Even at the height of the Troubles, when thousands of policemen, customs officials and soldiers patrolled both sides of its length, it was still very open. Terrorists moved freely across it, as did smugglers, workers, school pupils and tourists alike.

One of the central promises made by all political parties in the UK and Republic of Ireland during Brexit was that there would be no change to the border and the common travel area would continue to operate.

By the middle of 2019 this promise clearly cannot be honoured. The soft border is proving too difficult to monitor. Smuggling of illegal goods, especially fuel, has increased dramatically in the first twelve months after Brexit and the new visa system imposed on the UK by the EU is simply not working. Hundreds of people are crossing the border from Ireland into the UK without having passport or visa checks.

A large number of migrants, who had been living in Ireland before Brexit, have since taken the opportunity to move through to England, via Northern Ireland. The United Kingdom Independence Party has made the tightening of this 'open' border one of its major manifesto commitments for the 2020 election. They claim that the Government is continuing to miss its reduced immigration targets. In response, the Conservative government insists on border posts at a number of major crossing points. These are manned on the northern side by unarmed Borders Force officers and on the southern side by Irish customs officials.

The police have been more or less absent from the border

region since 2010, after the uneasy peace in Northern Ireland took hold. What was once 'bandit country' has returned to being a quiet, peaceful area, with only limited police presence from a few stations that operate only on a part-time basis. It is possible to drive the full length of the border and never encounter a police car, such is the freedom of movement. This reflects not only the positive aspects of the peace dividend, but also the fact that the police service is still regarded with great suspicion in rural areas and is generally not welcome in the remote Republican communities that run the length of the border.

British Army soldiers, who manned static observation posts on hillsides overlooking the border during the 1980s and 1990s, and patrolled the area routinely by helicopter, have mostly returned to England. Those remaining are now confined to barracks in Northern Ireland, with no role in internal security there.

The challenge of maintaining a more secure border falls to the police service, which has been reduced in number from over 13,000 in 1990 to less than 7,000 regulars and reserves in 2020. Although the Patten reforms have seen a rise in Catholic officers joining the new organisation, it is still a long way from being trusted completely in society and remains the only fully armed police force in Britain. Their return to high-profile border duties presents Republican dissidents with the perfect opportunity to rejuvenate their campaign, and the new border posts, which rely heavily on technology and remote security, are exactly the vulnerable target array they need.

~

On New Year's Day 2020, in a coordinated attack, bombs explode at a number of cross-border checkpoints, killing several policemen and border-force officers and wounding others, as well as a number of civilians. Terrorists attack checkpoints on many occasions over the following two months with small arms and rocket-propelled grenades. The Chief Constable has no choice but to establish protected and 'hardened' checkpoints, of a style similar to those used during the Troubles. Once again, the border begins to take on the hallmarks of a disputed frontier.

Dissident Republicans are determined to face down this increase in security-force activity. Police cars are no longer safe in the border area and are vulnerable to attack; they are replaced by a fleet of armoured Land Rovers. The single police helicopter is supplemented by Army helicopters from Aldergrove and an additional 1,000 armed police officers are brought in from England as a short-term measure to underpin the surge.

During a St Patrick's Day parade in Forkhill, on 17 March 2020, community police officers are attacked by dissident terrorists, with a female officer killed and a male colleague kidnapped. That second officer, a Catholic, is subsequently executed; his body is found dumped on the southern side of the border, near the small village of Jonesborough. This is the spot where in 1989 the Provisional IRA killed two senior policemen who were returning from a routine meeting on cross-border liaison at an Irish police station in Dundalk. The Republicans have made their point. The border is once more returning to a no-go area and lawless zone. Precisely the nightmare scenario that politicians on all sides in London, Dublin and Belfast, have feared the most.

The Prime Minister agonises over the decision to deploy military force to support the police in Northern Ireland. Both the Secretaries of State for Defence and Northern Ireland urge caution. In Belfast, the First Minister calls for military personnel to be deployed in the short term and extra resources to allow the police to recruit additional manpower. It would take at least twelve months before they could be recruited, trained and deployed and the police need the support there and then. The Deputy First Minister calls for calm in Republican communities and opposes any increase in policing numbers; she also wants no 'Brits' to be seen on the streets. She suggests that it would be better for the police to withdraw once more from the border. Unionists are outraged and their senior leaders, along with Catholic Nationalist politicians, attend the funerals of the dead police officers in a show of support.

Reluctantly, the Prime Minister agrees to deploy UK special forces and intelligence-gathering equipment on operations to degrade the dissident leadership command and control. These missions, carried out under the command of the police special-operations branch, result in the deaths of several high-profile dissidents in the border areas. A number of alleged leaders in Belfast are arrested for questioning. The funerals of the terrorists provoke large street protests across Northern Ireland, while senior Republican politicians attend the funerals, appealing for calm within the communities. Sinn Fein offices in border towns are attacked and ransacked with the Irish word *fhealltóir*, meaning 'traitor', daubed on the walls and doors.

The Easter Rising commemorative demonstrations in the middle of April 2020 attract large crowds to a number of towns either side of the border. Republican activists take to the streets in military uniforms and balaclavas. A number of videos appear on social media showing terrorist active-service units patrolling with weapons in prominent border locations. The message is quite clear: 'We have taken control.'

The British Army puts its units in Northern Ireland on standby and armed soldiers patrol the entrances to their barracks. In England, more than 10,000 soldiers from 16 Air Assault Brigade, including Parachute Regiment battalions and Marines from 3 Commando Brigade, are also brought up to 48 hours notice to move for potential deployment into the rural border areas to provide protection for the police service.

They are put through a series of rapid training exercises, only to find that the Army no longer has large stocks of public-order equipment. All they have immediately available is helmets, rifles and body armour, the other equipment having been sold off years earlier as part of defence cuts. The Chief Constable makes it clear that he can not accept the support of armed soldiers in such a fashion. COBRA sits at the end of April and directs the Attorney General to prepare Emergency Powers legislation to be brought before Parliament to authorise military deployments to support the civil powers in Northern Ireland.

On the southern side of the border, politicans condemn the British military action and also appeal for calm. The Irish Prime Minister flies to Brussels to hold emergency talks with the EU High Representative for Foreign and Security Policy and asks her to intervene with the British. He also seeks assistance from the European Police Office, requesting independent police officers from Europe to monitor the Northern Irish police response, from the southern side of the border. Irish Army units from Finner Camp on the north-west coast of Ireland are also mobilised to bolster security at Irish police stations close to the border and reassure local communities. By the beginning of May, Northern Ireland is edging closer to the brink. The soft border has hardened in less than twelve months.

The escalation of the threat level in England, combined with the terrorist attacks in Northern Ireland, causes the security services to stretch beyond breaking point. MI5 has lost much of its corporate memory capacity; the old guard who understood

London and Londonderry have been replaced by a younger, more fashionable generation of operators; a combination of educated elites and cosmopolitan activists who have proved themselves more than capable of handling complex field operations, but are less able to understand the old structures and ideologies that are emerging as the new threats.

A lack of recruits from ethnic minorities has made it extremely difficult to penetrate extremist groups in the UK and the growing numbers of returning jihadists are impossible to track and monitor. Reductions in funding to groups supporting the various Home Office 'Prevent' initiatives have seen raw intelligence almost dry up. The large Irish communities across England have long since ceased to be of interest to the security services. The two groups now presenting major credible threats to security are not well understood.

Perhaps too much time and resource has gone into monitoring and penetrating the Eastern European gangs at home, while MI6 have been busy recruiting and handling agents across the Middle East and North Africa, and trying to get a handle on what is going on in Moscow, Tehran, Beijing and Pyonyang. Indeed, the organisation is still recovering from the very public sacking of its chief, a former Army officer, after an operation to obtain sensitive intelligence on the EU Brexit negotiating strategy was uncovered in Brussels.

Metropolitan Police resources have to be deployed outside London to support other police forces, where specialist firearms units have been cut as a result of spending reductions. In the north of England, undercover policing units are struggling to cope with the increase in surveillance requests from drugs-squad officers and the National Crime Agency. In several cities, criminal and terrorist investigations are being undertaken by military police officers, seconded from the UK Armed Forces.

The amount of data being produced by the government's intelligence communicators at GCHQ is overwhelming. The age-old problem of too much intelligence and too few analysts has returned. Police officers brought in off the beat are being put to work sifting through thousands of emails, Facebook messages and WhatsApp conversations, trying to get on top of the increasingly blurred intelligence picture.

For all their undoubted benefits, the Internet and computer processing are fast becoming the enemy of the decision makers. Police and the security service are overwhelmed by inputs. All this information is being stored on huge banks of computer servers and shared on a multitude of overloaded IT platforms and data networks, on mobile smartphones and tablets. Few if any of the operators can remember their own passwords, let alone think up a different one for each computer and phone app.

The Home Secretary is painfully aware of the challenge posed by the open border between England and Scotland. Monthly summits with the Scottish Interior Minister have not borne fruit. The Scot is adamant that this is not their problem and there is little reassurance to be given. Scottish policing and security priorities do not include their border. Their focus is on ensuring compliance with EU procedures, rules and regulations on free movement in order to accelerate their accession to full-member status. The Scots are determined to demonstrate their credentials as willing Europeans and do not concern themselves with the unintended consequences affecting England. Revenge is indeed a dish best served cold.

The National Security Council meets in mid-April to consider the matter of border security. It is clear that something needs to be seen to be done ahead of the general election. The Prime Minister's SPADs have made it abundantly clear that there are a number of vulnerable Conservative marginal seats at risk from both Labour and UKIP in the north of England and in the border region. Polling data is clear enough, they say, and what is needed is a very public move to demonstrate willingness to deal with both the drugs and the migrant issues. The Defence Secretary, having reluctantly agreed to stand up Army units for potential deployment to the Irish border, is now being lobbied by the Home Secretary to provide forces to the Scottish border.

The Chief of Defence Staff makes it clear in a letter to the Service Chiefs, leaked to the *Daily Telegraph*, that as far as the Regular Army is concerned, the cupboard is bare. The cuts in Army numbers in 2010 have seen the regular component drop to 80,000. This is exacerbated by the loss of 8,000 soldiers transferred to the fledgling Scottish Defence Forces. A further 15,000 soldiers are unable to deploy as a result of medical conditions, long-term injuries or ongoing training. Thousands of soldiers are deployed overseas on a myriad defence engagement tasks and exercises, another 10,000 are stood by for Northern Ireland, and even more are set against standing UK, legacy EU and NATO commitments.

With the burden of public duties in the early summer accounting for a further 5,000 soldiers, there are simply none left. There is no choice but to deploy manpower from the Navy and Air Force onto the border. They will be underpinned by some of the 6,000 non-specialist Army Reserves that have been partially mobilised to support this operation. They have taken over regular military patrols on the English border at weekends.

By the beginning of May, Hadrian's Wall is once again under the protection of a military garrison force. This time, though, it will not be Roman legionaries keeping a watchful eye across the border, nor indeed any other soldier, but 'a coalition of the unwilling' sailors and airmen drawn from naval stations and air bases across England. Mobilising at Otterburn military-training camp adjacent to the border, they are deployed across the north of England in battered and outdated fleets of Land Rovers culled from across the veteran military vehicle fleet.

They communicate using civilian handheld radios, because not enough of them can manage the overcomplicated and painfully limited Bowman radio system procured by the military. That multi-billion-pound system seldom works over any significant distance in the hilly Northumbrian countryside; the vehicles cannot be fitted with the radios because of health and safety issues, and even if they did have the Bowman, it could not communicate with police or emergency services radio systems and so would be redundant anyway.

All of this has been known about, albeit subsequently forgotten, since the same problems were identified during the foot and mouth crisis of 2001 and in subsequent civil–military operations undertaken in response to severe flooding across the UK. It seems that corporate memory in the Ministry of Defence has also fallen victim to the austerity cuts.

In the skies over the border, the operation is supported from the air by the Sentinel ground-surveillance aircraft. Fortunately, this asset, which was originally due to be culled in the defence cuts earlier in the decade, was reprieved. They are further supported by drones flying out of Air Force bases in Yorkshire. This allows the force to maintain a 24-hour watch of the border, particularly important at night, which is the favoured time for border interdiction in the rural areas.

Limitations on rules of engagement for this military force mean that they are unarmed and are only allowed to report suspicious vehicles and people. Ultimately, they must communicate with the police, who have the powers to arrest and detain as well as to seize goods. Liaison is improving, although the police chiefs remain frustrated that they are unable to direct the efforts of the service personnel, or their surveillance assets, because of the Byzantine arrangements for command and control that remain between the military and civilian agencies.

As this rainbow coalition of twenty-first-century warriors watches over a sleeping public by night, the jihadists monitor the military and civilian radio networks. They have already hacked into the police command-and-control network and have their own drones up overhead confirming the roads that the military have 'eyes on'. They make their decisions about which roads they can use overnight.

At about 2 a.m., a fleet of four transit vans emerges from a warehouse in Pollokshields, on the outskirts of Glasgow. They make their way down the 'A' roads towards the border. Reaching Langholm, they separate, two head for Kielder Forest and cross into England through a maze of forest tracks, rejoining the roads network near the old Roman fort at Vindolanda. The other two vans skirt the border and move eastwards, crossing over near Mindrum and making their way south through farm tracks that criss-cross the Cheviot Hills. By 7 a.m., the vans are moving south on the M6 and A1.

Each van is crewed by a driver and passenger, both of whom are unarmed. In the back are a mixture of harmless boxes of computer games and mobile-phone accessories. Their cover story is quite simple. They are on their way to sell their gear at the markets in London. They have receipts for the stuff in the back of the van, and the vehicles are registered to a company with a website that explains how they sell-on electronic entertainment equipment bought at government auctions. It all checks out. The vans have their

MOT certificates and are insured. There is no reason for them or these young men to raise suspicion.

The vans stop for fuel so they can complete the journey to London. The drivers buy coffees and snacks, and then continue their journeys. On their way south, they pass numerous police, military and emergency services vehicles also using the motorways.

The vans carry an additional precious cargo. Each is loaded with about 1,000 kilograms of commercial explosives and a large quantity of industrial smoke detectors. Their targets are the major electoral-counting centres in London at Alexandra Palace, Excel, and Olympia.

At each of these venues, hundreds of people are gathering to count the votes in the general elections. Political candidates from all parties will flock there in the hours after the polling stations close, in order to see how they have fared in the elections. Major broadcasters from the UK and across Europe will also be present, anxious to see how the British people have cast their votes in reaction to the events of the previous five years. Dozens of white transit vans are criss-crossing the capital, bringing in the ballot boxes from across London. It is a busy and frenetic evening, with the private security company guards at each location completely overwhelmed by the pace and the numbers of people and vehicles coming and going.

The police keep their distance, having done their work to secure and clear the venues earlier in the day. The senior media advisor to the Metropolitan Police Commissioner has made it clear that there is reputational risk in being associated with the 'balls up' that is the controlling of the count locations. Best to keep a safe distance away and use the defensive line that 'resources are now so stretched that the force cannot expect to be everywhere all the time'.

At about 1 a.m. on Friday, 8 May, the UK Foreign Secretary

gets into the back of his car to head for the count centre in North London. It has been a long, tough election and an uncomfortable four years criss-crossing the globe trying to make some sense of Britain's new place in the world. As the lightly armoured Jaguar car pulls up at Alexandra Palace, it joins a short queue of vehicles awaiting access. The Foreign Secretary is pleased to see the large numbers of transit vans delivering the votes to the count centre. He is hopeful of an increased majority and also to be back home in bed by 6 a.m.

Neither he nor anyone else notices the white transit van that has made its way down from the north of England and pulls in discreetly behind the Jaguar. That van may be carrying no votes, nevertheless, its deadly cargo will have a far more significant political impact than any other vehicle on its way to a count that night.

CHAPTER 9

OPERATION IMPERFECT
STORM
The European Dilemma

*The era out to 2040 will be a time of transition; this is
likely to be characterised by instability, both in the relations
between states, and in the relations between groups within
states. During this timeframe the world is likely to face the
reality of a changing climate, rapid population growth,
resource scarcity, resurgence in ideology, and shifts in global
power from West to East. No state, group or individual can
meet these challenges in isolation, only collective responses
will be sufficient. Hence, the struggle to establish an effective
system of global governance, capable of responding to these
challenges, will be a central theme of the era. Globalisation,
global inequality, climate change and technological innovation will affect the lives of everyone on the planet. There
will be constant tension between greater interdependence
between states, groups and individuals and intensifying
competition between them. Dependence on complex global
systems, such as global supply chains for resources, is likely
to increase the risk of systemic failures.*

Global Strategic Trends – Out to 2040
(4th Edition)[37]

The History

Large-scale incursions and insurgencies driven from MENA towards Europe are nothing new, nor are the forces that create the conditions for such incursions. Demographic shifts, economic and political dislocation, territorial ambitions, and religious expansionism can be traced back as early as the third century BC and the Second Punic War between 218 and 201 BC. Famously, Carthaginian general Hannibal established a North African presence in what is today southern Spain, focused on modern-day Cartagena. In 217 BC, supported by a curious amalgam of Gallic tribes, Hannibal twice defeated the armies of the Roman Republic at the battles of Trebbia and Trasimene. In 216 BC, the fall of Rome itself seemed imminent when Hannibal inflicted a crushing defeat on the Roman armies at the Battle of Cannae, but failed to follow-up his victory. This enabled Publius Cornelius Scipio Africanus to employ a distraction strategy by attacking the Carthaginian base in Spain at Carthago Nova.

Between the eleventh and fourteenth centuries, successive hordes of Christian pilgrims from Europe sought to impose 'outremer' on the Levant. The Crusades were often little more than European-inspired genocide on the Arab people, as the Great Orders of Christendom such as the Knights Templar put Islam to the sword in the name of Christ. A brutal experience for Arabs that is still, in turn, seared into the mindset of contemporary Arabism.

Between AD 711 and 718, the Ummayid Conquest of Hispania took place and established the Ummayid Caliphate. Local leaders embraced Islam, and Arabic became the official language of the southern half of Spain for some 800 years.

Over the intervening centuries Muslim emirates were established, whilst the period was continually pockmarked by tensions with Christian Europe, which included one expedition to Spain by the Holy Roman Emperor, Charlemagne. The last Muslim or Moorish emirate was not expelled from Spain until 1492, after the victory of the armies of Ferdinand of Aragon and Isabella of Castille, a conquest that helped to forge modern Spain.

In south-eastern Europe, the fall of Constantinople to Islamic forces in 1453 ended a series of wars between the Byzantine Empire and Christian Western Europe, which can be traced back to the First Crusade of 1095 and the seizing of Jerusalem by Christian forces in 1099. With the sacking of Constantinople and the creation of Istanbul, the ensuing centuries saw several attempts by the Ottoman Empire to spread Islam across Europe. The peak of Ottoman power was in 1529 with the siege of Vienna. However, Ottoman incursions into south-eastern and central Europe continued until 1683, when the forces of Suleiman the Magnificent were finally defeated at the Battle of Vienna.

In more recent times, the collapse of the Ottoman Empire was followed by the bungled attempts by the British and French to build a Westphalian-style state structure to replace Turkish dominion during the Interbellum of 1918–1939. With the eclipse of Europe's two imperial powers in the wake of the Second World War, the founding of the State of Israel in 1948, and superpower competition across the region for much of the Cold War, the Middle East has continued to be the crucible for a deadly contest between faith, ideas and power.

That contest continues today, as the post-colonial aspiration that found its expression in pan-Arab nationalism has been eroded by a complex mix of demography, demagoguery and decline. Today, the Middle East is again trapped in a vice between the confessional competition of Shia and Sunni, regional-strategic competitors such as Iran and Saudi Arabia, and the new geopolitical struggle between the fading liberal West and resurgent liberal powers such as China and Russia, all of which are stirred by the seemingly endless and intractable Israeli-Palestinian struggle, itself a metaphor for the failure of the West in the Middle East. The tragedy of Syria is but the surface of a deep cauldron of hate, ambition and contest that shows no sign of abating.

The signs of those struggles for hegemony by Arabs, Europeans and others are apparent today in the structures, faiths, and ethnicities of peoples across Europe and the Middle East and North Africa. Together such legacies reinforce what is in essence a symbiotic set of relationships that over recent decades has been reinforced by globalisation and the mass movement of peoples.

The Build-Up

This is also a story of Europe's political and economic weakness and the generation of strategically illiterate and inept leaders spawned by the very idea of 'Europe'. The economic decline of southern Europe pre-dates the 2008 financial collapse and the 2010 Eurozone crash. Inefficient states across the region have demonstrated repeatedly an inability to reform public sectors, which continues to this day. State structures are vulnerable. Spain in 2015 had a budget deficit of 5.1 per cent of gross domestic product (GDP), well above the 3 per cent debt to GDP ratio established as 'law' by the 1991 EU Maastricht Treaty. Not only that, but public debt accounts for 99 per cent of GDP, with Madrid having to service enormous interest payments to the detriment of public services, most notably security and defence.[38]

Italy is in an even worse condition. Europe's fourth largest economy saw public debt in 2016 at a record 133 per cent of GDP with a growth rate of 0.3 per cent. Indeed, the Italian economy did not grow at all between 1999, when Italy joined the single currency, and 2014. Greece is the worst-off of all the southern European states, with a public debt that stands at an unsustainable 177 per cent of GDP. The December 2016 fall of Prime Minister Renzi following a popular rejection of his attempts to streamline Italy's self-paralysing political system suggests little will change in either Italy or across much of the Eurozone. A situation made far worse by the 2017 collapse of a major Italian bank.

Even France, Europe's third biggest economy and second military power, has a public debt to GDP ratio of 96.1 per cent, although the UK is only marginally better at 89.6 per cent. The May 2017 presidential elections simply confirm France's political reality; a country uneasy with itself, and uneasy with much of the world around it. These realities reflect fundamental structural weaknesses in the respective economies of the three countries that make it ever more difficult for Madrid and Rome to invest in security and Defence Forces equipped for the challenges of today. According to the International Institute for Strategic Studies (IISS), in 2015 Italy spent 1.1 per cent of GDP on defence, whilst Spain spent 0.9 per cent and both on static economies.[39]

Even those relatively modest levels of defence investment are finessed by including the costs of both the Carabinieri and the Guardia Civil respectively in the figures declared by both countries. Therefore, any likelihood that Italy and

Spain will meet the NATO guideline of 2 per cent GDP to be invested in defence 'within a decade', with 20 per cent of that investment to be made on new defence equipment, is remote.[40]

To make matters worse, at a meeting of Eurozone finance ministers in May 2016, it was agreed in principle to commence debt mutualisation in late 2017 or early 2018, in other words, after the September 2017 German federal elections. This will involve the further transfers of huge amounts of taxpayers' money from the north and west of Europe to the south and east of Europe. Not only will such transfers continue to restrict economic growth, but Germany will insist that debtor states aim to remain within the Maastricht convergence criterion of compiling budget deficits of no more than 3 per cent GDP. This will likely further constrict expenditure on security and defence across much of southern Europe.

When compared with British defence investment, the figures for most southern European states raise even more concerns. Whilst many British commentators point to flaws and weaknesses in the 2015 Strategic Defence and Security Review, Britain is far better placed.[41] According to IISS, in 2016 Britain was still the world's fourth-biggest defence investor, spending some $56.2 billion or 2 per cent GDP, compared with France, which spent $46.8 billion (1.9 per cent GDP) in 2016, and Germany which spent $36.6 billion or 1.1 per cent GDP. Equally, the economic consequences of the June 2016 decision by British voters to quit the EU are as yet unclear, and could further constrict Britain's investment in security and defence.

Structural European decline is exacerbated by similar, if not worse, structural weakness in states across a MENA already weakened by the Syrian War, the 2011 Arab Spring, or a toxic combination of both. Egypt, the most populous state in the Middle East, has a level of public indebtedness that totalled 90.5 per cent GDP in 2015, and an unemployment rate of 12.7 per cent, with much of that joblessness affecting young people. Jordan bears a similar burden, with Amman facing a public debt-to-GDP ratio of 89 per cent in 2015, and unlike Britain (for example) few means to sustain such a debt over the medium-to-long term.

On top of that, the unemployment rate in Jordan is some 15 per cent, with again much of that unemployment affecting the youth population. Add to Jordan's burdens the enforced need to cope with huge numbers of refugees from the Syrian war, as well as a large Palestinian refugee population, and Jordan is at best a precarious state. The same instability also applies to Lebanon, which also labours under public debt that represents some 133 per cent GDP.

Whilst the figures vary from state to state, Algeria, Libya, Tunisia, and Morocco can all, in one way or another, be described as precarious states. And, whilst population growth has flattened in recent years, a past rapid rise in the population across MENA will continue to have political consequences.

For example, the youth population of 18–25 year olds is not projected to peak at 100 million people until 2035. Between 1950 and 2000 the population of the Middle East and North Africa soared from 92 million to 349 million, a year-on-year growth rate of 3.7 per cent.[42] Critical public services such as education have simply failed to meet the challenge posed by such a population bubble. Even today, education remains focused in many countries across the region on exerting political control and on preparing future elite bureaucrats. Few if any countries have education systems designed to better prepare the mass of the population for the challenges of a globalised world.[43]

The parlous situation of the state is even more marked in Sub-Saharan Africa. According to *The Economist*, a 'high variant' projection by the United Nations suggests that by 2050 the population of Sub-Saharan Africa will rise to 2.7 billion, or 25 per cent of the projected world population.

If African states continue to face challenges they seem incapable of surmounting, such as mass famine, desertification, and elite corruption, there is little doubt that populations will continue to seek to move across borders and in very large numbers.

In June 2016, a report by the United Nations High Commissioner for Refugees (UNHCR) pointed to the growing pressure-cooker effect that mass migration is having on states and regions.[44] There are a record 65.3 million forcibly displaced people worldwide, roughly the same as the population of the United Kingdom, of which 21.3 million are refugees. These figures are unlikely to fall anytime soon. Indeed, the EU alone received 1,321,560 asylum claims in 2015, not including the many illegal and irregular migrants that have entered Europe over the past five years, many of whom come from countries where violent extremism is rife.

The Scenario

The Middle-East Meltdown

Friday, 8 May 2020. It is Ramadan in the dusty, Egyptian city of Mansoura, capital of the Dakahlia Governate. Home to almost 500,000 people, Mansoura sits roughly at the centre of an isosceles triangle with the distance between

Alexandria and Port Said providing the base, whilst Cairo sits at the apex. The literal translation of Mansoura from Arabic is 'victory', named after the 1219 Muslim defeat of France's Louis IX and the disastrous Seventh Crusade. Today, Mansoura is regarded by many conservative Egyptians as the spiritual home of the Muslim Brotherhood, which remains a powerful political and spiritual influence in the city.

For some months following the 2016 fall of Aleppo and the 2017 sacking of Idlib, foreign jihadis have been making their way through Mansoura, passing from one safe house to another as they traverse from northern Syria and Iraq, where Islamic State is close to defeat, west towards Libya, Tunisia, Algeria and Morocco, in the hope of creating a new Caliphate. The city is tense. Or, to be more precise, the Governor and the Egyptian Army are tense. On one hand, Cairo has aided the Islamists by creating a 'green corridor' in an effort to move them on west through Egypt. On the other hand, Cairo is all too aware of the growing influence of the Islamists in the Egyptian Army and fears a Muslim Brotherhood that is gaining ground once more in the provinces.

To make matters worse, for the past two years the Egyptian economy has deteriorated markedly, with ordinary Egyptians struggling to survive. In the cities, at least on the surface of what is a tightly controlled society, this growing political rupture in society is not so evident. However, in the conservative Sunni heartlands tensions are simmering, much like the early summer heat.

Since ousting Egypt's one and only elected president, the Muslim Brotherhood's Mohamed Morsi, back in 2013, former General now President Abdel Fattah el-Sisi has been attempting to buy off opposition by improving living standards. His strategy is similar to that employed by China's Communist Party leadership in the wake of the 1989 Tiananmen Square massacre.

In China it worked, but in Egypt it did not.

In 2017 President Sisi reflated the economy and for a time it seemed as though the gamble might pay off. However, the 2018 collapse of Italian banks, triggering the second Eurozone debt crisis, robbed Sisi of a key EU market. Forced to rescue Italy and stop a run on all southern European banks, political leaders in the ten states that actually pay for the EU demanded that the EU and its member-states drastically and dramatically cut all the aid and development upon which much of Sisi's gamble was reliant.

Since the EU cut off the aid, the Gulf States led by Saudi Arabia have offered some help, but they too are concerned by growing dissent against the mix of kings, emirs and sheikhs who run the Gulf Cooperation Council, and the growing regional-strategic threat posed by Iran, with its Russian and increasingly Turkish backers. Ankara in 2017 proved that confession is no barrier to power, as Sunni Turkey joined forces with Sunni Syria, Shia Iran and Putin's Russia to forge a new anti-Western bloc. Not only that, but the return of Iranian and Iraqi oil onto an already saturated oil market has suppressed the price of Saudi crude below $20 per barrel for over three years.

Bereft of donors, unable to meet the needs of its people, Egypt is fast becoming an economic basket case.

As the faithful leave the mosque after Friday prayers on 8 May 2020, a fight breaks out between Mohamed and Abdallah, a distant cousin, over some money owed by the former to the latter. Unfortunately, Mohammed is a radical member of the Muslim Brotherhood, and Abdallah a soldier. In the midst of the fight, Abdallah pulls out a revolver and shoots Mohammed dead. With people already unhappy and fractious due to the fast, a mob soon forms around Abdallah. He is manhandled to the ground and then taken to a nearby lamppost, where he is strung up and lynched.

Cairo reacts to what it thinks is the long-expected start of a Muslim Brotherhood coup. In 2014 the Army had stormed Mansoura University to arrest what the high command believed to be hard-line Islamist supporters of Morsi. Now the Army is again ordered into Mansoura in strength. A stand-off begins with members of the Muslim Brotherhood in the mosque where Mohammed was praying the day before. A fearful Cairo orders the Army to go into the mosque and arrest those it calls the ringleaders of a planned coup.

The lieutenant-colonel in charge orders his troops to prepare the assault. Nothing happens. Not one of his soldiers moves. He orders them again to enter the mosque. Nothing happens. Having not been paid for weeks, and with their ranks increasingly subverted by members of the Brotherhood, rank-and-file soldiers simply refuse to fire on their fellow Egyptians.

As news of the mutiny is passed on, regiment after regiment lays down its arms. Finally, a little-known Special Forces officer issues a proclamation that spreads rapidly, calling on troops to arrest President Sisi in the name of deposed President Morsi and the Egyptian people. Riots break out across the Nile delta and they extend quickly up the Nile valley. Soon after, Alexandria and Cairo are taken by forces led by units of the Army, which swear allegiance to President Morsi. Worryingly, a few also swear allegiance to the now-dead leader of Islamic State, Abu Bakr al-Baghdadi.

As Egypt stumbles, topples and then falls, similar movements spring up in Libya, Tunisia, Algeria and Morocco. It is clear that a series of already very shaky governments are about to fall and the West meets in crisis in Brussels to decide what to do about it. They meet first at the new NATO HQ in Zaventem, and then in the EU Council of Ministers' building. Little is agreed, not least because a resurgent Russia warns the West not to interfere in the Middle East and despatches its strengthened Mediterranean Fleet to underscore Moscow's intent. Greece, Hungary and Italy, all three of whom have become reliant on Russian loans and energy, block agreement in both the Alliance and the Union.

As the crisis intensifies, President Trump's United States and its European allies discuss the evacuation of their nationals, many of whom are holidaymakers. They also consider taking the matter to the United Nations Security Council (UNSC). However, given the tense relationships that exist between the US, Britain and France on one side, and China and Russia on the other side of an increasingly fraught geopolitical situation, there is little chance that any UNSC Resolution could be agreed that would permit the West to intervene. In any case, President Trump is up for re-election and his close relationship with President Putin makes him less convinced that failing American strength should be committed to a fight that, for him, is essentially a European problem.

Furthermore, since the June 2016 decision by Britain to quit the European Union, much political energy has been spent in Europe on a bad-tempered set of negotiations over the UK's departure from the EU. There is little love lost between Berlin, London and Paris, and even less strategic unity of purpose and effort. Nevertheless, after several days of bartering, some form of agreement is eventually reached to evacuate Western nationals and a much-circumscribed

Crisis Activation Order is issued by NATO's North Atlantic Council. Sadly, such is the parlous state of several European navies, most notably the Italian Navy, it falls upon the Americans, British and French to carry out the evacuations.

By late June 2020, chaos reigns across the Middle East and North Africa, as government after government falls. However, it is not just the forces of chaos at work. Iran sees an opportunity to launch wave after wave of terrorist attacks against Israel through its proxy Hezbollah. At one point Israel places the Israeli Defence Force (IDF) on full alert, including its nuclear arsenal at Dimona, as Tel Aviv fears Tehran might seek to turn the crisis into a full-scale war. On 25 June 2020, Western forces land in Libya to begin evacuation operations. Russia and much of the Muslim world react in anger, most notably the 'Arab Street', the volatile underclass of Arabian society, who are led to believe by radical Islamic preachers that the West is about to use the crisis to re-establish colonies across the region. At the same time, Russia begins a major cyber, disinformation, and destabilisation hybrid-warfare campaign against Poland and the Baltic States.

China's Moment

At 0325 hours on 26 June, the USS *John C. Stennis*, a 103,000-ton, nuclear-powered American fleet aircraft carrier, enters the disputed South China Sea at the centre of a full carrier strike group to conduct a freedom of navigation operation in strength.

As recently as June 2016, the US and Chinese navies had conducted a joint tactical-manoeuvre exercise in the North Pacific. However, since a ruling by the International

Tribunal for the Law of the Sea in favour of the Philippines, and against Beijing's claim that China has exclusive territorial rights to over eighty per cent of the South China Sea, relations had deteriorated sharply, as China moved rapidly to exert its influence over the area by force. Between 2016 and 2020, China had strengthened its forces on several artificial islands it had constructed to act as military bases.

This 'string of pearls' now act as Chinese sentinels to control access to the South China Sea. One such 'sentinel' is Fiery Cross Reef; completed in 2017, the island is now fully equipped with a military airstrip and a 5,000-tonne sea-berth. Beijing's strategic aims are fivefold: to create a military capability on the disputed Spratly Islands, which at a stroke would end sovereignty disputes with the Philippines and Vietnam; to control the oil and gas resources believed to lie under the Spratly Islands; to reinforce China's self-proclaimed Air Defence Identification Zone; to extend Beijing's self-proclaimed Exclusive Economic Zone (EEZ) right across the South China Sea; and in time to tip the strategic balance against the US and Japan. It is that balance that the USS *John C. Stennis* is seeking to uphold.

Fiery Cross, or *Crann Tara*, is aptly named. A Fiery Cross was a medieval Scottish device used to summon the clans in the event of danger. It was a half-burnt wooden cross soaked in blood and used as a signal to the clans of the revenge by fire and blood that awaited those that did not answer the summons. Revenge is fast coming. At 0425 hours, twenty-five Chinese J-16 *Shengyang* fighters, armed with advanced anti-ship technology, approach the US force with orders to engage. After repeated warnings to turn away, the US commander orders the Chinese aircraft to be engaged and 'downed'. Ten of them are quickly shot down by 'active countermeasures' and a further two are badly damaged. However, eight aircraft continue their attack and before they can be destroyed, an ageing Aegis-class cruiser, the USS *Mobile Bay*, is struck by several missiles and sinks with heavy loss of life. A full-blown crisis in the Asia-Pacific is now underway.

Beijing does not back down. China is determined to ensure that it becomes the dominant strategic power in East and possibly South Asia and having witnessed the crisis in the Middle East believes now is the moment to act. After years of sequestration and a gridlocked Congress, which has prevented the Pentagon embarking on sound long-term defence planning, the United States is no longer able to engage effectively in three simultaneous crises in Asia-Pacific, the Middle East and Europe. The Trump presidency, far from rebuilding the US armed forces, has been long on rhetoric and short on action, not least because President Trump has spent much of his time fighting attempts by his many enemies in Congress to have him impeached. Knowing this, Beijing has built up its military power patiently and relentlessly, intimidating its neighbours, and challenging the post-Cold War Western order. Consequently, for some time the world has stood on the brink of a new age of 'might is right' hyper-competition. It is about to step over the brink. China is also all too aware of what President Putin is planning next.

As the crisis in Asia-Pacific deepens, the US is forced to respond in force. However, American action is only likely to prevail if Washington commits the bulk of its forces to Asia-Pacific. These include forces either stationed in Europe, or earmarked for the defence of Europe.

The Russian Gambit

On 1 July, as American forces head south, power and information networks begin to crash in the Baltic States and across much of Central and Eastern Europe. Russian military exercises underway in and around the Kola Peninsula, Kaliningrad and Belarus, on the Ukrainian border and in the Black Sea, suddenly intensify and expand. Hybrid warfare intensifies in the Baltic States as so-called 'little green men' – masked soldiers in unmarked green uniforms – are reported seizing vital installations. The 4,000 NATO troops stationed since 2017 in the Baltic States as part of the Alliance's forward presence are ordered to react by the Strategic Allied Commander, Europe (SACEUR), together with their Estonian, Latvian, and Lithuanian colleagues. However, NATO forces are stretched thin and kept off balance by sabotaged roads and bridges and jammed communications. Quickly non-linear warfare, as the Russians call hybrid warfare, begins to turn into real warfare, as the equivalent of four army corps, or 120,000 troops, in the Western Military Oblast begin to move into NATO territory.

The North Atlantic Council (NAC) meets in emergency session and reluctantly puts both the Very High Readiness Joint Task Force (VJTF) of some 5,000 troops, and the enhanced NATO Response Force (eNRF) of some 35,000 troops on Notice to Move. The NAC also orders the nine Graduated Response Force headquarters to stand by, including the British-led Allied Rapid Reaction Corps (ARRC).

However, the hard military-strategic truth is that the VJTF Notice to Move will realistically require some five to seven days, whilst the eNRF will require at least thirty to forty-five days. And, whilst on paper NATO has a further 180 battalions to call upon as part of its wider force structure, many of them are ill equipped, lack critical logistics, and are unable to move, having been maintained at a lower level of readiness for several years, and exercised only occasionally with other NATO forces. In any case, NATO nations are deeply divided over which threat should take priority: Russia's threat to the eastern flank of the Alliance or the growing danger from the south.

The most optimistic planning scenarios suggest that the bulk of NATO's Defence Forces will require from 60 to 180 days' Notice to Move, and even longer between Notice to Move and Notice to Action. Either way, many of the forces of the southern Allies already have their eyes firmly fixed on the deteriorating situation to the south of the Mediterranean, as irregular migration flows suddenly accelerate, and the threat from Islamic State grows.

As the NAC meets, the Kremlin begins to talk of NATO aggression and cites entirely fictional violations of Russian air, sea, land, and cyberspace. Suddenly, Russian forces seize land either side of the Lithuanian and Polish borders between Kaliningrad and Belarus along the so-called Suwalki Gap, over some sixty-five kilometres in length. Moscow cites the failure of both Vilnius and Warsaw to agree guaranteed Russian land access to Kaliningrad as justification for its 'legitimate' actions. Russian forces also build up on the Estonian border, claiming the need to protect the new corridor, and give all NATO forces five days to leave.

The NAC meets again in emergency session and at Poland and Lithuania's request finally issues an ultimatum to Moscow, albeit one in which Germany and Italy insert a holding clause calling for further talks. Unless Russian forces are withdrawn from NATO territory in forty-eight hours, the Alliance will declare a breach of Article 5 of the Washington Treaty and invoke collective defence.

Russia immediately responds by putting its Intermediate Nuclear Forces (INF) treaty-breaching *Iskander M* and *Kalibr* short- and medium-range nuclear weapons on full alert, thus threatening a nuclear attack on European cities, and calls the action 'nuclear de-escalation'. However, Moscow is careful not to place all its Strategic Rocket Forces on alert, as that would imply an impending threat against continental North America. Skilfully, Moscow is exploiting Trump's long-held ambivalence about America's commitment to the defence of Europe. In the wake of the NAC meeting, the Kremlin cites a vital Russian need to consolidate a 'peace buffer' between Russia and a 'clearly aggressive NATO'.

Conventional deterrence fails, as Russian *Spetsnaz*, naval infantry and airmobile forces move to seize vital areas of the three Baltic States. Estonian, Latvian and Lithuanian forces, together with their NATO allies, put up a brief, effective and deadly fight, but with Russian forces massing in strength, it is clear that even if the VJTF or the eNRF can be fully deployed, they are no match for the Russian forces in the area of operations (AO). Worse, NATO's conventional air power is in any case unable to overcome Russian anti-access/ area denial (A2/AD) capabilities that were strengthened immeasurably by the 2015 stationing of the *Voronezh* radar system in Kaliningrad.

Suddenly, faced with a massive crisis in Asia-Pacific, President Trump, in characteristically blunt language, says to the Europeans: 'We Americans are busy. You Europeans sort it out!' But the European forces are too hollowed out, lack key enablers and vital logistics, and their leaders are too lacking in political will to respond in force. President Putin knows full well that having overcome NATO's conventional deterrent, the Alliance faces a long war to recover the Baltic States and many Western European leaders simply lack the resolve to confront such a terrible choice between war and peace. History remains, after all, eloquent in Europe.

On 10 July, having achieved his military objectives, President Putin calls a ceasefire. Seizing the moment, Putin calls a much-weakened Chancellor Merkel and tells her that his 'limited correction' is over, that Russia is now content with the new strategic 'balance' in Europe, and that Moscow has no more territorial ambitions. He laments the fact that European leaders did not heed his warnings about NATO and EU enlargement, and the threat the twin enlargements posed to Russia. He even offers to compensate the families of the 224 NATO force members killed during Russia's 'corrective' operation.

At the same time, President Putin offers Chancellor Merkel a stark choice. It is the same choice Britain and France faced in 1939 over the defence of Poland. Having already traded space, does she really want to fight a war over a long period of time, and at great cost to Germany, to recover the Baltic States?

Merkel is faced with an appalling dilemma, for which neither she nor contemporary Germany is prepared. London and Paris obfuscate and bluster, but do nothing. With US forces committed to Asia-Pacific, southern Europeans either impotent or desperately trying to engage with the deteriorating situation in the Middle East and North Africa, Washington is too over-stretched to respond in force in any of the three theatres in which major conflict has broken out.[45]

Moreover, NATO Europeans are too weak and divided to act as effective first responders, whilst the Trump White House will not risk a nuclear confrontation with Russia over the Baltic States, much though Trump denounces Russia's actions and speaks of 'betrayal'. The EU's European Council goes into emergency session to impose punitive sanctions on Russia, but it is all too little too late. NATO's bluff has been well and truly called, and from Putin's perspective the sanctions are merely a price worth paying, given the surge of popularity he enjoys in Russia, however brief. The EU is humiliated. NATO is a spent force. By the end of July 2020, the Baltic States are once again firmly under Russian control, almost a century to the day since they declared their independence in the wake of the First World War.

Chaos, Criminality and Caliphate

Europe's tragedy is synchronicity. By early 2020, the situation in North Africa is dire. The small European force that landed in Libya in June has been beaten back with significant loss of life by a mix of local militias and jihadis. Hundreds of European nationals are trapped in Tunisia and Morocco, where the situation is little better than in Libya. Some are held as hostages by criminal gangs, who threaten to sell them on to newly formed Islamist groups, which are in turn being reinforced by battle-hardened jihadis arriving daily from the collapsed Raqqa Caliphate. Beheadings of captured Westerners begin.

In the ensuing chaos, it is criminal gangs that prove best adapted to exploit the situation. For years now various groups affiliated to both al-Qaeda and Islamic State have been working with criminal gangs to exploit the mass migration of mainly black Africans from Sub-Saharan Africa. As the crisis unfolds, there are some 800,000 souls trapped in North Africa seeking to gain illicit entry into the European Union. These already desperate people are driven even deeper into despair as the last vestige of state authority collapses around them.

Compounding this situation, after the sacking of Aleppo and Idlib in 2017 Turkey had allowed Syrian and other refugees and migrants to move unimpeded towards Greece and Europe. The migration crisis has been raging unabated for three years, as more than 3 million have entered Europe illegally between 2017 and 2019.

Seeing an opportunity, Ayman al-Zawahiri, Osama bin Laden's successor and leader of al-Qaeda, orders his network to make contact with the Islamic State leadership now established in Mansoura and seek common cause. Zawahiri offers an outlandish but compelling vision to ISIS leaders. He tells them at a secret and hastily convened conference, of which British Intelligence is aware but which GCHQ cannot pinpoint, that the moment has come to establish a Grand Caliphate, not just in the Middle East and North Africa, but also in Europe.

His vision is to unify the various Sunni Islamist groups by recreating in southern Europe, in the name of the Prophet, the Ummayad Caliphate of the eighth century. However, he wants to go further than simply the reconquest of 'Hispania'. His ambition is to do to the Christian world what Islamic State has already done to the apostate symbols of the Roman Empire in Palmyra – destroy them completely. In other words, as he states to his inner group, his ultimate aim is an attack on both Istanbul and Rome to destroy the hated vestiges of Roman, Byzantine, Crusader/Christian civilisations by 'ripping out the hearts of the beasts' and uniting all true believers.

As a peace-offering to Islamic State leaders, Zawahiri proposes creating a new force that will act as the vanguard for the new European Caliphate, called the Islamic State of

Europe, or ISE. He also points to the vital importance of the Caliphate in North Africa, reminding his audience that the Golden Age of Islam coincided with the establishment of the Abbasid Caliphate across North Africa in the eighth century AD, the third of the great Caliphates established following the death of the Prophet. Zawahiri says the dawning of the 'new golden age of Islam' is now at hand.

His proposed strategy has several elements, all of which are fantasy but also have some grounding in truth, particularly in Zawahiri's very *parti pris* world view. Both al-Qaeda and Islamic State have used the uncontrolled migrant flows to establish some 40,000 foreign fighters back in Europe, who have been established as 'sleepers', ready to be activated at any time. Zawahiri suggests that both al-Qaeda and Islamic State must learn the lessons of Taliban and al-Qaeda operations in Afghanistan, and Islamic State in Syria and Iraq. If Islamic State of Europe seeks to act like a conventional military force, it will be crushed by 'Crusader' air power.

Zawahiri also says he has been studying Russia's use of what the Crusaders call hybrid warfare. ISE will use disinformation, disruption and destruction to create in the minds of the Crusaders a sense of hopelessness, disrupt any response and/or any attempt to reinforce a response.

al-Qaeda has also been quietly establishing links with migrant groups in Italy, Greece and Spain. Angered by their treatment by Europeans, some of them are prepared to act with ISE to establish armed clusters, which come the hour will join together to create the Great European Caliphate. His network has also been working with criminals in Russia, Eastern and Western Europe and the Balkans, to move significant supplies of small arms and explosives across open borders. 'With the Great Crusader America distracted and the Little Crusader Europe in chaos, it is now time for revenge to be enacted on all the Crusader peoples, on the way to the creation of a new "umma" and the Great Caliphate that will rid the world of infidels and apostates.'

From the outset, the plan is doomed to fail, not least because Zawahiri assumes that 'all good Muslims will rise up to join the Caliphate'. His surrogates in Europe have also wildly exaggerated the numbers of refugees willing to act in concert with ISE. He fails utterly to understand that the massive majority of 'good Muslims' in Europe want nothing to do with him or his creed of hate. However, the 'Z Plan', as it becomes known, possesses sufficient reality and sufficient thugs to cause immense damage, social upheaval, and the loss of social cohesion in European states already sensitised by repeated terrorist attacks and the Russian threat to the east.

For all the madness of the 'Z Plan', the failure of EU member-states to come up with a realistic strategy to manage the mass-migration flows from its south and south-east has left millions of desperate, angry people festering in hopelessness either side of the Mediterranean. The prospect of an EU Common Asylum Policy is as far off as it was back in 2015, when first discussed. Racism abounds in Europe, as the indigenous population grows ever more nervous about the influx, and the changes the influx is already imposing on societies and public and social services. Only ten EU member-states are bearing the brunt of ninety per cent of the migration flow, and since 2017 most of them have closed their borders. Central and Eastern European EU member-states will have little or nothing to do with any migration, and in early 2020 Britain finally left the EU and also closed its borders to migrants.

Suddenly, with Northern and Western Europe weakened by the huge transfers of taxpayers' money in the form of

Eurobonds by the European Central Bank, in an increasingly desperate attempt to keep indebted Eastern and Southern European states from bankruptcy, the Eurozone again crashes as the markets hike the cost of borrowing. The 2016 Brexit vote was only the beginning; the 'European Project' for ever-closer union is in tatters as the Eurozone begins to fall apart and millions of Europeans are cast into poverty. Brussels is hated and mainstream politicians are despised . . . everywhere.

Populist politicians are the winners. They offer cheap and easy solutions to angry people. In 2017, Marine Le Pen's Front National only narrowly fails to take the Elysée in the French presidential elections. By 2020 she is well on the way to being elected as the French president. *Alternatif für Deutschland* did spectacularly well in the September 2017 German federal elections. The sinister and anti-Islamic Pegida movement is also making progress in Belgium, Germany, and the Netherlands. After the Brexit promise to reduce immigration is revealed to be a sham, and inward migration to the UK helps push population towards the 70 million mark in 2020.

However, it is in Greece, Italy and Spain where populism is at its most charged. In 2019, the nominally left-wing Syriza government is thrown out of office in elections that see a far-right coalition around Golden Dawn elected. In Italy, Beppe Grillo's Five Star Movement ejects the Rome government and the coalition that replaces it calls for a Brexit-style EU referendum to take place in 2022. Similar demands come from the new Unidos Podemos government in Madrid, determined to confront and frustrate what is seen as an increasingly dictatorial Brussels elite, and end the politics of austerity.

It is also Southern Europe where the effects of Europe's never-ending crisis are most keenly felt. Trapped between

Berlin-inspired and ECB-implemented austerity, and the servicing of enormous government debt, public services across Southern Europe are close to collapse. Infrastructure is crumbling and public servants are depressed and under-supported. This lack of investment is nowhere more apparent than in police services and armed forces across the region, most notably in rural and coastal communities in southern Italy, Spain and Greece.

In early August, migration flows suddenly surge. Hundreds of thousands are put in horribly overcrowded boats along the North African coast and forced to set out for Europe. Tens of thousands drown and the EU's recently strengthened external-border force is soon overwhelmed, whilst Western navies in the region fare little better. For example, the Royal Navy discovers to its cost that the serial underfunding of both its sea-control and sea-presence missions has left it with far too few ships to cover the sea space now being filled with the bodies of drowned migrants, let alone deal with the powerful Russian Northern and Mediterranean fleets.

There is also a growing migrant surge from the Levant that threatens to destabilise Turkey. Confronted with a major Kurdish insurgency in its eastern provinces, already host to some 4 million refugees and irregular migrants, and following the June 2016 Islamic State attack on Istanbul Airport, and the July 2016 failed coup, Ankara has become steadily more distant from its NATO Allies. Turkey acts for itself and in August begins expelling huge numbers of migrants from Turkey towards the Greek island of Lesbos.

As the newcomers are sent to already overcrowded detention centres and holding camps, trouble flares between groups, and the Greek authorities steadily lose control. Reports emerge that armed Islamist gangs are taking command of a large number of camps and have begun the systematic murder of local officials, as well as EU and UN personnel.

On Monday, 14 September 2020, and at the start of the new Islamic year, bomb and machine-gun attacks begin on rail and road infrastructure across southern Europe, and suicide bombers attack Athens, Madrid, and Rome Fiumicino airports. What is believed to be 100 jihadis open fire on the faithful and tourists in the Vatican, murder the Swiss Guard, then seal off the Vatican from the rest of Rome and prepare for a long siege. Semtex explosives smuggled into the Vatican in backpacks are placed in the Basilica and detonated, and the dome of St Peter's collapses.

A little-known Islamist, claims to be the friend of a now-dead, one-time al-Qaeda leader Said al-Adel (real name Mohammed Ibrahim Makkawi, a former colonel in the Egyptian Army) and announces in St Peter's the creation of the Islamic State of Europe. Bizarrely, he speaks with a southern English accent. He then begins to publicly behead hostages in front of the shattered Basilica.

The Mont Blanc road tunnel, together with the Frejus, Gotthard, and Simplon rail tunnels are also attacked, as are the main motorway tunnels at Gotthard in Switzerland and Brenner in Austria. Similar attacks take place at the Parthenon in Athens, which is partially destroyed, and against Eastern Orthodox churches and monasteries from Sinai to Istanbul, to Athens and beyond. Suicide bombers attack the Amsterdam, Berlin, London and Paris metro systems, whilst a suicide bomber detonates an enormous truck bomb outside the Justus Lipsius and new Berlaymont buildings in Brussels, destroying both structures.

Initially, Greece, Italy and Spain are overwhelmed, whilst other European countries are still reeling from the Russian seizure of the Baltic States. However, the attacks then pause, unable to maintain their own spectacular momentum. A fundamental flaw in the 'Z Plan' soon becomes apparent. Ayman al-Zawahiri had assumed that many millions of Muslims across Europe, both citizens and refugees, would rise up. They do not. Instead, Muslim citizens begin to work with hard-pressed police and intelligence services as they construct a picture of the situation.

For the moment, Islamists and their affiliates 'control' much of the Middle East and North Africa, which in reality is little more than armed anarchy, tens of thousands of Africans, Arabs, and Europeans are dead, and huge swathes of Greece, southern Italy and southern Spain are subject to bands of armed thugs, as state authority has all but collapsed. Meanwhile in Eastern Europe, Russian forces have occupied the Baltic States, claiming to have 'liberated oppressed Russian speakers' and to have restored an 'essential' security balance in Europe. In the South China Sea, a shooting war continues. It looks as if the Third World War is imminent.

Operation Imperfect Storm

Given that Russia has ceased its aggression with the seizure of the Baltic States, it is decided by Europe's leaders now meeting in almost permanent crisis mode that apart from the punitive and punishing economic sanctions that are slapped on Moscow, the recovery of Estonia, Latvia and Lithuania will have to wait. It is also decided that the United States will focus on challenging and containing China in the South China Sea, with the assistance of Australia, Japan, the Philippines, South Korea and not without a certain historical irony, Vietnam.

For Europeans, the first mission is to trap the Islamists and other armed gangs roaming around southern Europe. Collectively, they recognise that their aggressive Brexit 'strategy' has been a mistake leading to mutual impoverishment and weakening. They finally begin to act as allies in a major crisis. Thankfully, throughout the Brexit fracas, London and Paris have continued to develop a powerful Combined Joint Expeditionary Force (CJEF), and the UK-North European Joint Expeditionary Force (JEF) has also maintained some momentum.

It is also agreed to use the Headquarters of the Allied Rapid Reaction Corps (HQARRC) to command and control three forces operating under the command of the Deputy Supreme Allied Commander Europe (DSACEUR), but in his dual-hatted capacity as EU force commander. This is because it is decided that Operation Imperfect Storm will be EU-flagged. Privately, the Russians assure the Germans that they will do nothing to hinder this operation, so long as no effort is made to remove them from the Baltic states.

In late September 2020, air strikes begin against various camps being used as bases by Islamic State and affiliated forces across Southern Europe. Special Operations Forces move in to capture designated leaders, with naval and amphibious forces proving vital, as the two British heavy aircraft carriers HMS *Queen Elizabeth* and HMS *Prince of Wales*, together with the French aircraft carrier the *Charles de Gaulle*, carry out air strikes against targets across Southern Europe.

Steadily, Allied forces advance and begin to bottle up insurgents in the three countries, before offering them a choice – surrender or die. Whilst hard-core Islamic State fighters opt for the latter and try to draw EU and partner-forces into towns for street-to-street fighting, and launch a series of suicide attacks, many of the forces and groups affiliated to Islamic State either surrender or simply melt away. By mid-October the insurgency is, by and large, over.

Dealing with Islamic State in the chaos that is now rampant across much of the Middle East and North Africa proves more difficult. Britain takes the lead by expanding its existing Gulf Strategy, which British diplomats jokingly call the 'Lawrence of Arabia' strategy. With British and American support, a new pan-Arab force is developed, based on the Saudi-led Arab Rapid Reaction Force. Much of the force is made up of Egyptian, Jordanian, Tunisian, Moroccan and other former elements of the respective armies of those countries.

In November 2020, they first drive down the Nile Valley towards Mansoura. The coalition enjoys some strange bedfellows brought together by Western diplomacy. Israel's Mossad helps with intelligence, whilst the Israeli Defence Forces protect the eastern and northern flank of the advancing Arab force.

Iran is persuaded to suspend its anti-Saudi operations in the Gulf on the basis that 'my enemy's enemy is my friend', and even for the moment halts its proxy war against Israel. The loathing of Islamic State by all the states involved is enough to forge a form of *de facto* alliance. Islamic State and its Muslim Brotherhood associates quickly collapse when faced with organised force and decide to make one last stand not far from Mansoura. They choose poorly, for it is the site where Field Marshal Bernard Law Montgomery's Eighth British Army fought in November 1942 and defeated Field Marshal Erwin Rommel's Afrika Korps, at the second Battle of El Alamein.

The sense of history being repeated is reinforced when in late November 2020 the situation in Asia-Pacific begins to stabilise as China pulls back from the brink of all-out war.

A powerful US, Canadian and European expeditionary force under NATO command, again supported by carrier strike aircraft, lands near Casablanca. The landing beaches are not far from where Allied forces had landed in November 1942 as part of Operation Torch.

Operation Torch was an attempt to bottle up Rommel's forces. In the ensuing three weeks that is exactly what happens as the Arab force, supported by land-based air power from Cyprus, drives westward past Tobruk and Benghazi, whilst the Western force drives east toward Tripoli. As the forces advance they are joined by Berber and other elements fed up with the presence of Islamic State in their midst. And, both forces hug the coast to enable both logistics and sea power to supply and re-supply the force.

On 15 December 2020, the two forces meet on the dusty road between Tripoli and Sirte. There is also a certain irony in this meeting, because Sirte was the town that Islamic State established in late 2017 as its base of operations for launching and controlling attacks in Spain and Italy. As the two forces advance, the first high-level political conference begins in Paris to plot the rebuilding of states across the Middle East and North Africa and what to do with the large numbers of young Arab and African men roaming at large across Europe.

The Assessment

The great crisis of 2020 revealed a whole series of failures long in the making by Britain and its allies. For too long British and other political leaders and policymakers refused to acknowledge the approaching danger. Through a toxic combination of wishful thinking, inadequate or misplaced investments and endemic short-termism in London, Brussels and elsewhere, both the EU and NATO are destabilised at the outset of the crisis, and remain off-balance and behind events until the Americans are finally able and willing to give their full attention to the situation. A Britain mired in Brexit effectively ceases to act as one of the world's top-five economic and military powers and opts instead for a strange mix of strategic political correctness, which essentially turns grand strategy on its head. Far from generating immense means in pursuit of large ends via well-considered ways, far too little is done far too late, and with far too little effect.

In reality, there is indeed a palpable gap between what could happen and the capacity and capability of the West to respond. This bigger strategic picture is missing from the 2016 NATO Warsaw Summit, because no leader wants to face such a scenario or indeed the lacunae that inspire it. The basic assumption upon which both NATO and the EU operate is thus profoundly flawed. The first-responder mul-tinational Very High Readiness Joint Task Force (VJTF) and enhanced NATO Response Force (eNRF) both imply a strategy that in turn presupposes the Americans will always be 'there', able to act like the US Seventh Cavalry in those western movies of old. The US rides over the horizon with a heavy force to save Eastern European 'homesteaders' from Russian aggression, which is held and then pinned in place by NATO's initial response. As for the EU, it has dem-onstrated no meaningful capacity or capability to deal with such a crisis, or crises of any magnitude.

As for Britain, years of defence pretence expose the British armed forces is dangerously hollowed-out, with insufficient reserves or means of regeneration, simply unable to meet many of the challenges thrown at them. For years Westminster and Whitehall have believed their own propaganda: that Britain is a top-five world economic and military power; that its intelligence and armed forces are world leaders; and that Britain is an indispensable player in world and European security. The crisis of 2020 makes it clear that Britain can just about defend itself, if Britain is not the main target for attack.

CHAPTER 10

CONCLUSION

Cold War Legacies

When General Sir John Hackett and his co-authors published *The Third World War* in 1978, their book made a firm impression among Western military academies and staff colleges – and was doubtless read very closely by analysts in the then Soviet Union and Warsaw Pact. For those serving in NATO's Armed Forces during the 1970s and 1980s the narrative device employed by Hackett was neither remote, fanciful nor exaggerated; their outlook was what lay at the heart of NATO planning and was the principal focus of national security strategy.

As the Cold War progressed from the late 1940s onwards, there had been no shortage of non-East/West security concerns around the world to occupy the minds and budgets of political leaders and military commanders. But if these concerns did not reflect or influence the security and stability of the European Central Front, then they were strategically peripheral. In other words, the 'deep and close' focus on the Central Front had a narrowing effect on strategic thought. In the UK, for example, it explained why the British military effort in Northern Ireland was always so problematic; it was never seen as core to national security interests largely because it was overshadowed by the Cold War.

Hackett's book also had a wider appeal, beyond its

professional military readership. A review published in the *Bulletin of the Atomic Scientists* in January 1980 – at a time when international security was judged to be at a very precarious 'seven minutes to midnight' – noted that *The Third World War* 'enjoyed astonishing popular success in Britain in 1978, and when serialised in several newspapers in the United States.' The reviewer, Irving Lerch, observed that Hackett had 'exploit[ed] the moment to expose the follies of military unpreparedness'. When in 1982 Hackett published a revised version of his book, Christopher Lehmann-Haupt, a reviewer for the *New York Times*, commended the work as 'a very high order of strategic thinking'. Lehmann-Haupt also saw the book as an illustration of the 'very basic message' voiced by the fourth-century Roman military writer Publius Flavius Vegetius Renatus: *Si vis pacem, para bellum* – 'If you want peace, prepare for war'.

This book *2020: World of War* emulates the approach taken by Hackett and his co-authors in several respects. We argue that cautious, well-reasoned worst-case analysis, far from being irresponsible, inflammatory or scare-mongering, can have a strategic agenda-setting function; insisting that security strategy must engage with the future, however unknown and unknowable that future might be. We also note that today, as in the late 1970s, it is all too tempting for strategic decision-makers to assume that the international security environment is more benign and less challenging than it actually is, often because it is politically expedient and financially cheaper to make such an assumption.

Hackett and his colleagues sought to engage with what could be Europe's strategic future, based on their long experience of war and peace. Yet they were not engaged in prophecy; their point was that it was necessary to engage with *the* future, rather than with *a* future. The inability to foresee the strategic future is not a deficiency, in *The Third*

World War or in any other strategic analysis; it is, instead, the defining characteristic of security strategy. Just as Hackett *et al.* might not even have imagined the global security environment forty years hence, so we might well argue that the world of 2057 is probably far beyond our current imagining. But the inability to imagine the future, at least not with any degree of accuracy and reliability, does not mean that we must wait passively for the future to arrive without making at least some effort at contingency planning.

It is here that Hackett's *The Third World War* makes arguably its strongest and most enduring contribution: 'We who have put this book together know very well that the only forecast that can be made with any confidence of the course and outcome of another world war, should there be one, is that nothing will happen exactly as we have shown here. There is the possibility, however, that it could.'

For Hackett *et al.*, governmental reluctance to engage with the possibility of the outbreak of war in Europe was an egregious strategic error. Then, as now, government spending plans were under intense pressure. But then, as now, to assume that a 'strategic holiday' could be taken while government finances improved was wish fulfilment at its most naïve and could only end in 'early disaster'.[46] The same can, and must be said for the current inclination to suspend strategic planning and decision-making as far as possible until the international security environment reveals itself.

In other respects, however, *2020: World of War* differs importantly from Hackett's work. First, there is no longer any validity in the Cold War idea of a 'strategic periphery'; the challenges and scenarios discussed in this book are all central concerns in the national and international security debate, whereas just decades ago they would not have been. Second, rather than the 'military unpreparedness' mentioned by Lerch, we now perceive the problem to be much larger and wider; nothing less than *strategic* unpreparedness, across the whole of public policy. And third, we observe that the international security picture of the twenty-first century is unlikely to be organised by one salient, overriding strategic concern in anything like the way of the Cold War.

Many of the assumptions that underpinned *The Third World War* – the determination of the 'Marxist-Leninists', the 'inexorable advance of communism' and the 'essentially offensive' character of the Red Army – now seem anachronistic, if not self-evidently wrong. Hackett and his co-authors benefited from the fact that during the Cold War Western strategic analysis could afford to be largely concerned – even obsessed – with the prospect of a singular strategic moment: the breakdown of military stability in central Europe.

As we have shown in this book, this linear approach to strategic thinking and planning no longer corresponds closely enough to the international security realities of the early twenty-first century for it to provide a credible and durable framework for strategic analysis. In this regard Lerch now appears rather prescient in his criticism of Hackett for producing an overly structured account: 'their world is too simple, too neat, too predictable. This is the consequence of the analytical committee approach designed to generate a coherent and logical picture of events.' But if a 'picture of events' is too much to expect, then what can reasonably be said of the twenty-first-century international security environment?

Charting Unknowable Waters

2020: World of War offers expert analysis and insight into the evolving twenty-first-century international security landscape.

Our first essay – From Cold War to Hot Peace: the Russian Strategic Challenge – focuses on Russia's strategic capabilities and intentions in Europe and across the globe. We show that while there is some sense of continuum in Russian strategic ambition, there are also important departures from the Cold War past, not least that Russia's strategic outlook is no longer contained within an overarching strategic framework. Our second essay – 'Global Insecurity' – shows how the international security landscape has broadened far beyond the outlook of Cold War strategists. Our seven regional and thematic scenarios then show how uncertainty and tension around the world can result in challenges to national and international security strategies, in a variety of ways and at different levels of intensity.

Scenarios are not predictions; they are merely illustrations of plausible developments and a device with which to conduct the future-oriented strategic analysis that we believe is currently in such short supply. Well-reasoned, future-oriented analysis must be the basis of all effective strategic decision-making. Yet analysis should never be confused with decision and action. Strategy is a purposive activity; the linking point between national policy and practical action. Put another way, strategy is a connector; it provides public policy with the ways and means it needs for implementation and effect, and it provides practical action with the rationale it requires to be respectable and credible. As *2020: World of War* clearly shows, however, this linking function has become far more difficult.

What security challenges might arise in the coming decades of the twenty-first century? Certainly, there are still those around the world who believe that 'might is right' and that coercion and violence can be used to achieve their goals. These governments, non-state actors and individuals can

often display impressive strategic patience, firm in the belief
that they have time on their side, and they should not, therefore, be ignored. The only accurate answer to questions
concerning twenty-first-century international security is that
we cannot know.

Former US Secretary of Defense Donald Rumsfeld has
been widely ridiculed, most often for a brief comment made
in 2002 concerning allegations that the Iraqi government had
been involved in supplying weapons of mass destruction to
terrorist organisations. The inference was that Rumsfeld was
a confused septuagenarian who had become lost in his own
logic. What Rumsfeld actually said was this:

> *Reports that say that something hasn't happened are always
> interesting to me, because as we know, there are 'known knowns';
> there are things we know we know. We also know there are
> 'known unknowns'; that is to say we know there are some things
> we do not know. But there are also 'unknown unknowns' – the
> ones we don't know we don't know.* [47]

In the uncertain context of early twenty-first-century international security, Rumsfeld's brief comment probably offers
rather more strategic wisdom than many of his critics have
since been able to generate. The challenge currently faced
by governments and strategic planners is precisely that of
the 'unknown unknown'. It is one of not knowing – or even
being able to guess with any reliable degree of confidence
– what range and intensity of security threats and challenges
might be encountered in the short- to medium-term future.
Yet governments cannot afford to wait for these threats to
manifest themselves before taking action; they must somehow
prepare for what they cannot yet know.

The characteristics of twenty-first-century international

security are likely to be both incomplete and changeable. The problem for national strategy is, therefore, to find solutions to opaque and partially formed problems as they arise, and to be sufficiently adaptable to redirect strategic interest when circumstances change. But how can strategy be built upon such shifting sands and shallow foundations? It is one thing to insist that strategy should not simply repeat the 'known knowns', but it is rather more difficult to see how strategy can equip societies to meet what might be volatile, varied and unknowable. Put simply, how can strategy be 'future-proofed'?

Future-Proofing Strategy

A future-oriented security strategy makes several requirements, some conceptual and others more practical. The first requirement is to be aware of the dominance of traditional language and ideas where strategy is concerned. Security strategy continues to be based on a largely binary outlook – 'peace' versus 'war' – with the Cold War having been a tenuous compromise between the two. This can limit severely the scope and relevance of strategic analysis; there is little opportunity for manoeuvre between these two poles, yet it is in that murky space that many of the twenty-first century's security challenges seem to lie. Our response to security challenges then narrows; if a crisis of some sort does not have the attributes or the intensity of large-scale 'war' then it is too tempting to assume that we are at 'peace' and to continue enjoying the 'strategic holiday' we believe we deserve. It is for this reason that this book is entitled *World of War* – to indicate that the overarching strategic challenge might be more of a continuum than a discreet moment or event.

The second requirement is a logical extension of the first.

Much of what is happening in the world today, and that which informs our scenarios, is new to a good deal of Western society and its political leadership and, just as importantly, is very often beyond the experience and competence of international institutions. The latter part of the twentieth century saw everything possible done to encourage globalisation and cooperation in the liberal international economic order and to exclude conflict and competition from world politics. In the process, war was dismissed as a means of resolving disputes and particularly as a means of exerting power over, and gaining control of, weaker neighbours. This was a laudable position to adopt, in principle, but it also represented the triumph of hope over experience. And the curious outcome was that the war/peace paradigm, which encourages a narrow, binary outlook on strategic challenges, was made even less useful by our having declared one half of it to be irrelevant. The second ingredient in a future-proofed strategy, then, is a willingness to see international security for what it *is* and might become, rather than for what we might *wish* it to be.

The third requirement is a reinvigorated strategic culture. This is most straightforwardly understood as the societal confidence and the institutional processes necessary to manage and deploy military force and other levers of national power and influence, all as components of a range of legitimate and effective policy instruments. Good, effective strategy cannot be achieved without the underpinning of a self-confident strategic culture, driven by the conviction that from time to time values and interests might have to be protected, and perhaps even enforced.

A responsible and mature strategic culture is one equipped to meet security challenges with the most appropriate selection of the available responses and one that has strategic patience; the ability to take and sustain a long view. These criteria are unlikely to be met by a society that considers all things 'strategic' to be regrettable at best, and deviant at worst. And a strategic culture must be more than declaratory. The all-too-tempting alternative to a serious, forward-looking, risk-taking strategic culture is the 'input culture', whereby political leaders are so conscious of the electoral cycle that they focus their 'strategic' time and attention on inputs for which they can claim short-term credit, rather than taking decisions that will have longer-term benefit.

Strategy can also be future-proofed in practical ways. In the first place, strategy requires the strong analytical base already mentioned. For though strategy requires bold decisions to be taken, analysis can do much to ensure that those decisions are not driven by prejudice, impulse or guesswork. Another important element of strategic analysis is to have the expertise – and indeed the political confidence and courage – to undertake politically inconvenient, but strategically vital, worst-case assessments of the sort we have undertaken here. Thereafter, strategy requires a range of policies and instruments to deal with a world in which not one, but many crises might erupt simultaneously.

Part of that requirement is for a full range of military capabilities – so-called 'hard power'. This is a matter both of having an effective, joint military force (infantry, armour, artillery, air power, sea power and cyber power), and of ensuring that these units are supported by key 'enablers' such as air- and sea-transport, real-time operational intelligence, and durable command and control systems. Unfortunately, many European countries currently fall far short of having enough deployable, effective and fully enabled armed forces.

Not all security challenges will require a military response, in whole or in part. It is for this reason that effective strategy requires the habit and the capacity for cross-governmental working involving all departments and agencies responsible for different levers of power and influence. And this spirit of cooperation and mutual self-help should extend much further, beyond national boundaries, to the maintenance of networks of alliances and partnerships committed to the pursuit, realisation and protection of shared values and interests.

But it should be borne in mind that an alliance is simply a mechanism; it is not a strategic response in its own right. In this respect, it is essential that NATO allies and EU member-states recognise the strategic significance of the transatlantic strategic contract and understand that this contract could be undermined as much by a United States displaying isolationist tendencies as by European countries with no discernible strategic culture and insufficient hard power.

Finally, strategy can be made fit for an uncertain future by rediscovering deterrence and by rethinking the purpose of innovation. Current and foreseeable challenges to the international security order require an intelligent reapplication of deterrence principles and techniques with which we have long been familiar. The basic principles of deterrence are unchanging: the imposition of intolerable cost, whether through defence and denial or by the threat of a punitive response, in order to dissuade an actual or potential adversary from adventurism or even all-out aggression. But the international security environment of the twenty-first century requires deterrence to be much more than strong defences and a declared promise to inflict violence by one means or another. An effective, future-oriented deterrence posture requires a range of capabilities (passive and active, military and non-military) in an 'adversary agnostic' posture that is both coherent and credible and which can be communicated unambiguously to any potential opponent or miscreant.

A more imaginative approach to innovation can improve the credibility of deterrence by enabling low-level, tactical decision-making and action. As well as pursuing 'game-changing' and disruptive technology and equipment, innovation should also be concerned with broadening the participation in strategy such that strategy can be implemented horizontally rather than hierarchically. It should be possible for high-quality analysis and assessment to be conducted as circumstances require. The credibility of a deterrent posture should be reinforced as soon as it comes into doubt, at even the lowest level.

Adaptability

Our essays and scenarios describe a range of security problems and challenges, actual and potential. *2020: World of War* also shows that today, some forty years since the publication of Hackett's *The Third World War*, international security is more complex, more diverse and much less predictable (if indeed it ever was predictable) than Hackett might have imagined. As a consequence, the response to international security challenges must be commensurately more intricate.

If they are to manage the international security environment effectively, policy-makers and strategists must have the capacity and the confidence to respond to security challenges with as much complexity and diversity as circumstances demand. In organisational terms, strategists must allow for a 'whole of government' response to security challenges around the world, involving much more than the projection of military force. National strategy must also be timely, offering a decisive engagement with security challenges as they arise, and occasionally with little or no warning.

National strategy in the early twenty-first century must be analytically robust; it should be goal-oriented and practically effective; it must be organisationally coherent, bringing together all necessary agencies and levers of government; it must encourage cooperation with allies and partners; and it must be timely. And if national strategy is to be valid and durable, then any decisions made and actions taken must be directly proportionate to the challenge.

Strategy requires decisions to be made and implemented which can involve very high levels of difficulty, political risk, physical danger and financial expense. Strategy involves the careful and proportionate use of ways and means to achieve clearly defined, lawful goals; anything else is at best an unplanned spasm and at worst a misuse of the mechanisms of government.

It is often said that strategy, in any sector, calls for agility, flexibility and versatility; meeting new challenges by using available resources to best effect. The metaphor of 'variable geometry' is often used; although the wings of an aircraft are solid objects, they can be reoriented to achieve different effects in different circumstances. At no point, of course, do they become anything other than aircraft wings. Ideas and metaphors of this sort are all suggestive of a drive for efficiency; improving our reaction to external challenges by making better, more imaginative use of what we already have.

But there is another term to consider that calls for a reassessment of what 'we' are and of how we go about things: *adaptability*. To be adaptable is to acknowledge that the best response to external change might at times be to change internally; to reconfigure familiar, well-used strategic techniques and assets and to be open to the possibility that new tools and procedures might be required, and to be able to do so again and again as circumstances demand.

The merits of strategic adaptability are set out in the following passage from the late Rafe Sagarin's *Learning from the Octopus*. Sagarin was a marine ecologist and environmental policy analyst at the University of Arizona and, earlier in his career, a science advisor in the US Congress during President George W. Bush's first administration. Amid the heightened security measures imposed after 9/11, Sagarin observed that biological adaptation and evolution might help to find better ways to 'fight terrorist attacks, natural disasters and disease.' The security problem might be more than simply managing the consequences of a natural disaster or anticipating the intentions of a threat actor. The security problem might also lie in the way society and government are configured to deal with security problems:

> For armies fighting a war, for health practitioners trying to ward off a flu pandemic, for first responders containing the damage from a natural disaster, for IT managers trying to protect a computer network, for resource managers trying to plan for a world dramatically altered by climate change, for CEOs worried about the next stock-market crash, and for any citizen worried about the effects of any of these potential threats, adaptability is essential. If we want to interact with the world at all (and in a world of seven billion people, we don't have much choice), having the ability to *change* how we interact with it is the only way we can survive.

Rafe Sagarin went on to observe that:

> Adaptability is fundamentally different from merely *reacting* to a crisis (which happens too late) or attempting to *predict*

the next crisis (which is almost certain to fail when complex ecological systems and human behaviours are involved). Adaptability controls the sweet spot between reaction and prediction, providing an inherent ability to respond efficiently to a wide range of potential challenges, not just those that are known or anticipated.[48]

Sagarin's 'adaptability' is the most convincing way for a future-oriented strategy to meet Rumsfeld's 'unknown unknowns'. It is not enough to say that since governments do not know how the international security environment will evolve over coming decades, they can only be expected to prepare for what they do know, or not prepare at all. The lack of foresight is nothing more than a statement of the obvious; governments have *never* been able to look into the future and it is inconceivable that they might recently have discovered how to do so.

Strategy has always been a form of organised, active ignorance and is likely to remain that way. Instead, the challenge lies in governments' capacity, confidence and courage to cope with uncertainty, to adapt internally and in conjunction with friends and allies and to act strategically without having all the information to hand they might need or wish. All that we can *know* of the twenty-first-century security environment is that we must engage with it.

SOURCE NOTES

Chapter 1. From Cold War to Hot Peace: The Russian Strategic Challenge

1   The cost of new military equipment is increasing at a rate of some 8% per annum above the rate of inflation.

Chapter 2. Strategy in Breadth: The Global Insecurity Complex

2   'Climate at a Glance: Global Time Series', NOAA National Centers for Environmental Information, December 2016: http://www.ncdc.noaa.gov/cag/.

3   Intergovernmental Panel on Climate Change: Working Group I, Climate Change 2013, *The Physical Science Basis*, Cambridge University Press, 2013, p. 77: http://www.climatechange2013.org/images/report/WG1AR5_ALL_FINAL.pdf.

4   IPCC, *The Physical Science Basis*, p. V.

5   'The biggest threat to Earth has been dismissed by Trump as a Chinese hoax', *UK Business Insider*, 11 November 2016: http://uk.businessinsider.com/donald-trump-climate-change-chinese-hoax-2016-11.

6   Annie Sneed, 'Yes, some extreme weather can be blamed on climate change', *Scientific American*, 2 January 2017: https://www.scientificamerican.com/article/yes-some-extreme-weather-can-be-blamed-on-climate-change/.

7   'World Day to Combat Desertification', United Nations: http://www.un.org/en/events/desertificationday/background.shtml.

8   'IFAD and desertification', International Fund for Agricultural Development: https://www.ifad.org/topic/overview/tags/desertification.

9   'Sea ice hits record lows', *Arctic Sea Ice News & Analysis*, US National Snow & Ice Data Center, 6 December 2016: http://nsidc.org/arcticseaicenews/.

10   'Frozen conflict', *The Economist*, 20 December 2014: http://www.economist.com/news/international/21636756-denmark-claims-north-pole-frozen-conflict.

11   UN Department of Economic and Social Affairs, Population Division, *World Population Prospects: The 2015 Revision: Key Findings & Advance Tables*, New York: UN, ESA/WP.241, 2015, pp. 1–2: https://esa.un.org/unpd/wpp/publications/files/key_findings_wpp_2015.pdf.

12   Ibid., pp. 3–4.

13   Ibid., p. 4.

14   Ibid., p. 6.

15   Ibid., Probabilistic Projections – various tables.

16   UN Department of Economic and Social Affairs, Population Division, *The World's Cities in 2016*, United Nations, 2016, ST/ESA/ SER.A/392: http://www.un.org/en/development/desa/population/publications/pdf/urbanization/the_worlds_cities_in_2016_data_booklet.pdf.

17   UN-Habitat, *World Cities Report 2016. Urbanization and Development: Emerging Futures*, Nairobi: UN-Habitat, 2016, p. 22: http://wcr.unhabitat.org/wp-content/

uploads/sites/16/2016/05/WCR-%20Full-Report-2016.pdf.

18   'Senior Israeli, Jordanian and Palestinian Representatives Sign Milestone Water Sharing Agreement', *The World Bank*, Press Release, 9 December 2013: http://www.worldbank.org/en/news/press-release/2013/12/09/senior-israel-jordanian-palestinian-representatives-water-sharing-agreement.

19   Wendy Barnaby, 'Do nations go to war over water?', quoted in Jack Shafer, 'The Water-War Myth', *Slate*, 2 April 2009: http://www.slate.com/articles/news_and_politics/press_box/2009/04/the_waterwar_myth.html.

20   World Economic Forum, *Global Risks Report 2016*, Geneva: World Economic Forum, 2016, p. 12: http://www3.weforum.org/docs/GRR/WEF_GRR16.pdf.

21   High Level Panel on Fragile States, *Ending conflict & building peace in Africa: a call to action*, African Development Bank Group 2014, p. 28: http://www.afdb.org/fileadmin/uploads/afdb/Documents/Project-and-Operations/Ending_Conflict_and_Building_Peace_in_Africa-_A_Call_to_Action.pdf.

22   Colin Gray, *Another Bloody Century: Future Warfare*, London: Phoenix, 2005, p. 83.

23   WEF, *Global Risks Report 2016*, p. 50.

24   UN Food and Agriculture Organization, *The State of Food Insecurity in the World*, Rome: UN FAO, 2015, p. 8: http://www.fao.org/3/a-i4646e.pdf.

25   UN Food and Agriculture Organization, *Regional Overview of Food Insecurity: Africa*, Rome: UN FAO, 2015, p. 21: http://www.fao.org/3/a-i4635e.pdf.

26   US Energy Information Administration, *International Energy Outlook 2016*, Washington D.C.: US Department of Energy, DOE/EIA-0484, 2016, Chapter 1: http://www.eia.gov/outlooks/ieo/world.cfm.

27   BP, *Statistical Review of World Energy*, 65th Edition, 2016: http://www.bp.com/en/global/corporate/energy-economics/statistical-review-of-world-energy.html.

28   World Health Organisation, *Global Tuberculosis Report 2016*, Geneva: WHO, 2016, p. 1: http://apps.who.int/iris/bitstream/10665/250441/1/9789241565394-eng.pdf?ua=1.

29   World Health Organisation, 'Drug-resistant TB: XDR-TB FAQ': http://www.who.int/tb/areas-of-work/drug-resistant-tb/xdr-tb-faq/en/.

30   'Last line antibiotics are failing', European Centre for Disease Prevention and Control, 18 November 2016: http://ecdc.europa.eu/en/press/news/_layouts/forms/News_DispForm.aspx?ID=1510&List=8db7286c-fe2d-476c-9133-18ff4cb1b568.

31   World Health Organisation, *Global Action Plan on Antimicrobial Resistance*, Geneva: WHO, 2015, p. vii: http://www.wpro.who.int/entity/drug_resistance/resources/global_action_plan_eng.pdf.

32   'Report of the World Summit for Social Development, March 1995', United Nations A/CONF.166.9, 12 April 1995, para. 19: http://www.un.org/documents/ga/conf166/aconf166-9.htm.

33   World Bank, 4 October 2015: http://www.worldbank.org/en/news/press-release/2015/10/04/world-bank-forecasts-global-poverty-to-fall-below-10-for-first-time-major-hurdles-remain-in-goal-to-end-poverty-by-2030.

34   World Bank, *Poverty and Shared Prosperity 2016: Taking on Inequality*, Washington, D.C.: IBRD/World Bank, 2016, p. 35: https://openknowledge.worldbank.org/bitstream/handle/10986/25078/9781464809583.pdf#page=55.

35   Oxfam, *Even it Up: Time to end Extreme Inequality*, Oxford: Oxfam, 2014, p. 32: https://www.oxfam.org/sites/www.oxfam.org/files/file_attachments/cr-even-it-up-extreme-inequality-291014-en.pdf.

36   US National Intelligence Council, *Global Trends 2025: A Transformed World*, Washington, D.C.: US Government Printing Office, November 2008, p. 54.

Chapter 9. Operation Imperfect Storm: The European Dilemma

37 https://www.gov.uk/government/uploads/system/uploads/attachment_data/file/33717GST_V9_Feb10.pdf.

38 See www.tradingeconomics.com for all government budget figures.

39 'The World Military Balance 2016', London: IISS, 2016.

40 Wales Summit Declaration: www.nato.int/cps/en/natohq/official_texts_112964.htm.

41 In November 2015 this author gave evidence to the House of Commons Defence Committee on the use of accounting techniques by the British Ministry of Defence to maintain the letter if not the spirit of 2% GDP defence expenditure as agreed at the 2014 NATO Wales Summit.

42 www.prb.org/Publications/People/2001PopulationTrendsandChallengesintheMiddleEastandNorthAfrica.aspx.

43 Patrick Clawson, 'Demography in the Middle East', March 2009: www.washington.institute.org/policy-analysis//view/demography-in-the-middle-east-population-growth-slowing-womens-situation-un.

44 See *The Economist*, 8 March 2014, 'Hopes that Africa's Dramatic Population Bulge May Create Prosperity Seem False': www.economist.com/news/middle-east-and-africa/.

44 UN Global Trends Report 2016: http://www.unhcr.org/uk/news/latest/2016/6/5763b65a4/global-forced-displacement-hits-record-high.html.

45 The current level of US forces in Europe is 1 divisional headquarters, 3 brigade combat teams, 6 fighter squadrons, 1 tanker squadron, 1 transport squadron, 1 Special Operations Forces transport squadron, 1 flagship and 4 AEGIS-class destroyers.

Chapter 10. Conclusion

46 General Sir John Hackett and others, *The Third World War: August 1985: A Future History*, London: Sidgwick & Jackson, 1978, p. 359.

47 Donald Rumsfeld, *Known and Unknown: A Memoir*, London, Sentinel, 2011, p. xiii.

48 Rafe Sagarin, *Learning from the Octopus: How Secrets from Nature Can Help Us Fight Terrorist Attacks, Natural Disasters and Disease*, New York: Basic Books, 2012, pp. xix, xxv.

INDEX